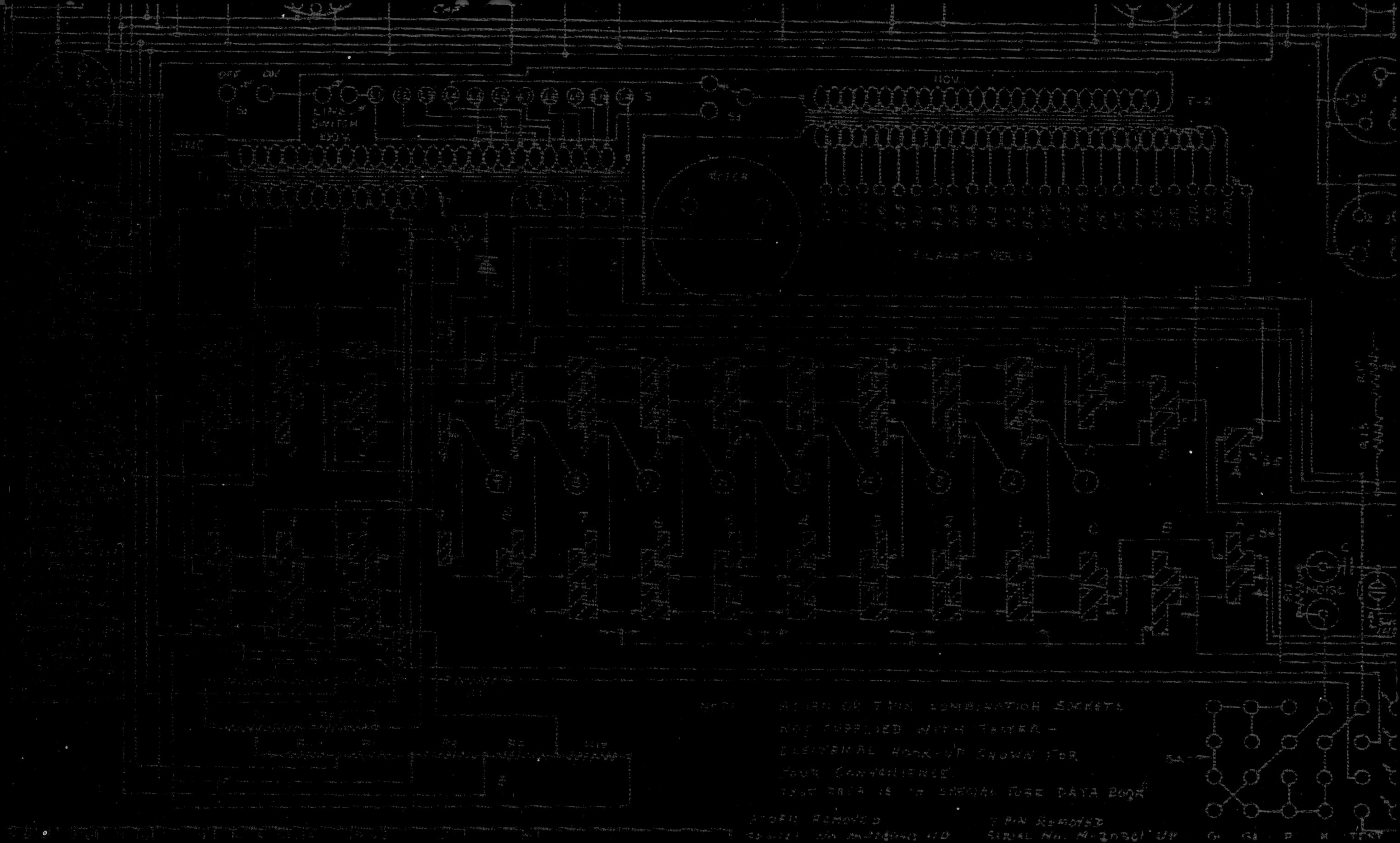
LINE SWITCH
METER
FILAMENT VOLTS
NOISE
OF THIS COMBINATION SOCKETS
NOT SUPPLIED WITH TESTER -
ELECTRICAL HOOK-UP SHOWN FOR
YOUR CONVENIENCE.
TEST DATA IS IN SPECIAL TUBE DATA BOOK

For the girls
– *Abba*

For Chief
– *J.S.*

THE ENGINEER

"KONSTRUKT"

by
BRIAN CHURILLA
and
JEREMY SHEPHERD

THE ENGINEER: KONSTRUKT

Written by BRIAN CHURILLA and JEREMY SHEPHERD
Illustrated by BRIAN CHURILLA
Colored by JEREMY SHEPHERD
Color Assistant LISA TRAN
Lettered by SEAN GLUMACE and JEFF POWELL

Published by **Archaia**

PJ Bickett, *President*
Mark Smylie, *Publisher*
Stephen Christy III, *Director of Development*
Mel Caylo, *Marketing Manager*
Brian Torney, *Associate Director, Creative Services*

Archaia Entertainment LLC
1680 Vine Street, Suite 912
Los Angeles, California, 90028
www.archaia.com

Write to:
editorial@archaia.com

ISBN: 1-932386-54-8
ISBN-13: 978-1-932386-54-7

FIRST PRINTING

10 9 8 7 6 5 4 3 2 1

Brian Churilla gives good monster.

That's as good a place to start as any.

* * *

I can't tell you much about Jeremy Shepherd. I don't think I've ever met him. But he does what he does well, as this volume will show you. THE ENGINEER is half Jeremy Shepherd, and no doubt I'm giving him short shrift, but I'm afraid I'm going to have to spend much of my space here talking about the drawing. Because that was where I started.

I first met Brian at an Emerald City Con in Seattle, where we were set up at adjoining tables. We had a good time talking, during the show, and the display art he had was compelling -- big, bold and imaginative. I picked up the first two issues of THE ENGINEER, and was entranced. I've seen a lot of people compare Brian's linework to Eric Powell and Mike Mignola, but there's more going on than just his inspirations. There's something ancient, primal and...in some strange way *aquatic* to Brian's visuals, as if he's haunted by visions of ancient hulking leviathans, lurking in deep ocean chasms, all battered, pitted exoskeleton or undulating tentacle, and he has no choice but to get these nightmares out onto paper, where they can be trapped. That sense of something old, hostile and *abyssal* informs THE ENGINEER, from the giant stone behemoth we meet right at the opening, to the bizarrely off-kilter crab-villagers to the gelatinous Lahar to the Witch Sisters, the creepiest trio of ass-faced, serpentine taskmistresses you'll ever meet.

And from the drawing, the next step is Jeremy's moody, absorbing colors, and then once you're wrapped in the world, the story...

The monsters had me from the first glance. And from there, I was sucked in to what Brian and Jeremy had...engineered. A world of mystic science holding back the destruction of all, a world where giant pipe organs play incomprehensible tunes that transport men across the realities, a world where one bitter, smart-assed ex-cosmonaut has to wrestle with his own fate while saving us all from an unknowably unpleasant extinction.

And the chickens. Did I mention the chickens? What the hell is up with *them?*

Anyway. The next time I saw Brian was at the Stumptown Comics Fest, where I picked up everything else he and Jeremy had available. I expect you'll want to, too. Because they – and THE ENGINEER – are just that good.

And it all starts with one unassailable truth.

* * *

Brian Churilla gives good monster.

But you don't need me to tell you that. You can see it.

And you'll find your way into Brian and Jeremy's world just fine from there...

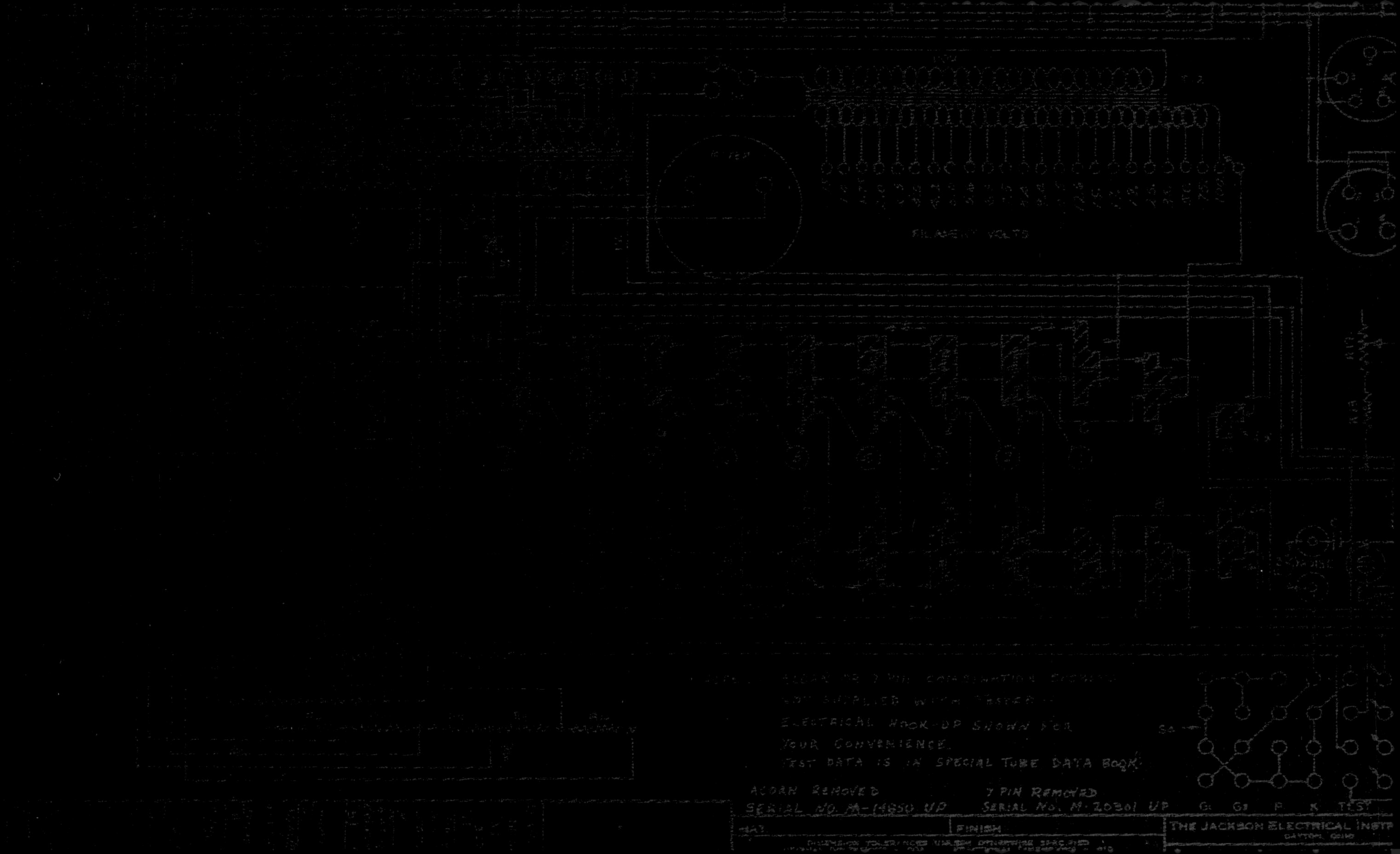
FILAMENT VOLTS
ELECTRICAL HOOK-UP SHOWN FOR
YOUR CONVENIENCE.
TEST DATA IS IN SPECIAL TUBE DATA BOOK.
ACORN REMOVED
SERIAL NO. M-14850 UP
7 PIN REMOVED
SERIAL NO. M-20301 UP
G1 G2 P K TEST
FINISH
THE JACKSON ELECTRICAL INSTR
DAYTON, OHIO

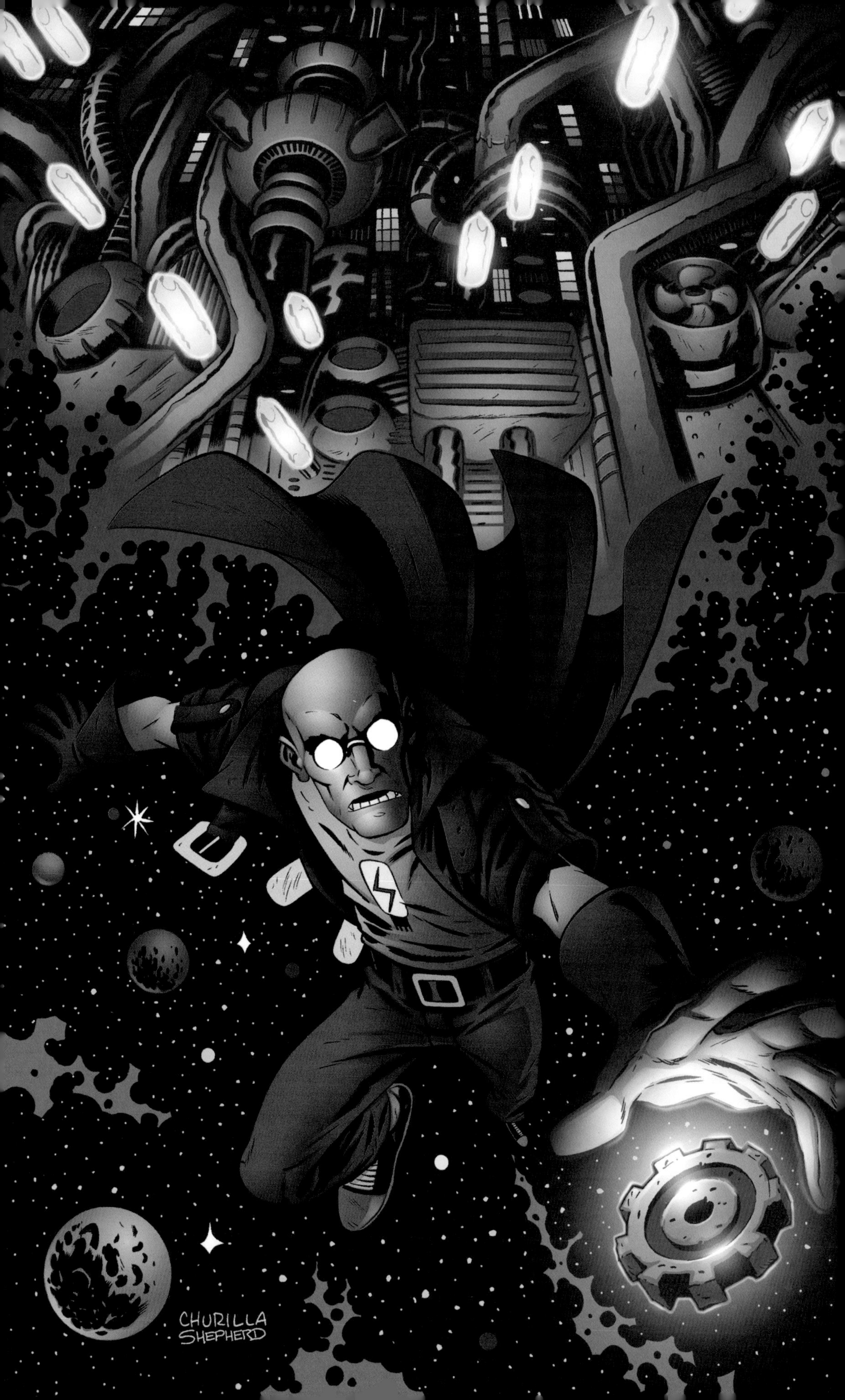
CHURILLA
SHEPHERD

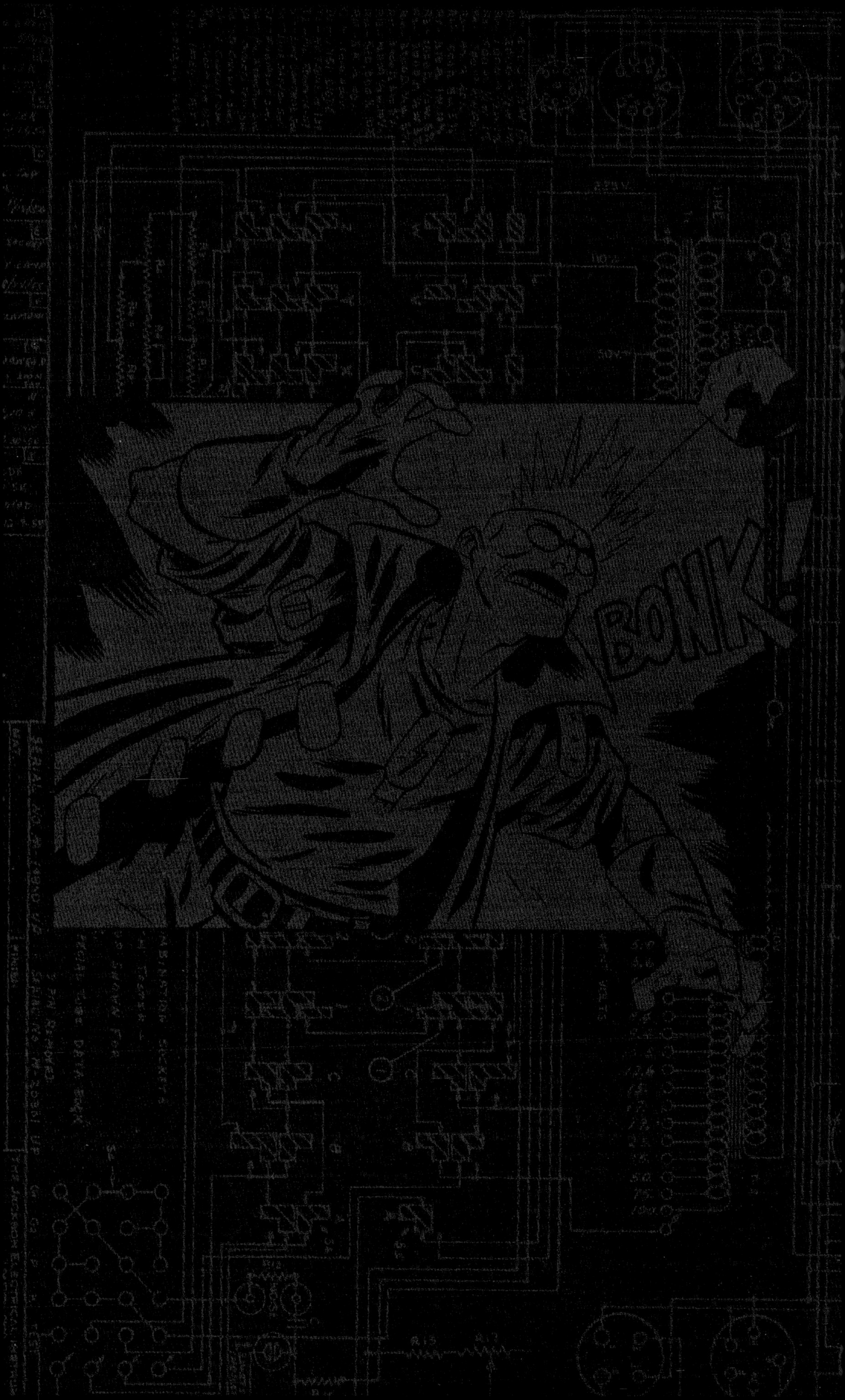
BONK!

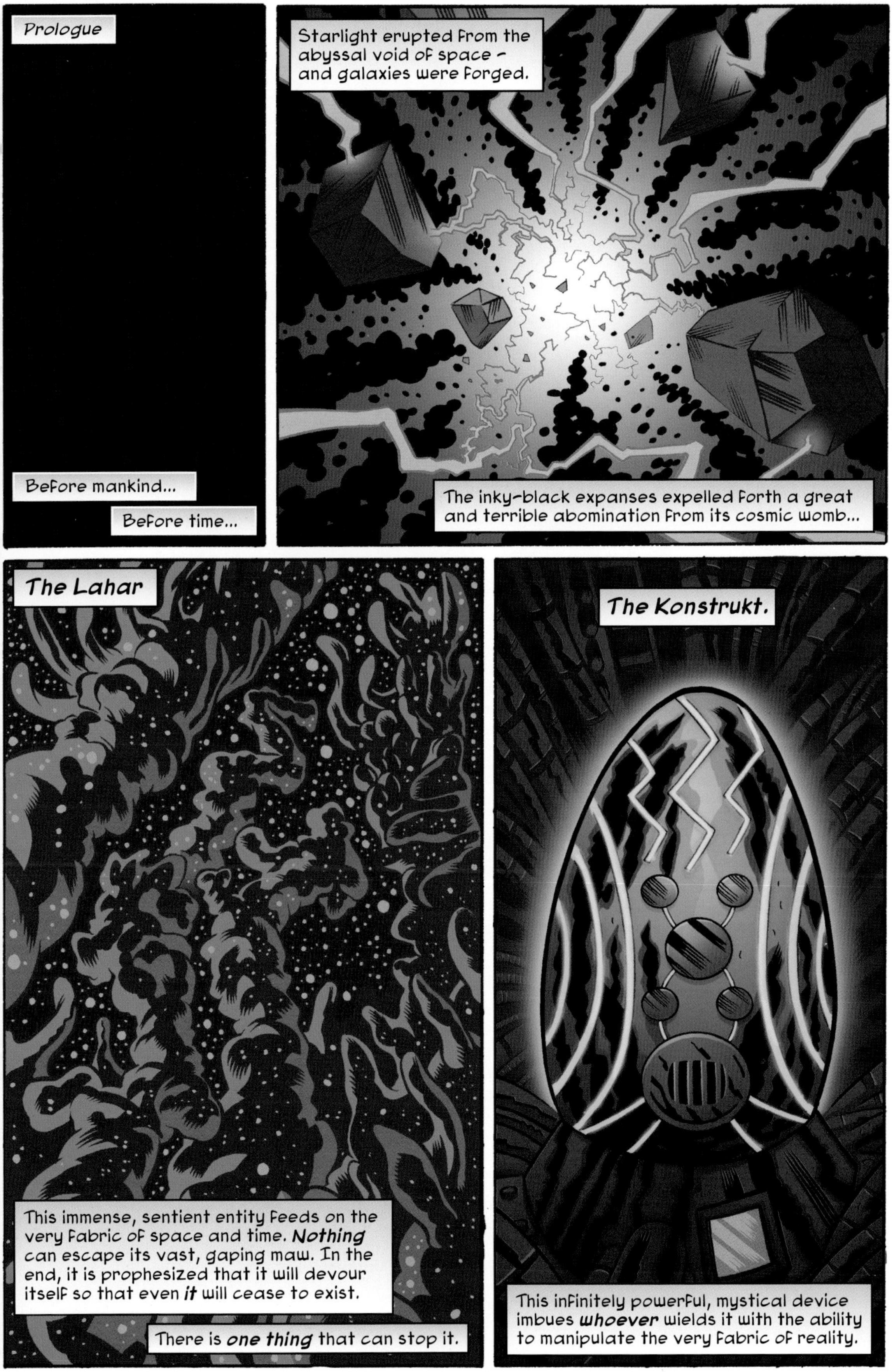
Prologue
Before mankind...
Before time...
Starlight erupted from the abyssal void of space - and galaxies were forged.
The inky-black expanses expelled forth a great and terrible abomination from its cosmic womb...
The Lahar
This immense, sentient entity feeds on the very fabric of space and time. **Nothing** can escape its vast, gaping maw. In the end, it is prophesized that it will devour itself so that even ***it*** will cease to exist.
There is ***one thing*** that can stop it.
The Konstrukt.
This infinitely powerful, mystical device imbues ***whoever*** wields it with the ability to manipulate the very fabric of reality.

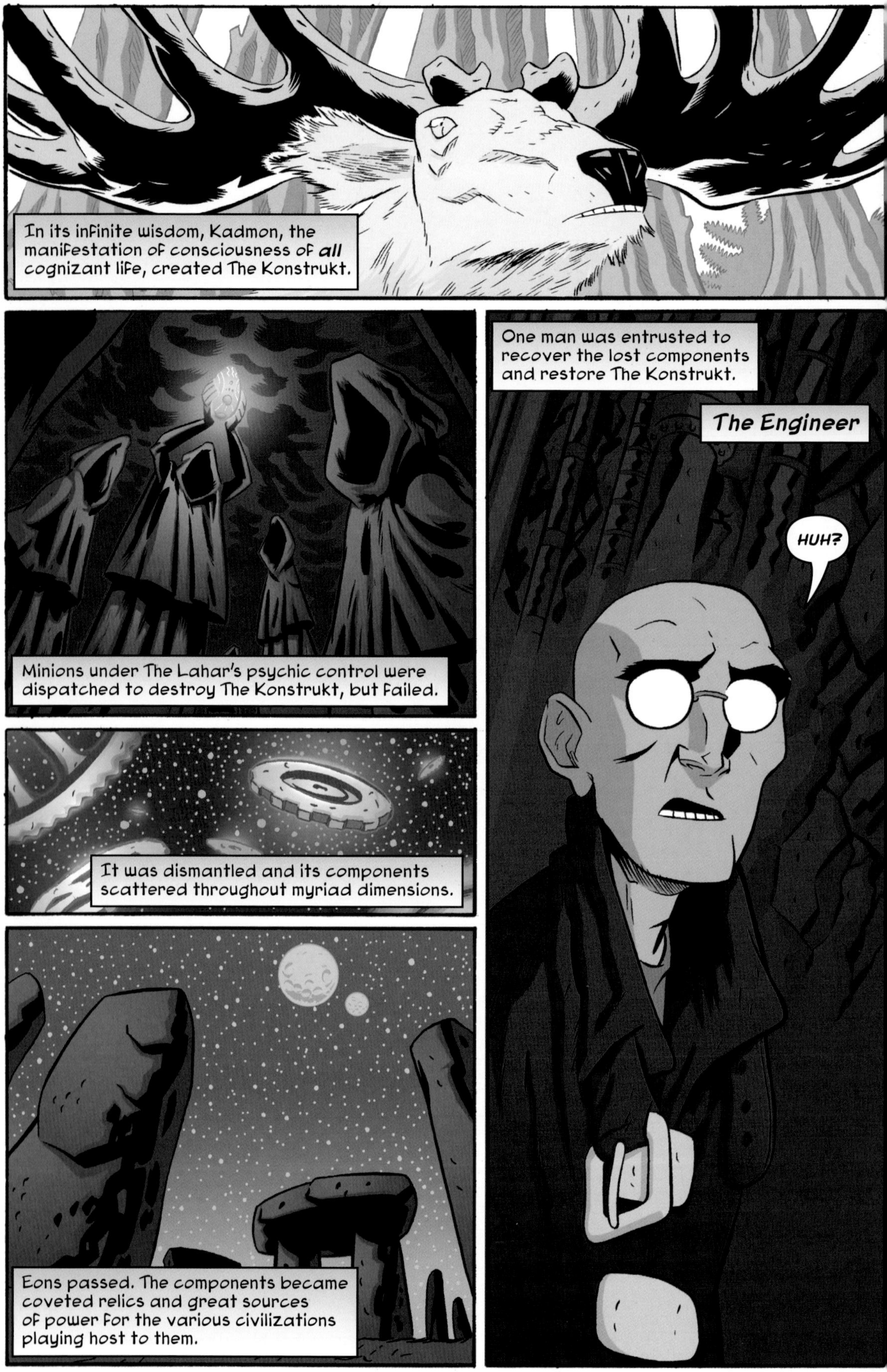
In its infinite wisdom, Kadmon, the manifestation of consciousness of *all* cognizant life, created The Konstrukt.
Minions under The Lahar's psychic control were dispatched to destroy The Konstrukt, but failed.
It was dismantled and its components scattered throughout myriad dimensions.
Eons passed. The components became coveted relics and great sources of power for the various civilizations playing host to them.
One man was entrusted to recover the lost components and restore The Konstrukt.
The Engineer
HUH?

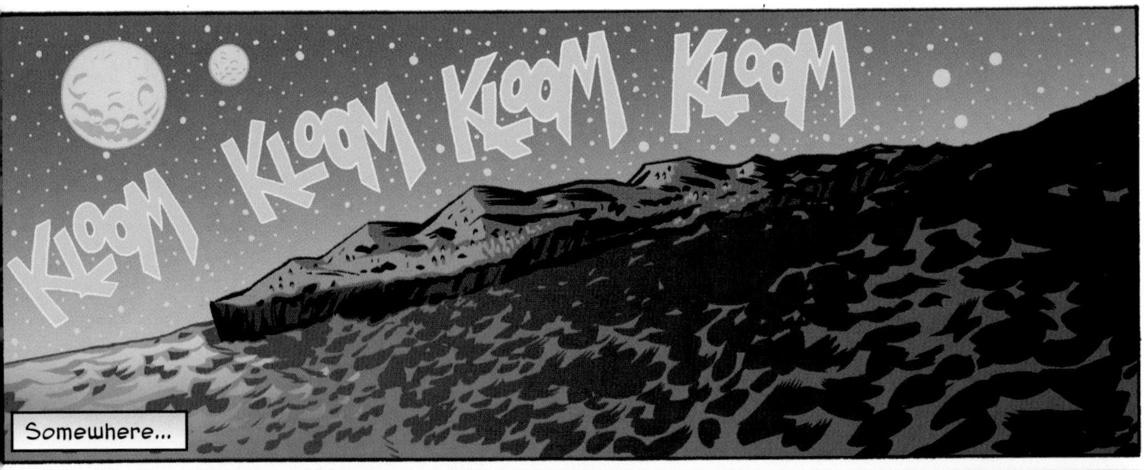
KLOOM KLOOM KLOOM KLOOM
Somewhere...

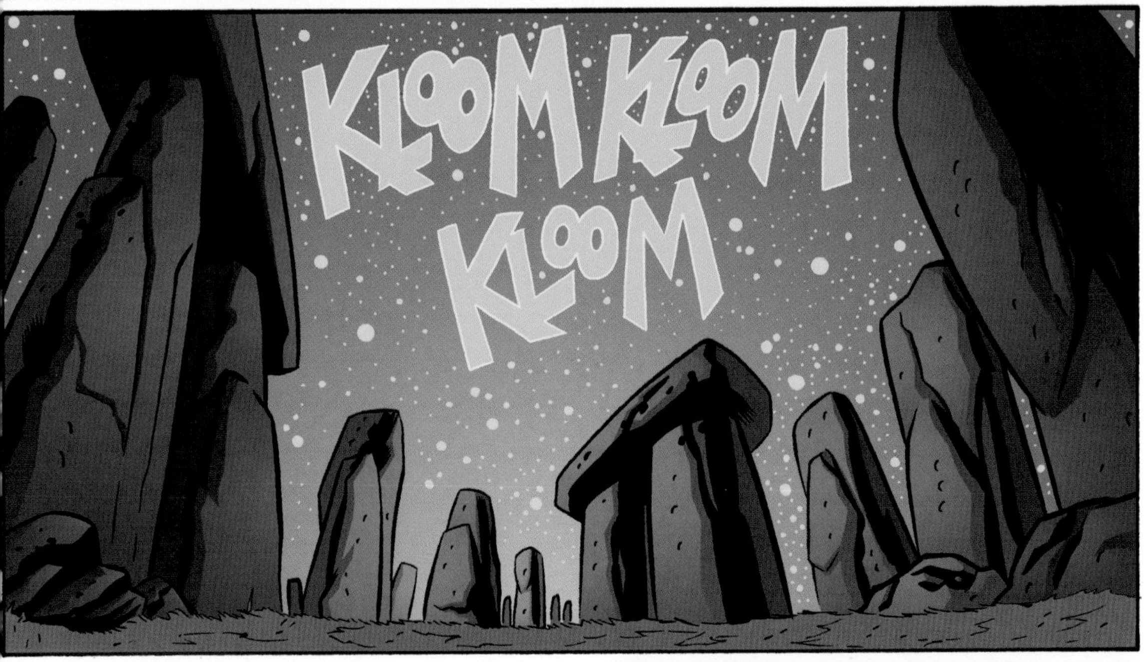
KLOOM KLOOM
KLOOM

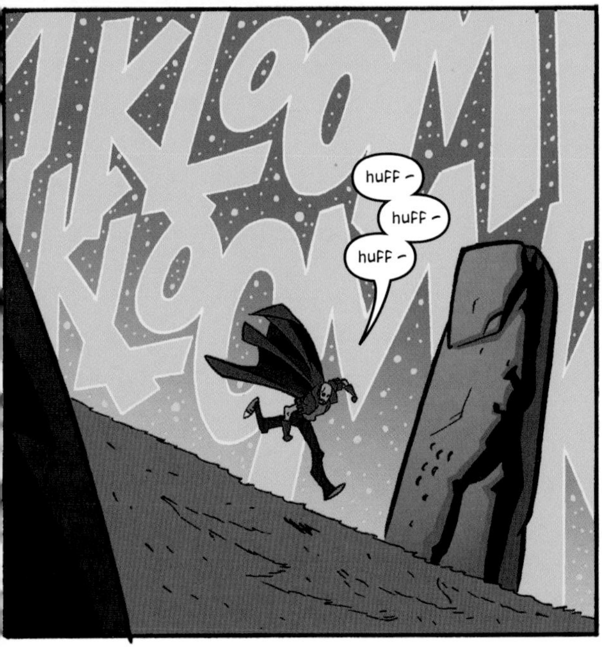
KLOOM
KLOOM
huff -
huff -
huff -

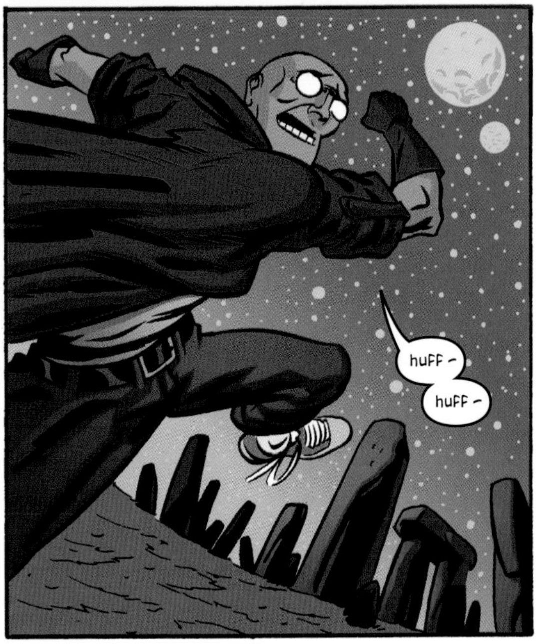
huff -
huff -

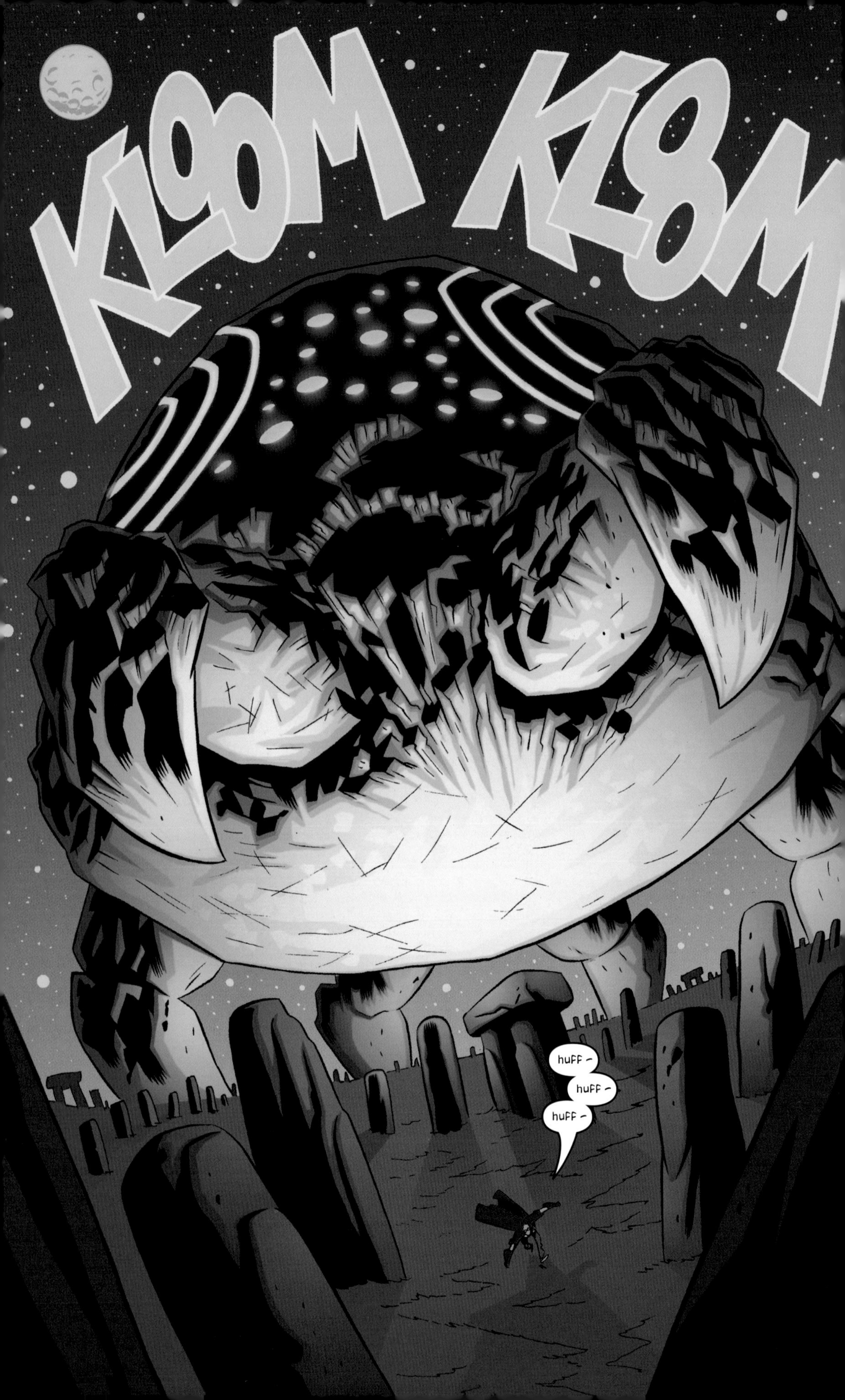
KLOOM KLOOM
huff -
huff -
huff -

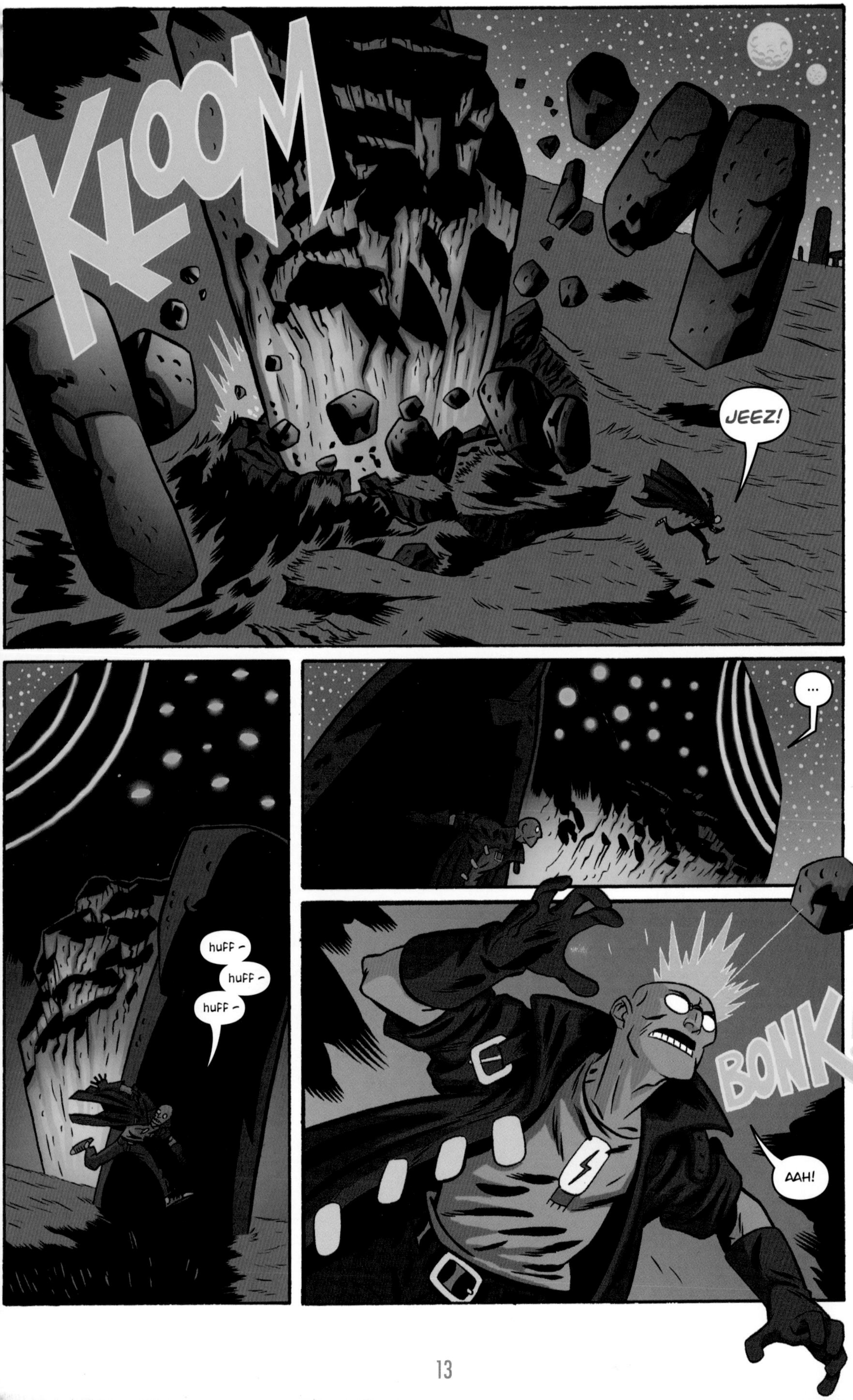
KLOOM
JEEZ!
huff -
huff -
huff -
...
BONK!
AAH!

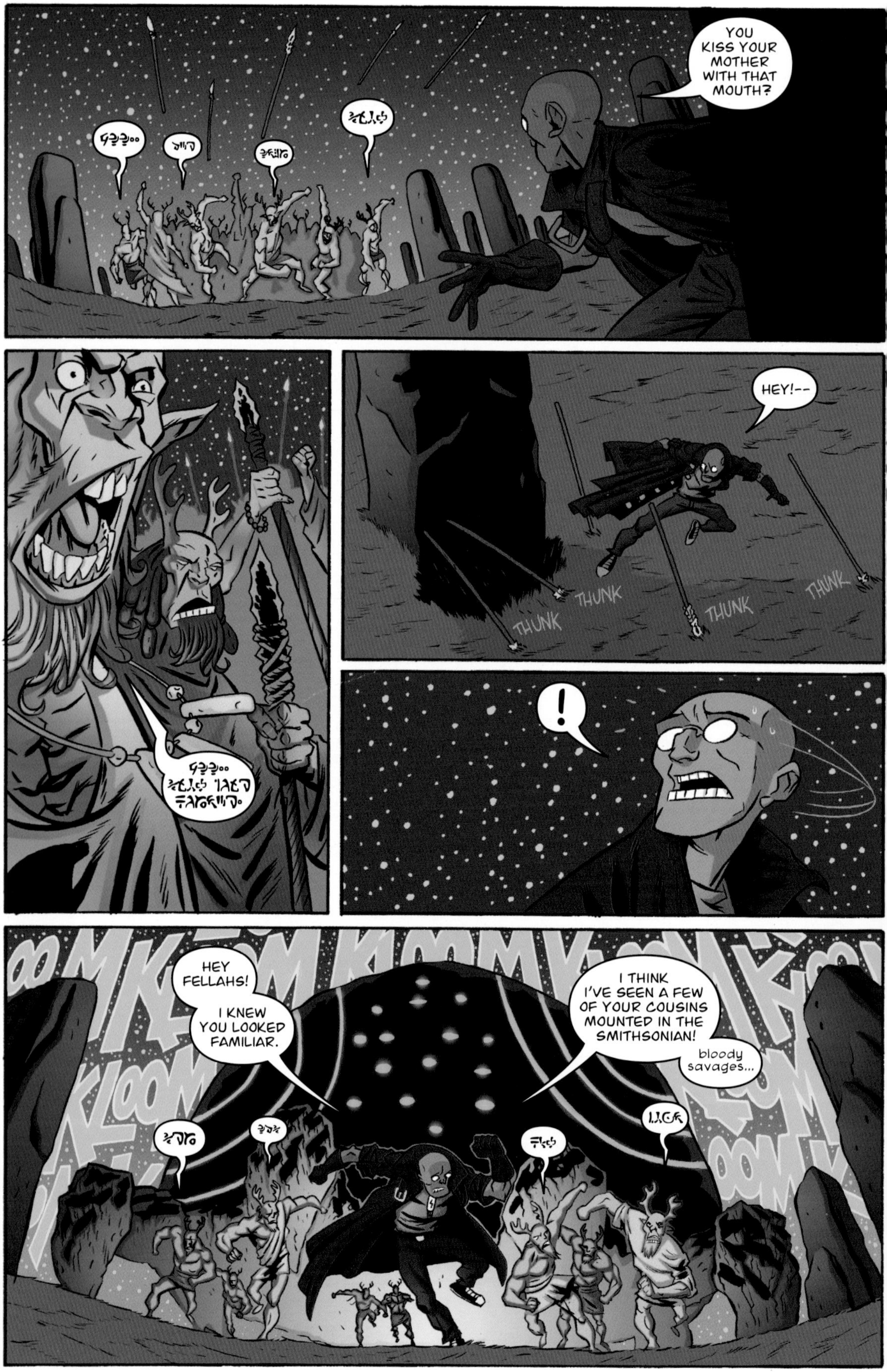
YOU KISS YOUR MOTHER WITH THAT MOUTH?
HEY!--
THUNK
THUNK
THUNK
THUNK
!
KLOOM
HEY FELLAHS!
I KNEW YOU LOOKED FAMILIAR.
I THINK I'VE SEEN A FEW OF YOUR COUSINS MOUNTED IN THE SMITHSONIAN!
bloody savages...

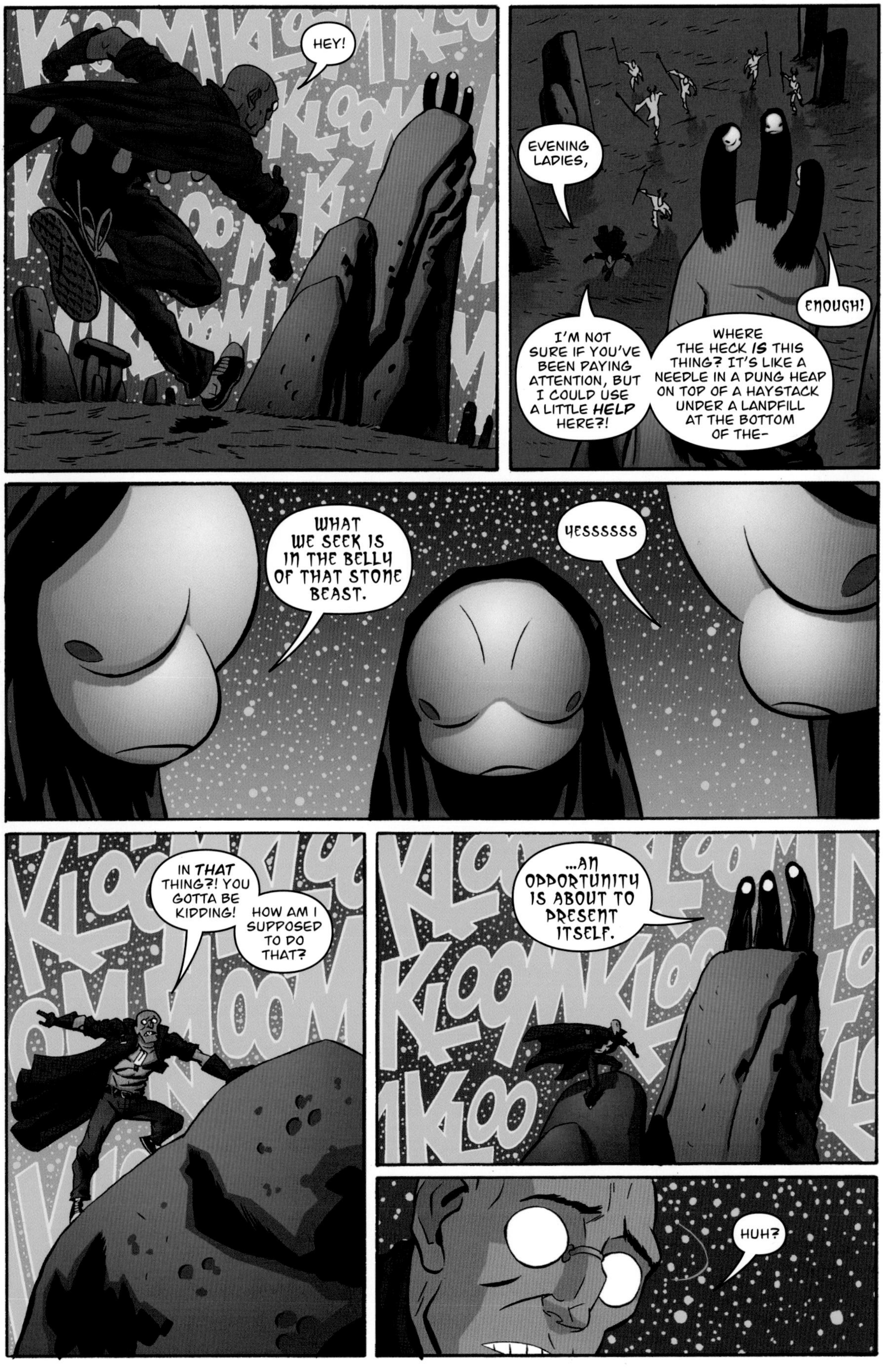
HEY!
EVENING LADIES,
I'M NOT SURE IF YOU'VE BEEN PAYING ATTENTION, BUT I COULD USE A LITTLE HELP HERE?!
WHERE THE HECK IS THIS THING? IT'S LIKE A NEEDLE IN A DUNG HEAP ON TOP OF A HAYSTACK UNDER A LANDFILL AT THE BOTTOM OF THE-
ENOUGH!
WHAT WE SEEK IS IN THE BELLY OF THAT STONE BEAST.
YESSSSSS
IN THAT THING?! YOU GOTTA BE KIDDING!
HOW AM I SUPPOSED TO DO THAT?
...AN OPPORTUNITY IS ABOUT TO PRESENT ITSELF.
HUH?

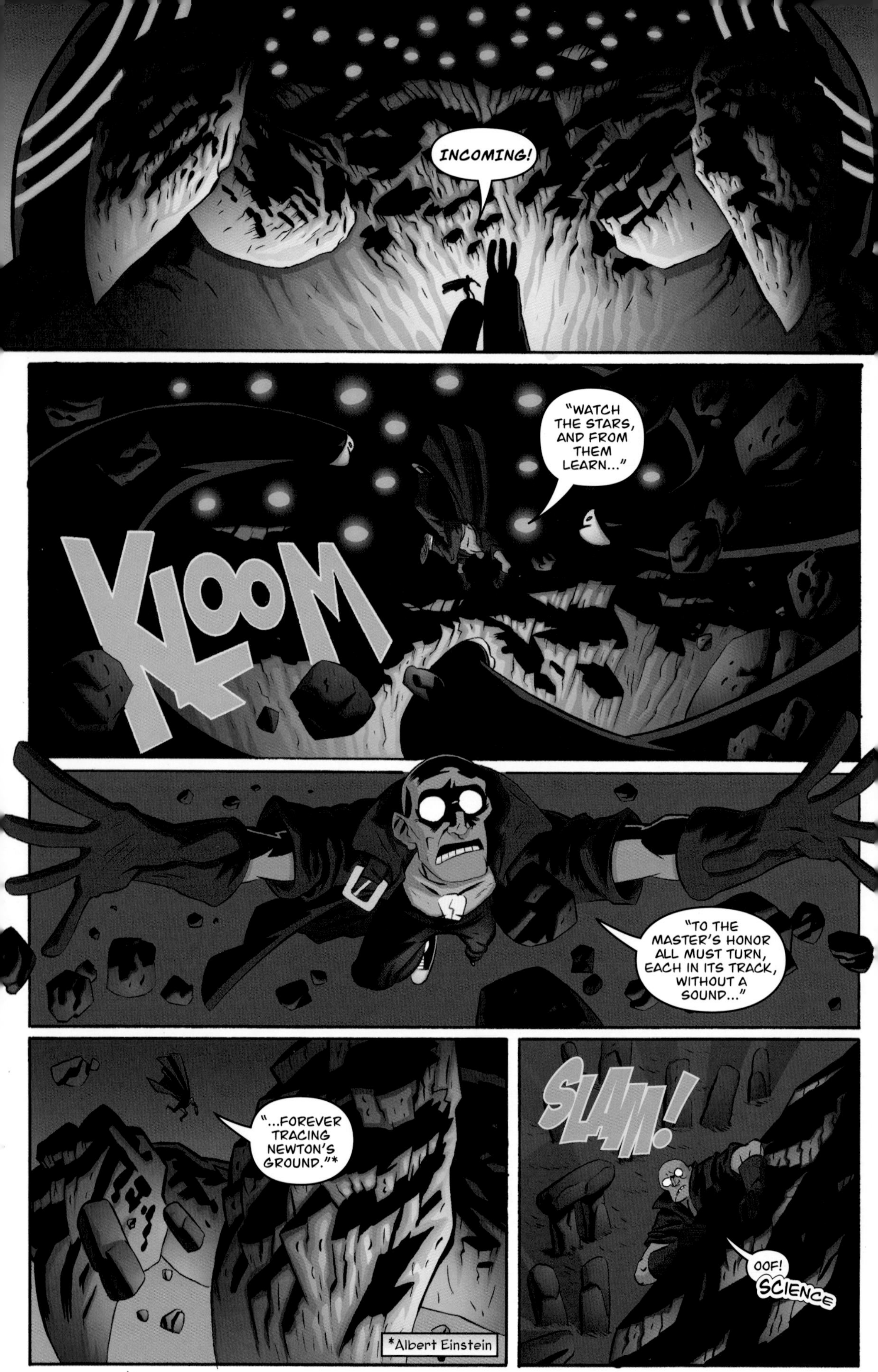
INCOMING!
KLOOM
"WATCH THE STARS, AND FROM THEM LEARN..."
"TO THE MASTER'S HONOR ALL MUST TURN, EACH IN ITS TRACK, WITHOUT A SOUND..."
"...FOREVER TRACING NEWTON'S GROUND."*
*Albert Einstein
SLAM!
OOF!
SCIENCE

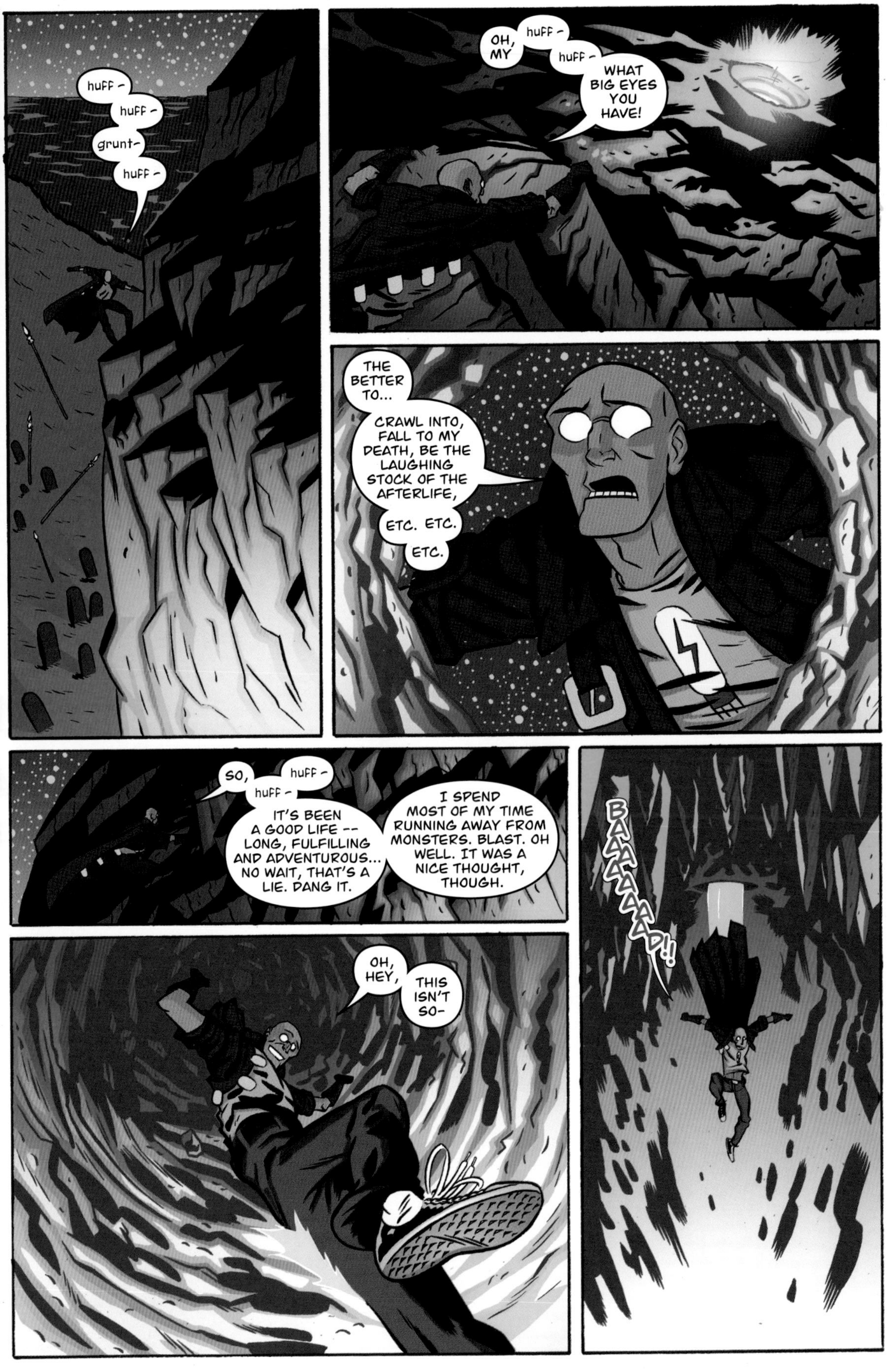
huff -
huff -
grunt-
huff -
OH, MY
huff -
huff -
WHAT BIG EYES YOU HAVE!
THE BETTER TO...
CRAWL INTO, FALL TO MY DEATH, BE THE LAUGHING STOCK OF THE AFTERLIFE,
ETC. ETC.
ETC.
SO,
huff -
huff -
IT'S BEEN A GOOD LIFE -- LONG, FULFILLING AND ADVENTUROUS... NO WAIT, THAT'S A LIE. DANG IT.
I SPEND MOST OF MY TIME RUNNING AWAY FROM MONSTERS. BLAST. OH WELL. IT WAS A NICE THOUGHT, THOUGH.
BAAAAAAAD!!
OH, HEY,
THIS ISN'T SO-

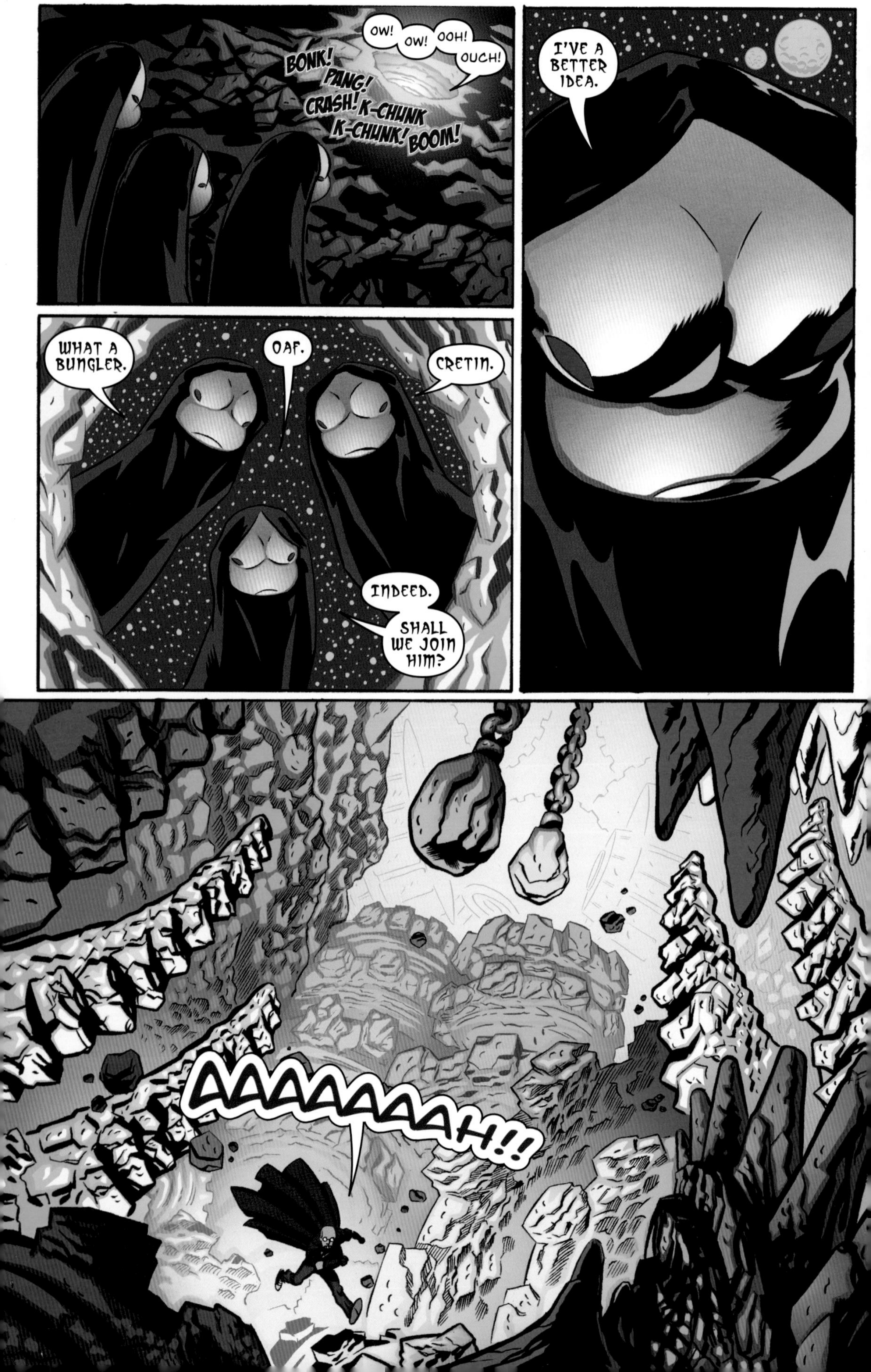
BONK! PANG! CRASH! K-CHUNK K-CHUNK! BOOM!
OW! OW! OOH! OUCH!
I'VE A BETTER IDEA.
WHAT A BUNGLER.
OAF.
CRETIN.
INDEED.
SHALL WE JOIN HIM?
AAAAAAAAH!!

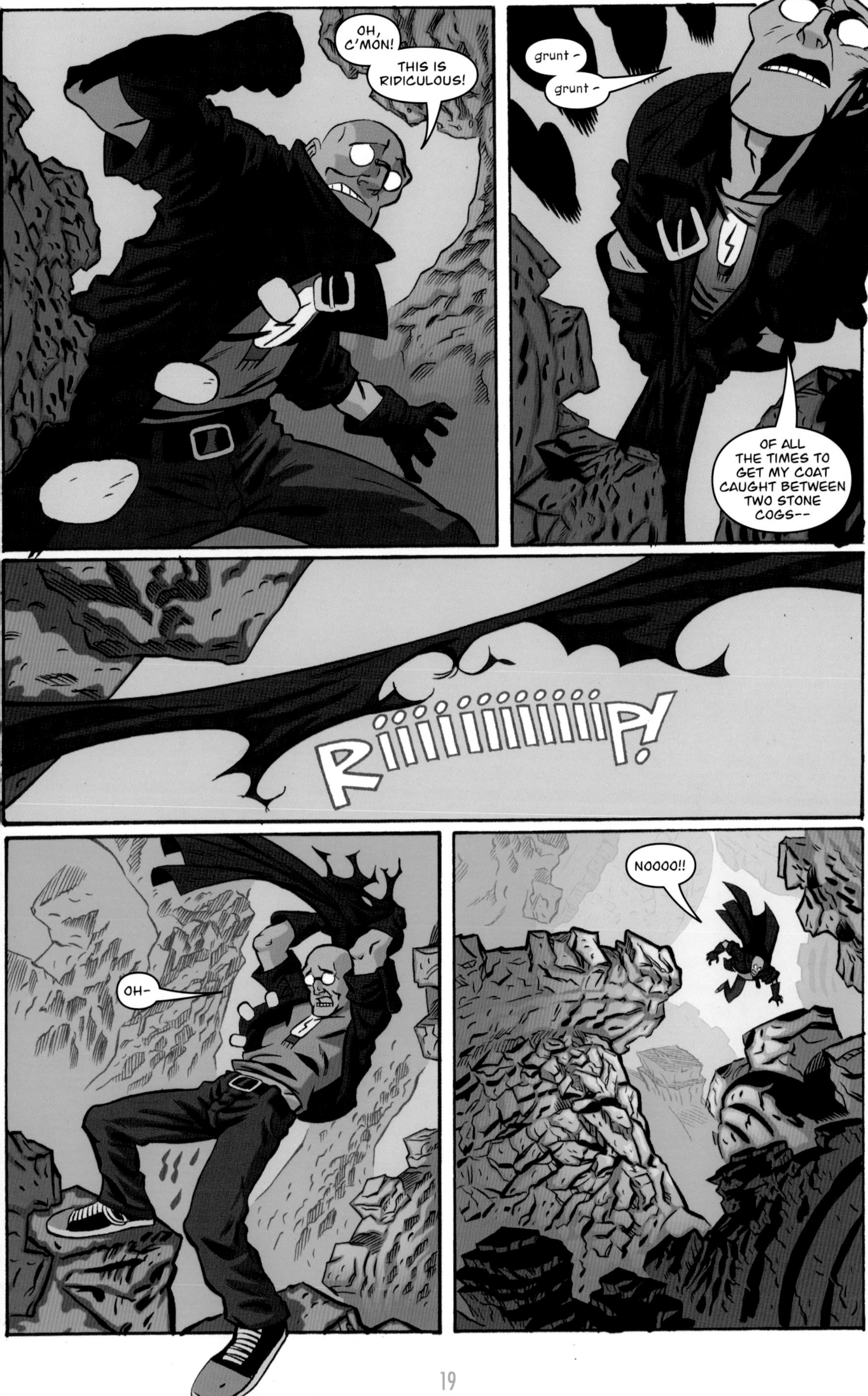
OH, C'MON!
THIS IS RIDICULOUS!
grunt -
grunt -
OF ALL THE TIMES TO GET MY COAT CAUGHT BETWEEN TWO STONE COGS--
RiiiiiiiiiiiP!
OH-
NOOOO!!

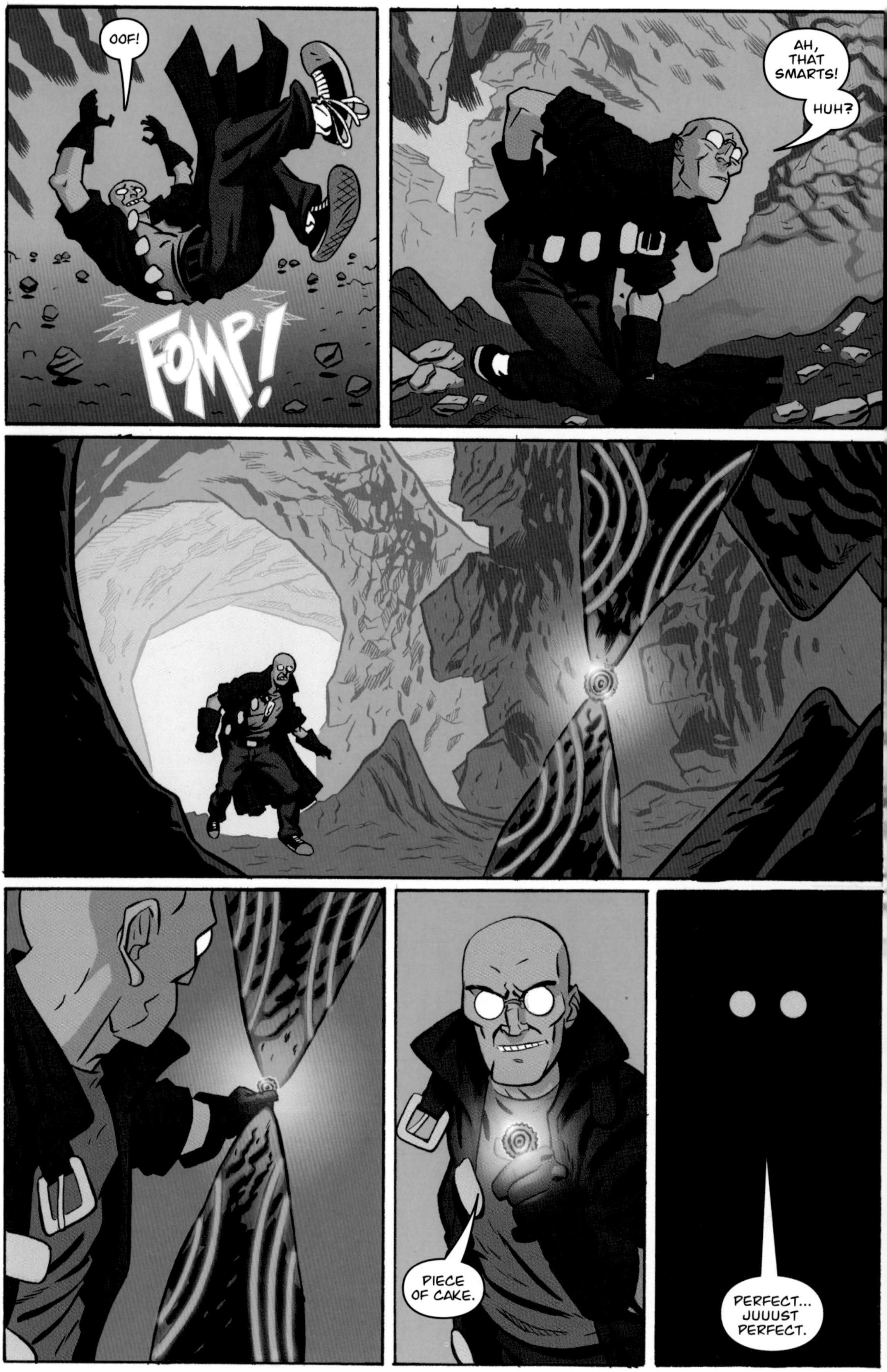
OOF!
FOMP!
AH, THAT SMARTS!
HUH?
PIECE OF CAKE.
PERFECT... JUUUST PERFECT.

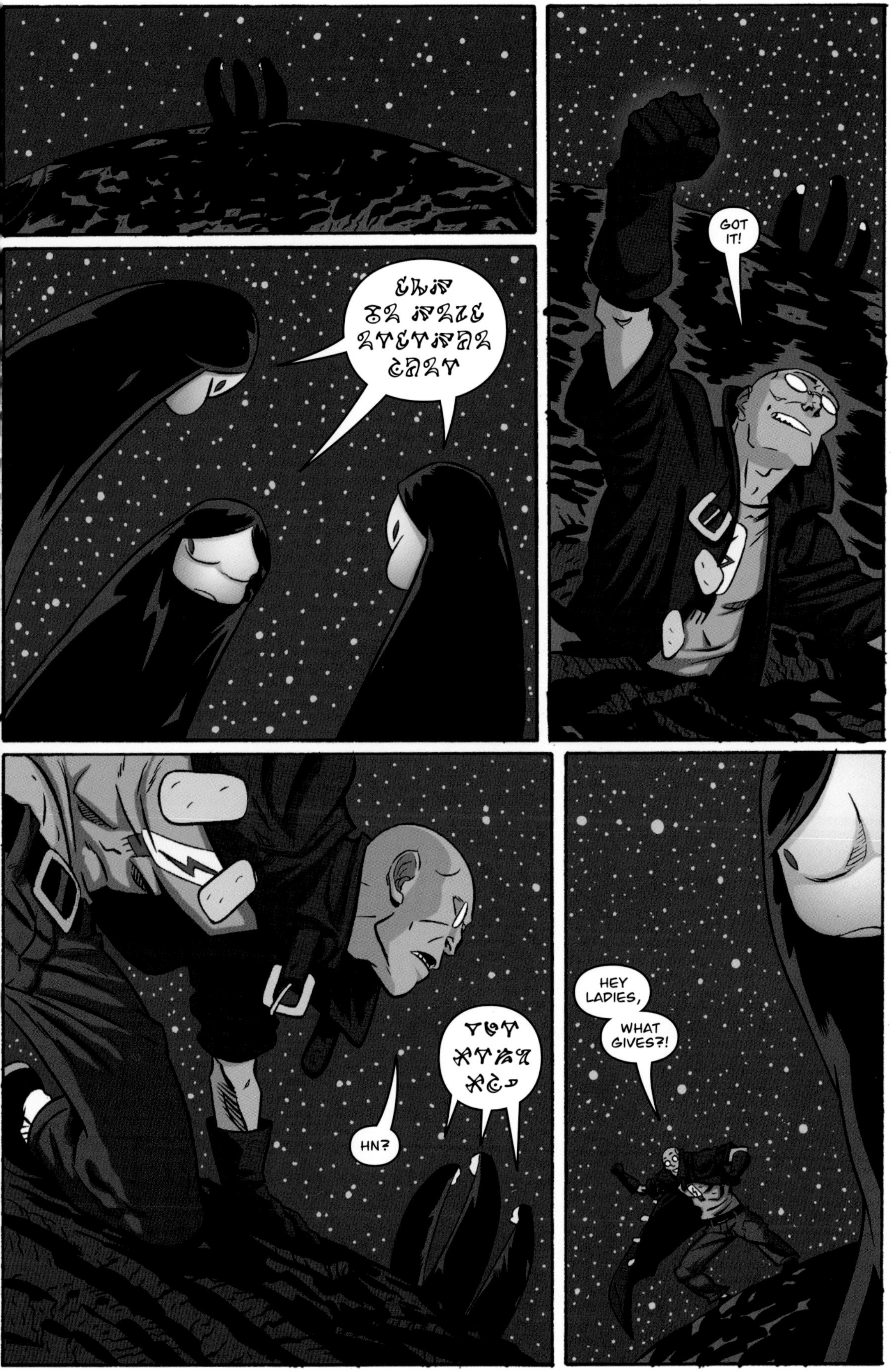
GOT IT!
HN?
HEY LADIES,
WHAT GIVES?!

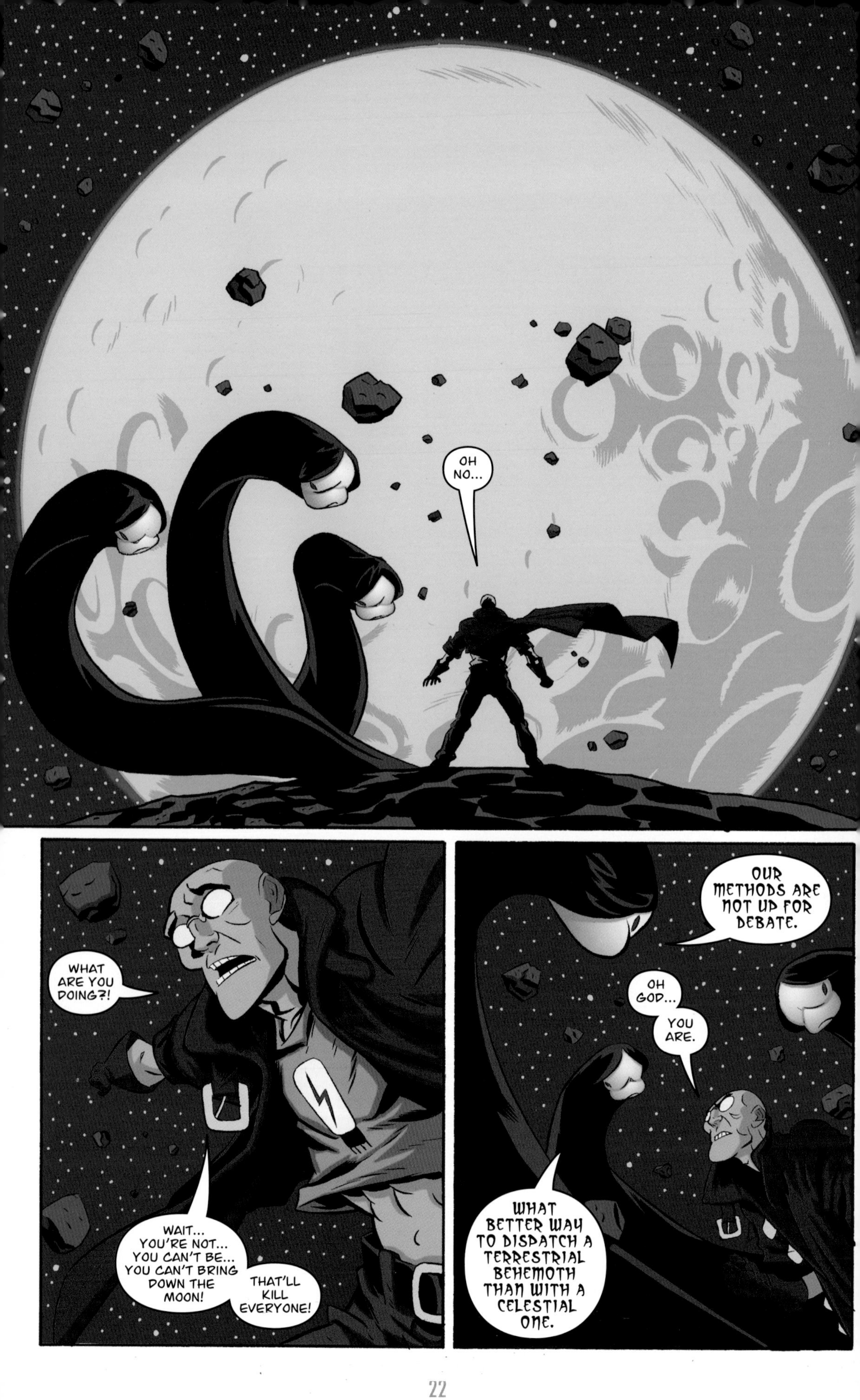
OH NO...
WHAT ARE YOU DOING?!
WAIT... YOU'RE NOT... YOU CAN'T BE... YOU CAN'T BRING DOWN THE MOON!
THAT'LL KILL EVERYONE!
OUR METHODS ARE NOT UP FOR DEBATE.
OH GOD...
YOU ARE.
WHAT BETTER WAY TO DISPATCH A TERRESTRIAL BEHEMOTH THAN WITH A CELESTIAL ONE.

PLOCK

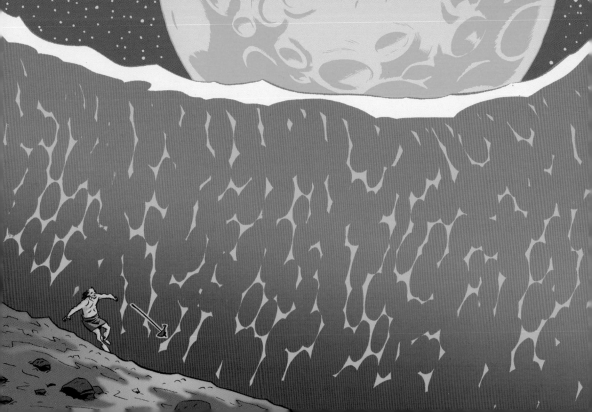

NO! PLEASE!

I GOT WHAT WE CAME FOR!

THIS IS INSANE! YOU HAVE TO STOP!

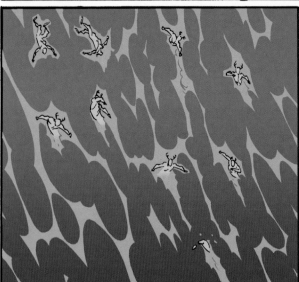

WAAAAA

YOU...YOU... MONSTERS!!!

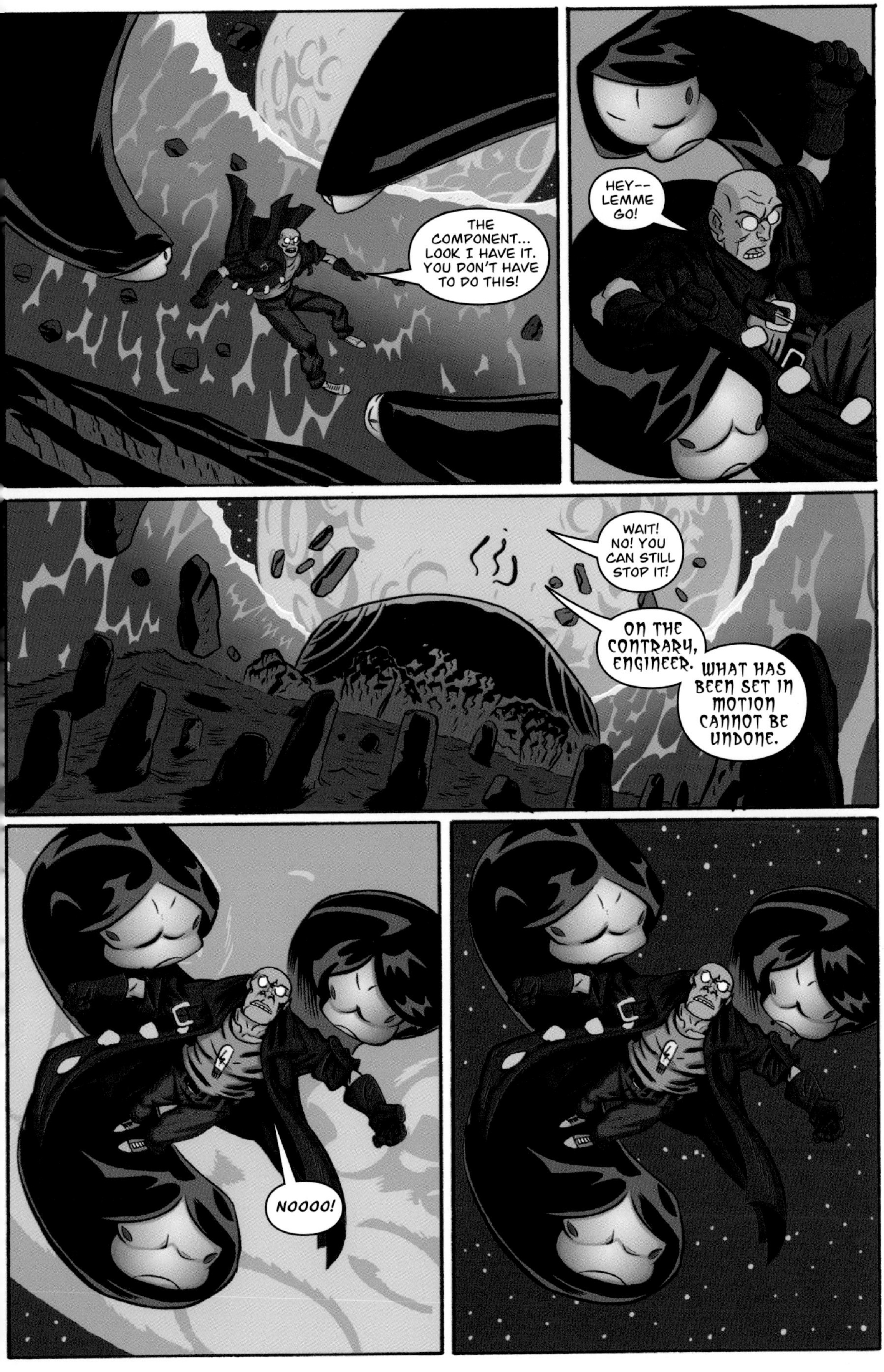
THE COMPONENT... LOOK I HAVE IT. YOU DON'T HAVE TO DO THIS!
HEY-- LEMME GO!
WAIT! NO! YOU CAN STILL STOP IT!
ON THE CONTRARY, ENGINEER.
WHAT HAS BEEN SET IN MOTION CANNOT BE UNDONE.
NOOOO!

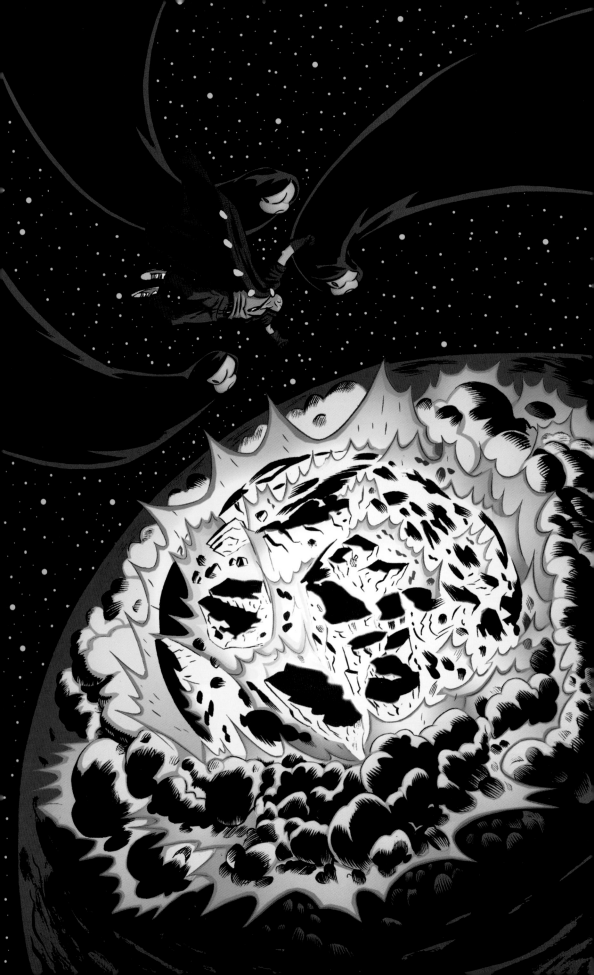

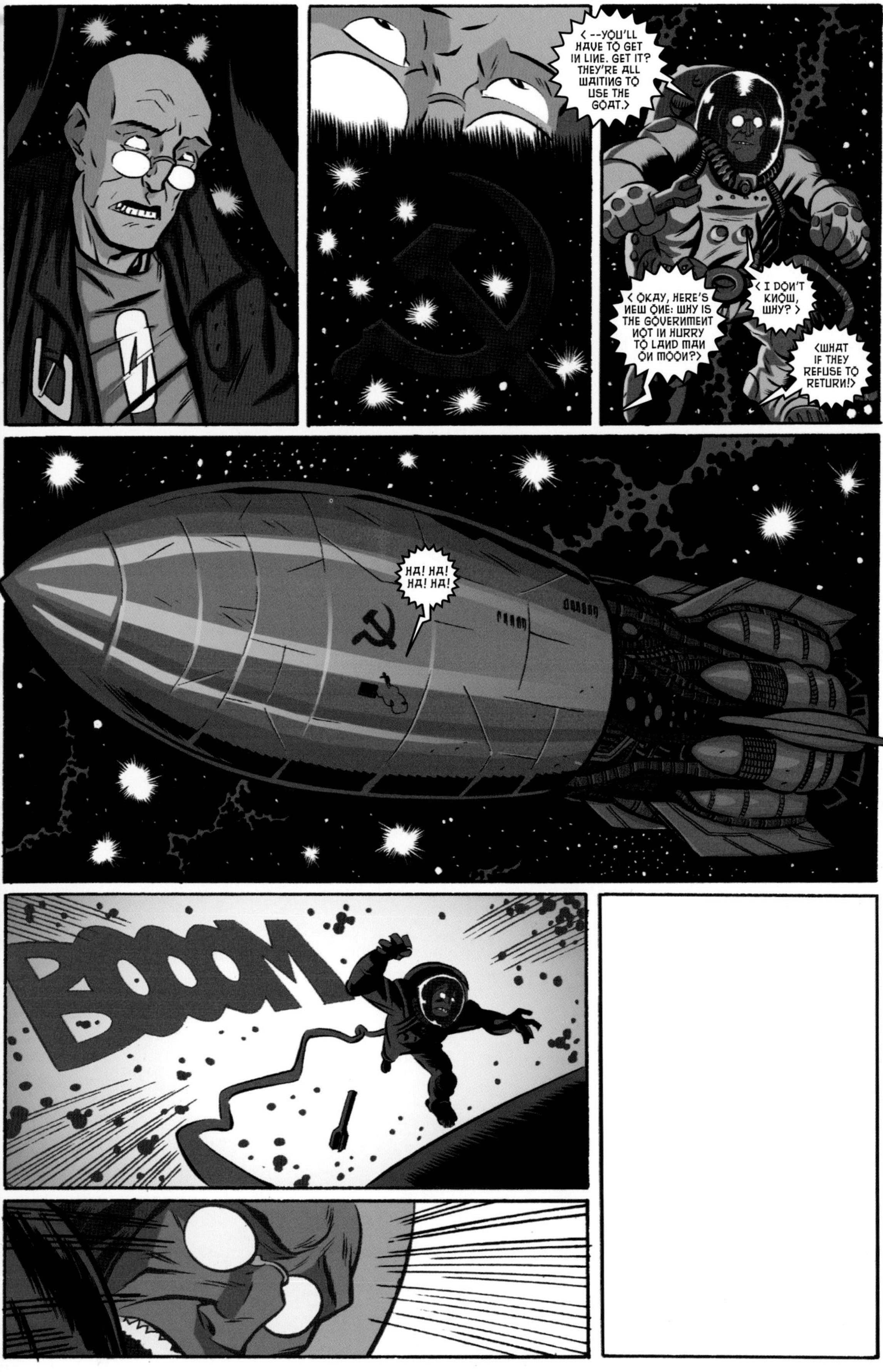
< --YOU'LL HAVE TO GET IN LINE. GET IT? THEY'RE ALL WAITING TO USE THE GOAT.>
< OKAY, HERE'S NEW ONE: WHY IS THE GOVERMENT NOT IN HURRY TO LAND MAN ON MOON?>
< I DON'T KNOW, WHY? >
<WHAT IF THEY REFUSE TO RETURN!>
HA! HA! HA! HA!
BOOOM

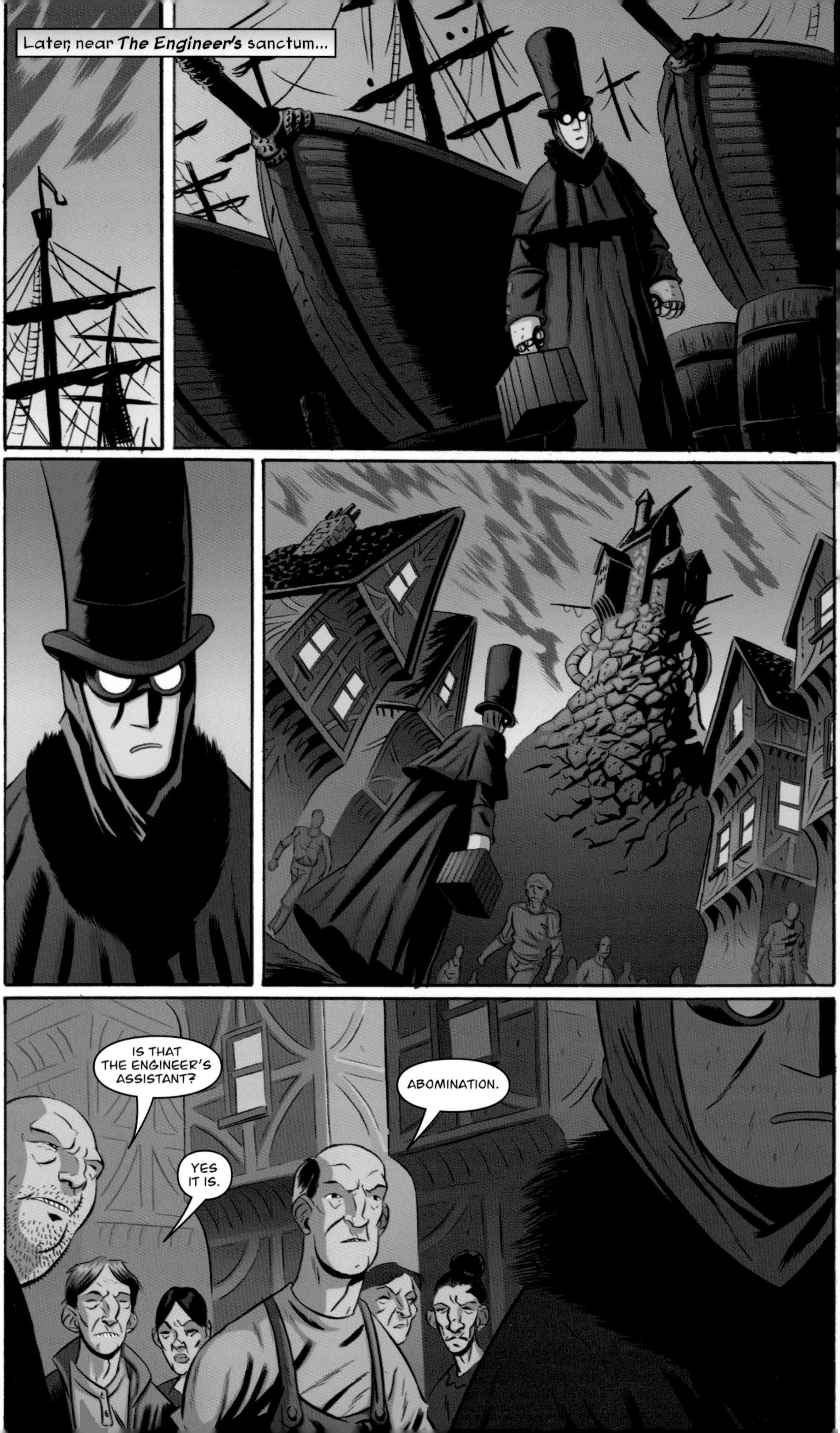
Later, near The Engineer's sanctum...
IS THAT THE ENGINEER'S ASSISTANT?
YES IT IS.
ABOMINATION.

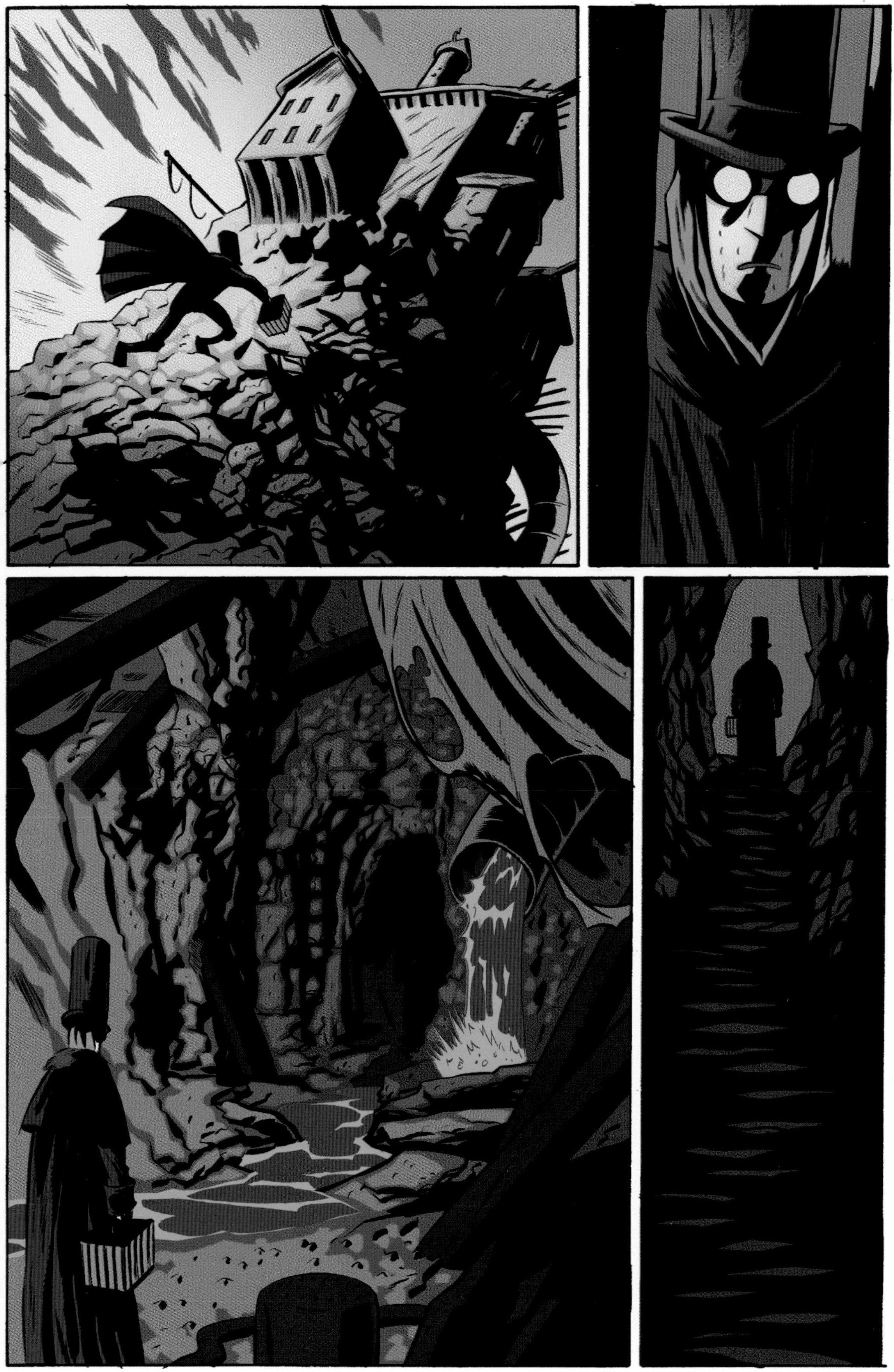

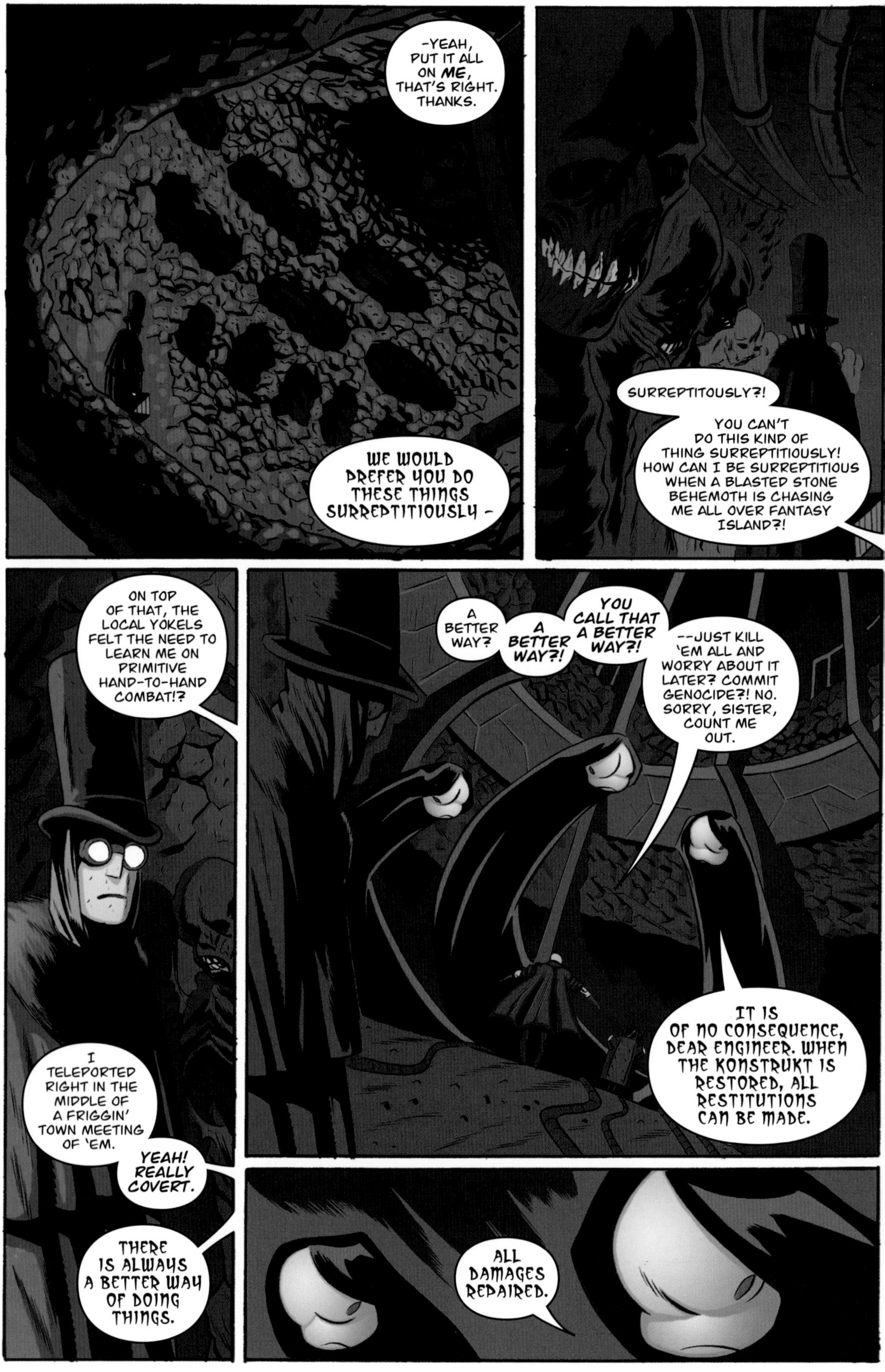
-YEAH, PUT IT ALL ON ME, THAT'S RIGHT. THANKS.
WE WOULD PREFER YOU DO THESE THINGS SURREPTITIOUSLY -
SURREPTITOUSLY?!
YOU CAN'T DO THIS KIND OF THING SURREPTITIOUSLY! HOW CAN I BE SURREPTITIOUS WHEN A BLASTED STONE BEHEMOTH IS CHASING ME ALL OVER FANTASY ISLAND?!
ON TOP OF THAT, THE LOCAL YOKELS FELT THE NEED TO LEARN ME ON PRIMITIVE HAND-TO-HAND COMBAT!?
I TELEPORTED RIGHT IN THE MIDDLE OF A FRIGGIN' TOWN MEETING OF 'EM.
YEAH! REALLY COVERT.
THERE IS ALWAYS A BETTER WAY OF DOING THINGS.
A BETTER WAY?
A BETTER WAY?!
YOU CALL THAT A BETTER WAY?!
--JUST KILL 'EM ALL AND WORRY ABOUT IT LATER? COMMIT GENOCIDE?! NO. SORRY, SISTER, COUNT ME OUT.
IT IS OF NO CONSEQUENCE, DEAR ENGINEER. WHEN THE KONSTRUKT IS RESTORED, ALL RESTITUTIONS CAN BE MADE.
ALL DAMAGES REPAIRED.

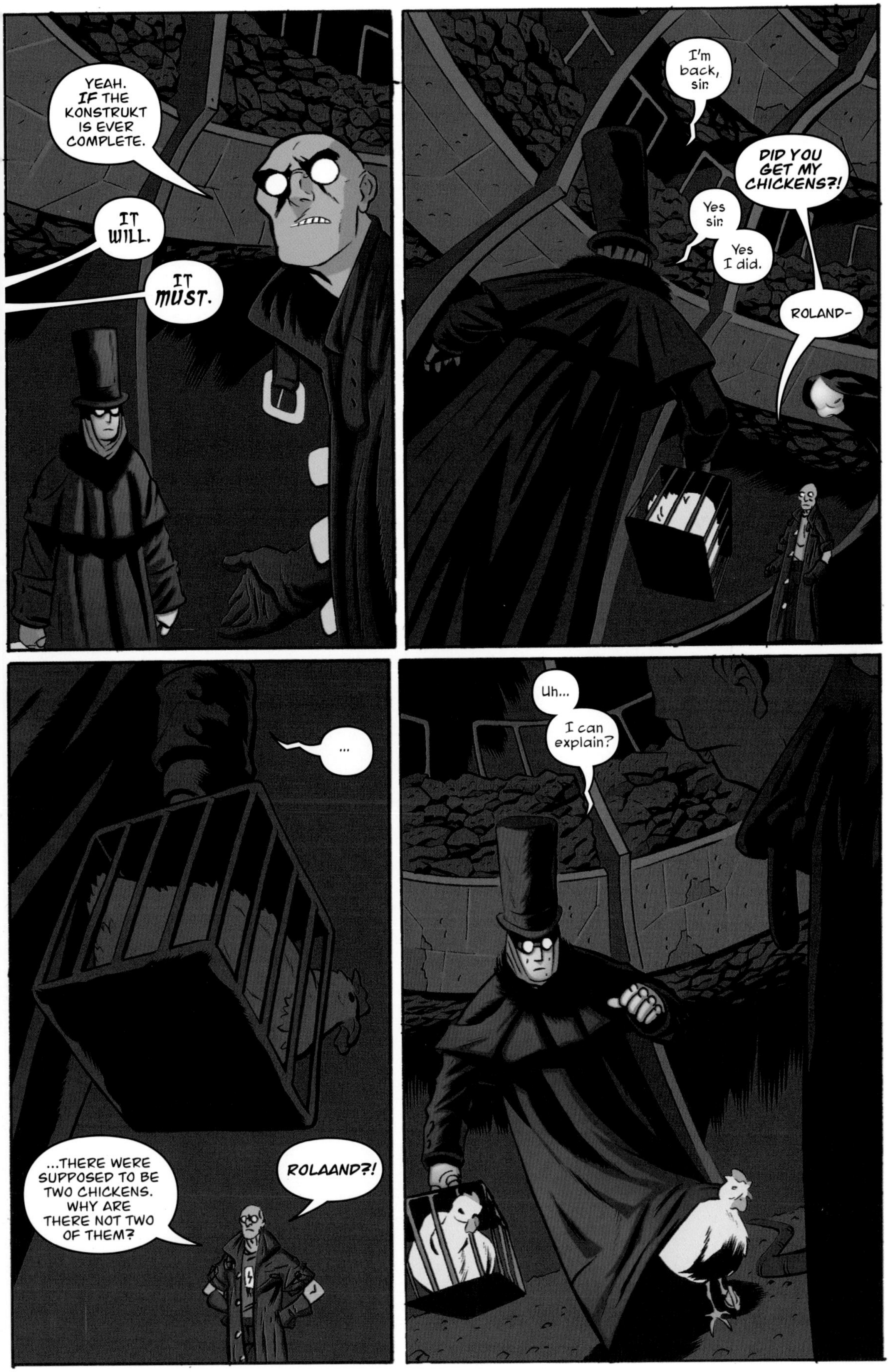
YEAH. IF THE KONSTRUKT IS EVER COMPLETE.
IT WILL.
IT MUST.
I'm back, sir.
DID YOU GET MY CHICKENS?!
Yes sir.
Yes I did.
ROLAND-
...
...THERE WERE SUPPOSED TO BE TWO CHICKENS. WHY ARE THERE NOT TWO OF THEM?
ROLAAND?!
Uh...
I can explain?

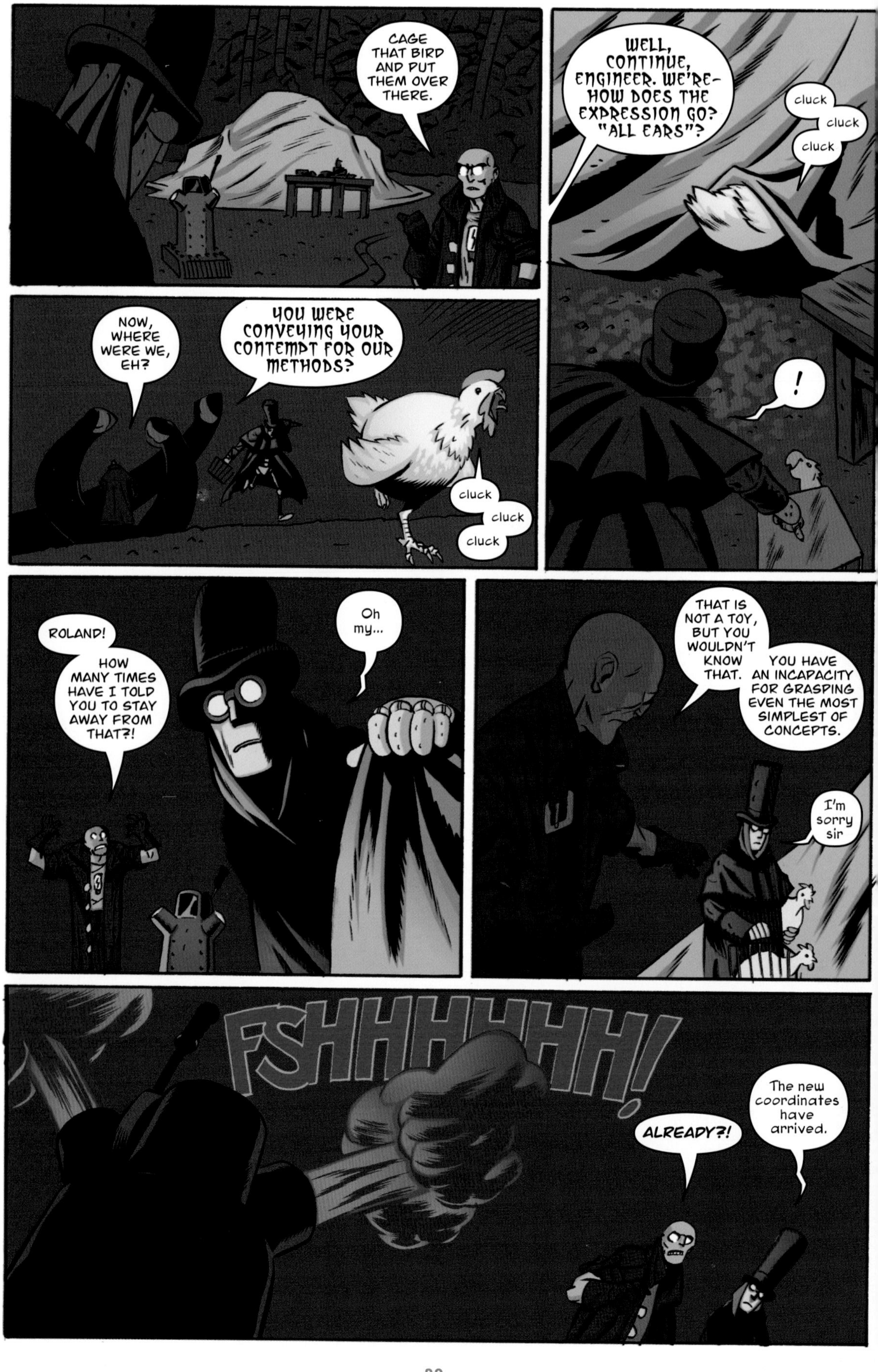
CAGE THAT BIRD AND PUT THEM OVER THERE.
WELL, CONTINUE, ENGINEER. WE'RE- HOW DOES THE EXPRESSION GO? "ALL EARS"?
cluck
cluck
cluck
NOW, WHERE WERE WE, EH?
YOU WERE CONVEYING YOUR CONTEMPT FOR OUR METHODS?
cluck
cluck
cluck
!
ROLAND!
HOW MANY TIMES HAVE I TOLD YOU TO STAY AWAY FROM THAT?!
Oh my...
THAT IS NOT A TOY, BUT YOU WOULDN'T KNOW THAT.
YOU HAVE AN INCAPACITY FOR GRASPING EVEN THE MOST SIMPLEST OF CONCEPTS.
I'm sorry sir
FSHHHHHH!
ALREADY?!
The new coordinates have arrived.

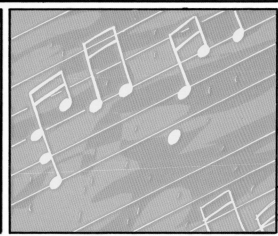

:POK:

I GUESS WE SHOULD GET STARTED.

AGREED.

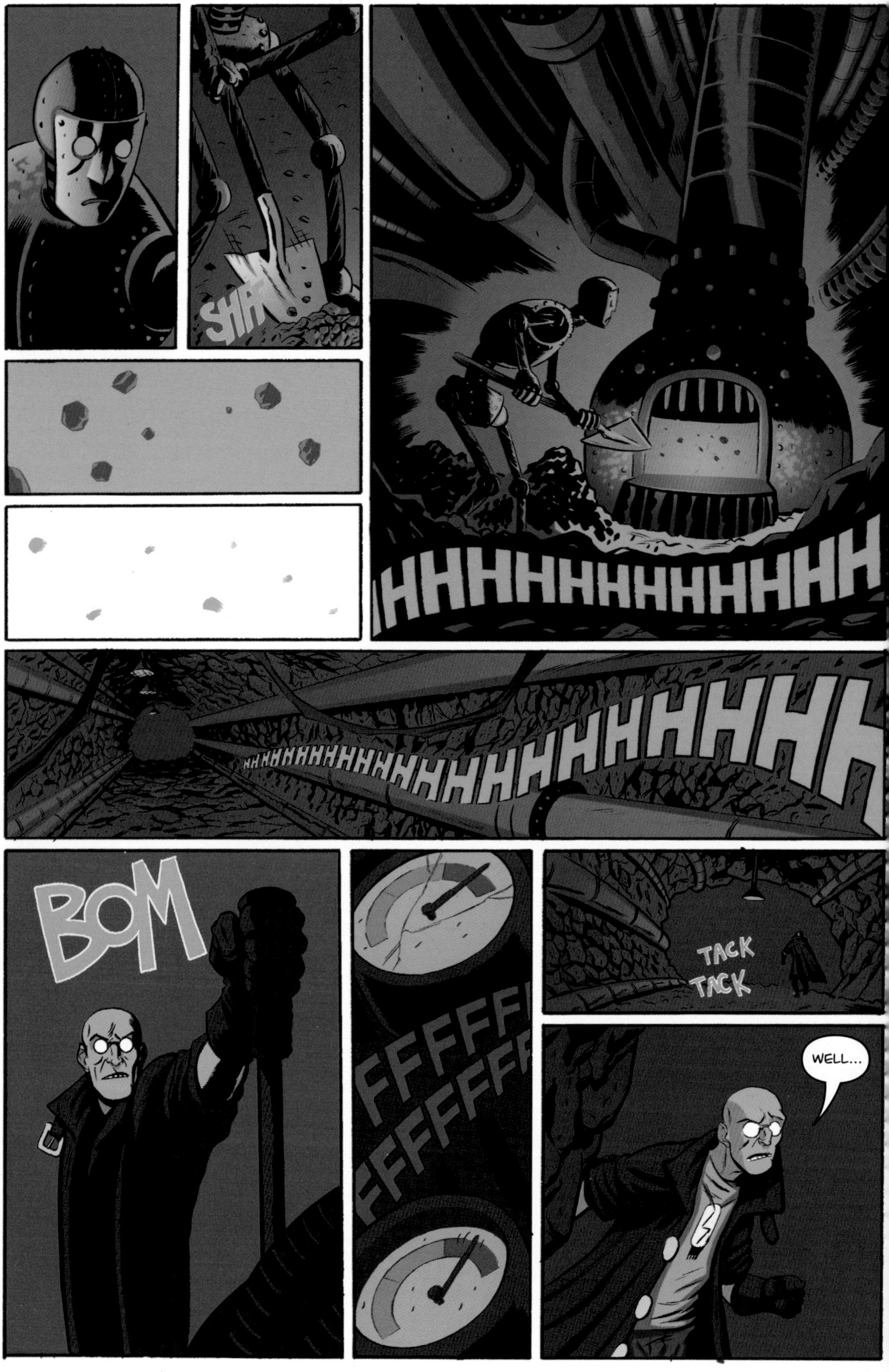
SHA
HHHHHHHHHHHHHHH
HHHHHHHHHHHHHHHHHHHHHHHHHHH
BOM
FFFFF
FFFFFF
TACK
TACK
WELL...

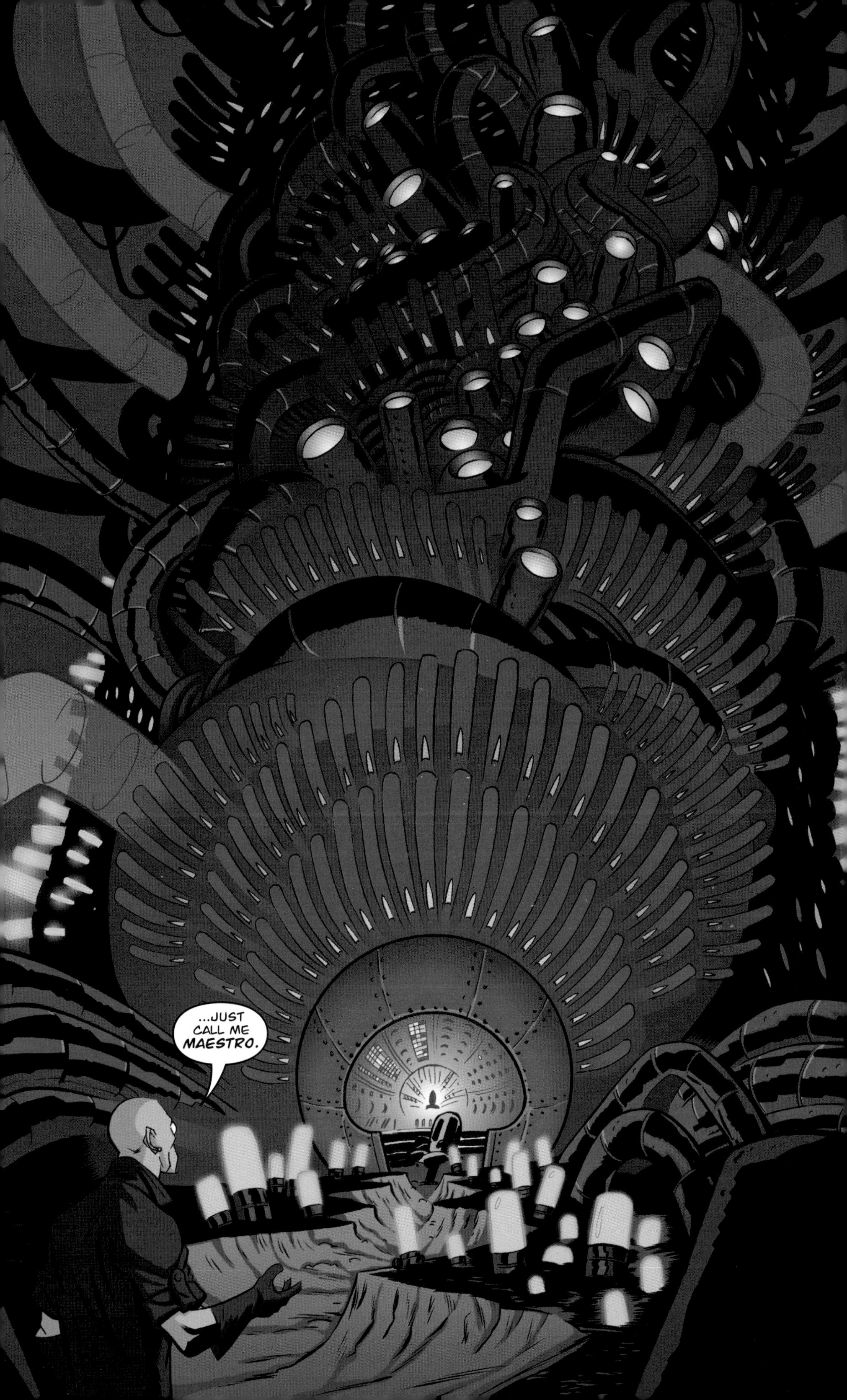
...JUST CALL ME MAESTRO.

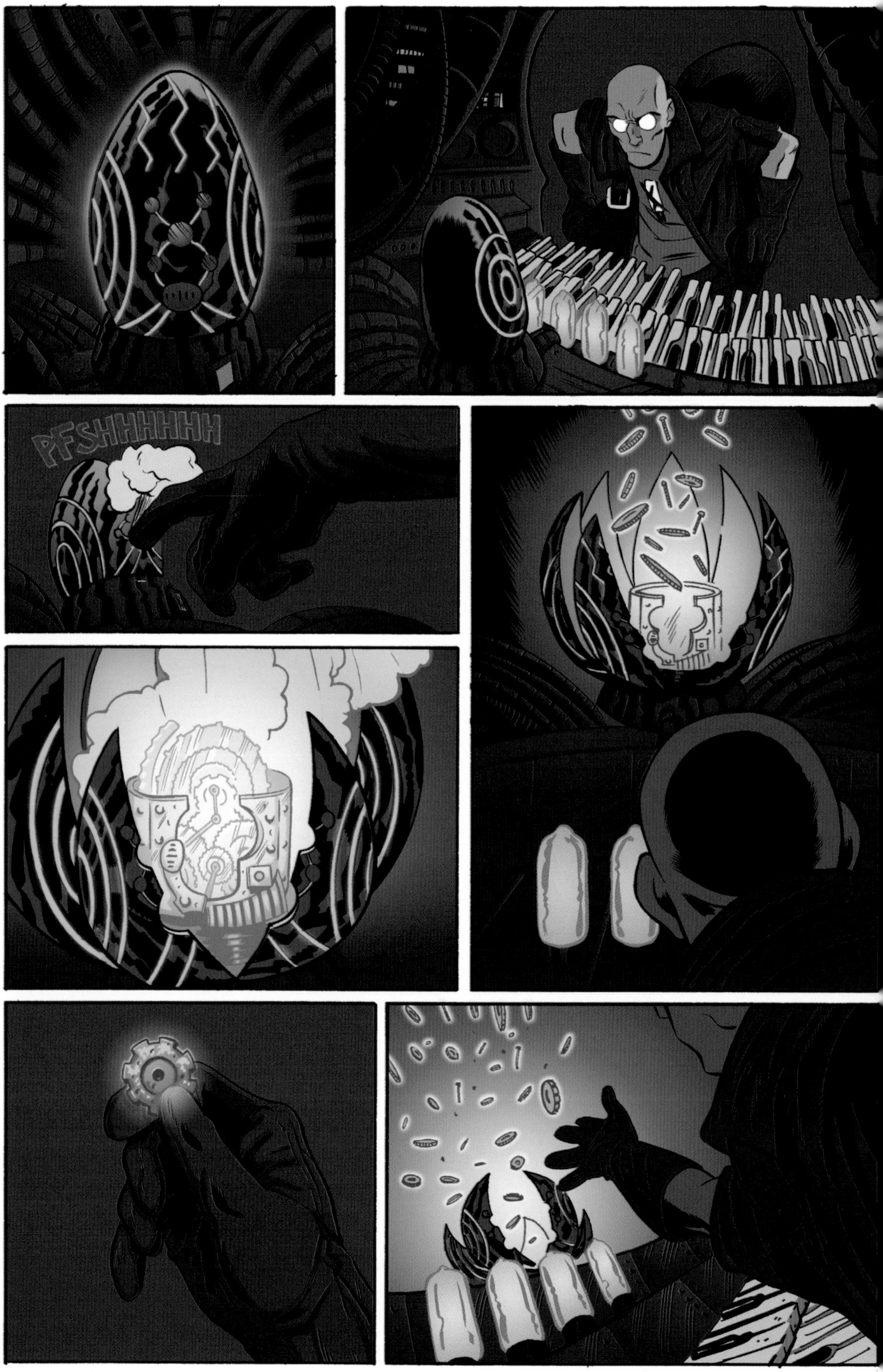
PFSHHHHHH

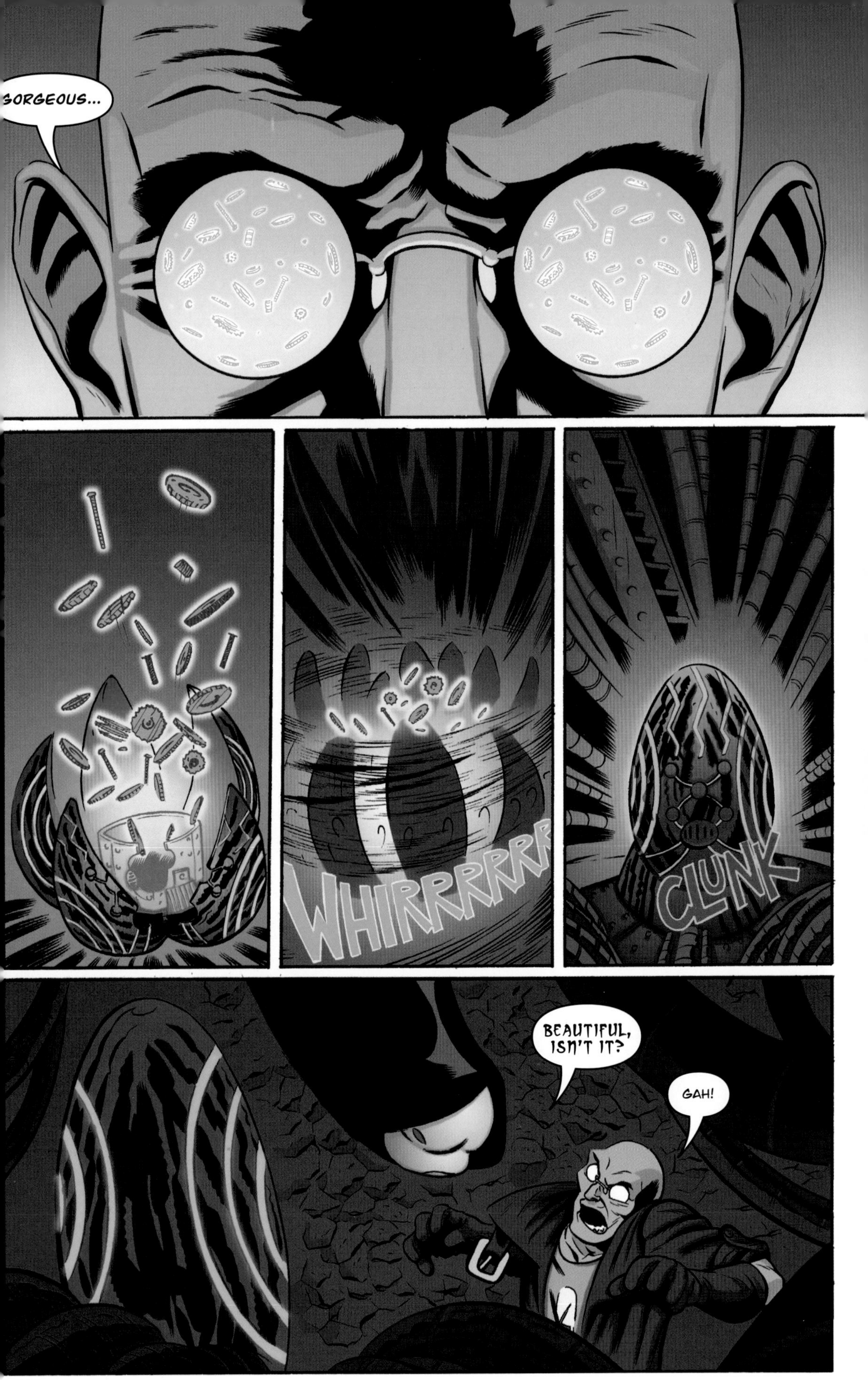
GORGEOUS...
WHIRRRRRR
CLUNK
BEAUTIFUL, ISN'T IT?
GAH!

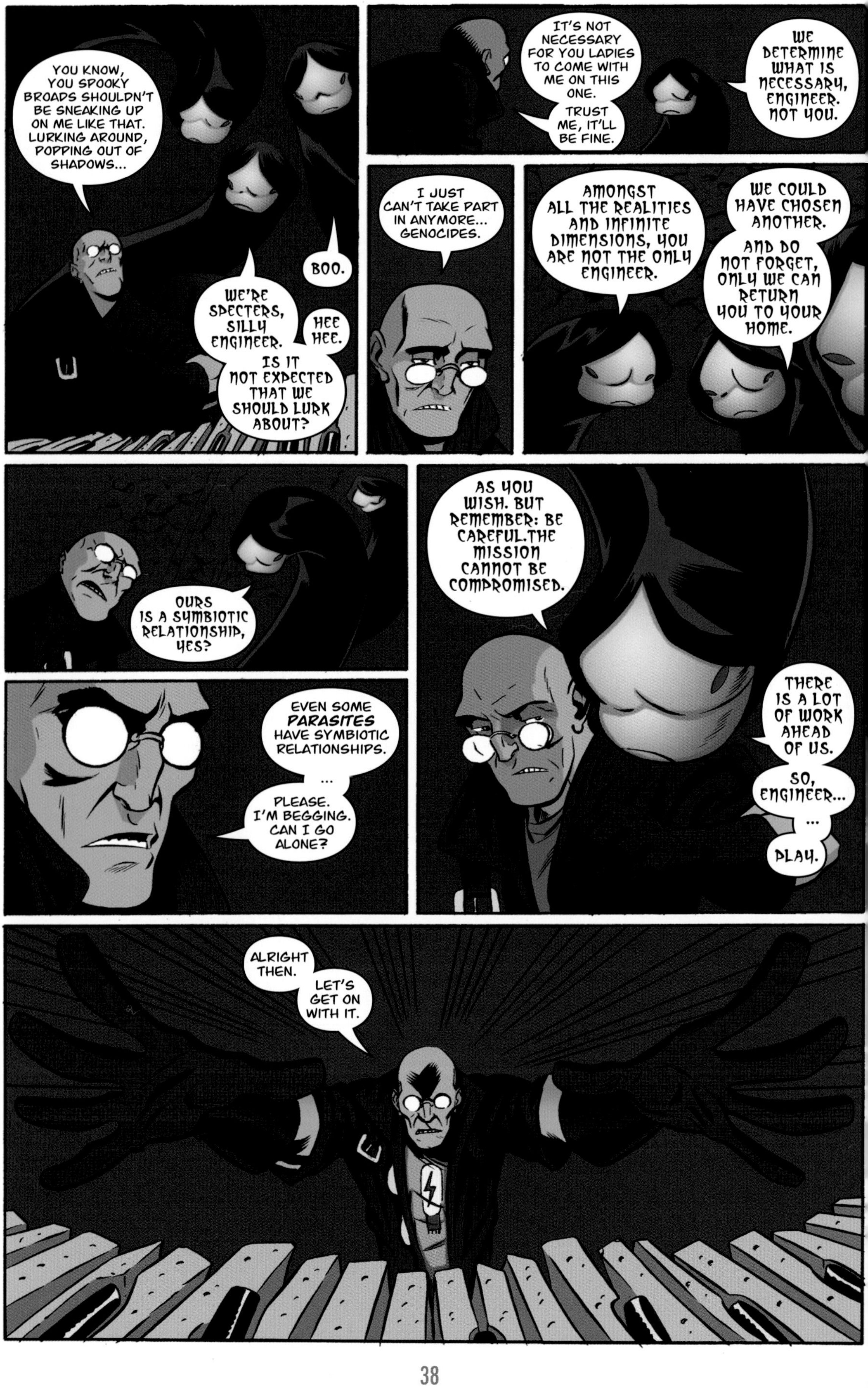
YOU KNOW, YOU SPOOKY BROADS SHOULDN'T BE SNEAKING UP ON ME LIKE THAT. LURKING AROUND, POPPING OUT OF SHADOWS...
BOO.
WE'RE SPECTERS, SILLY ENGINEER.
HEE HEE.
IS IT NOT EXPECTED THAT WE SHOULD LURK ABOUT?
IT'S NOT NECESSARY FOR YOU LADIES TO COME WITH ME ON THIS ONE.
TRUST ME, IT'LL BE FINE.
WE DETERMINE WHAT IS NECESSARY, ENGINEER. NOT YOU.
I JUST CAN'T TAKE PART IN ANYMORE... GENOCIDES.
AMONGST ALL THE REALITIES AND INFINITE DIMENSIONS, YOU ARE NOT THE ONLY ENGINEER.
WE COULD HAVE CHOSEN ANOTHER.
AND DO NOT FORGET, ONLY WE CAN RETURN YOU TO YOUR HOME.
OURS IS A SYMBIOTIC RELATIONSHIP, YES?
EVEN SOME PARASITES HAVE SYMBIOTIC RELATIONSHIPS.
...
PLEASE. I'M BEGGING. CAN I GO ALONE?
AS YOU WISH. BUT REMEMBER: BE CAREFUL.THE MISSION CANNOT BE COMPROMISED.
THERE IS A LOT OF WORK AHEAD OF US.
SO, ENGINEER...
...
PLAY.
ALRIGHT THEN.
LET'S GET ON WITH IT.

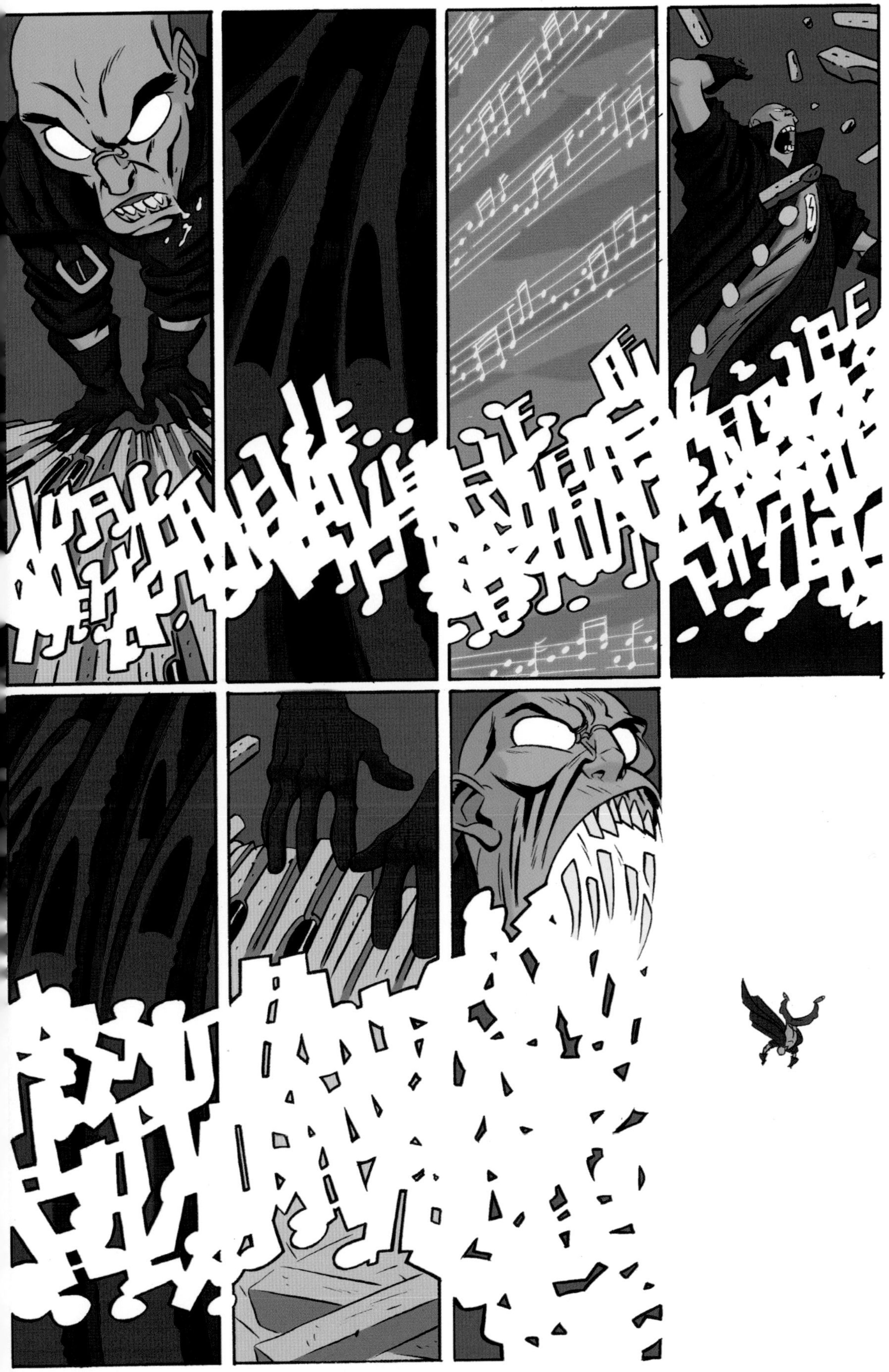

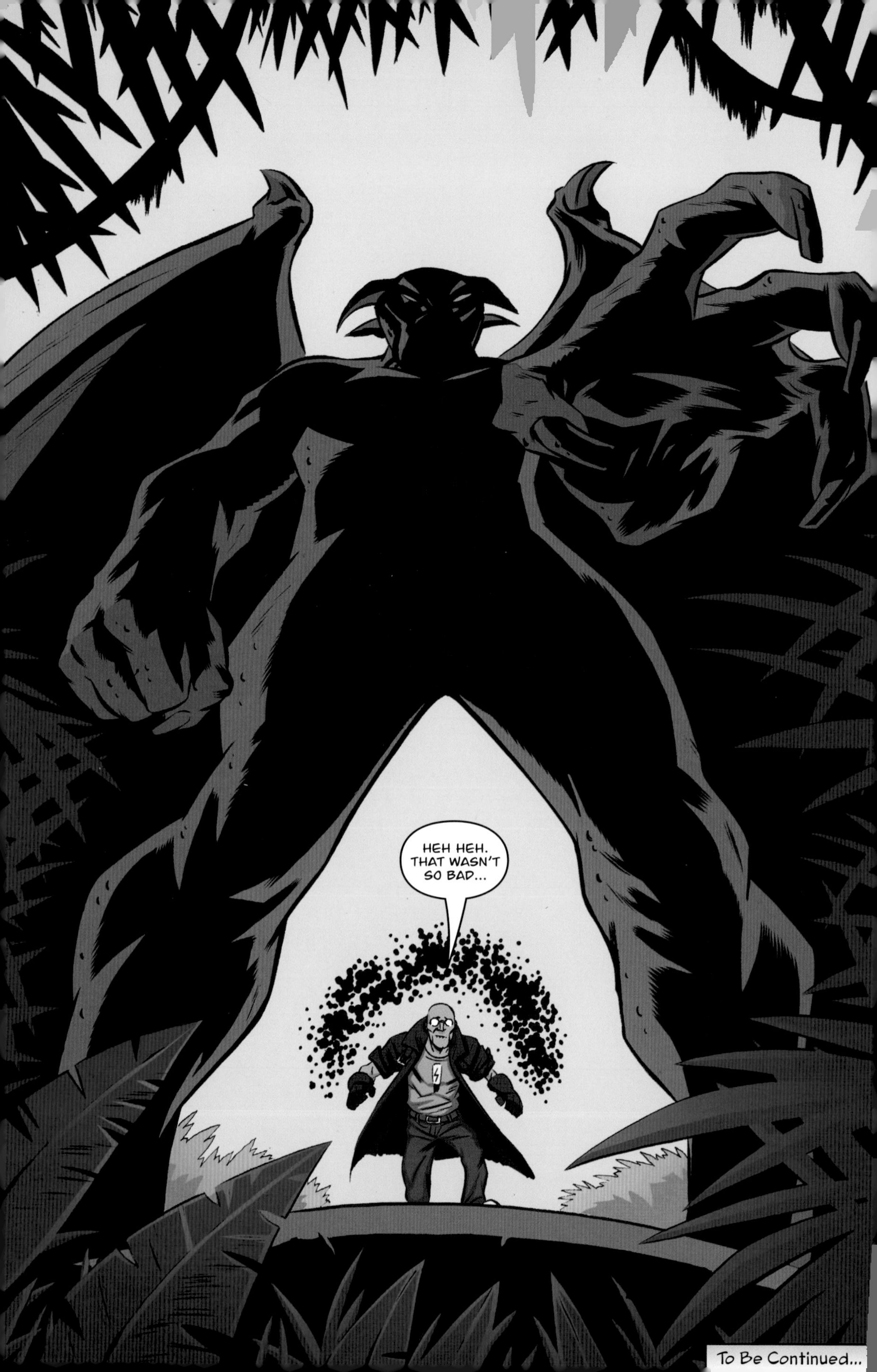
HEH HEH. THAT WASN'T SO BAD...
To Be Continued...

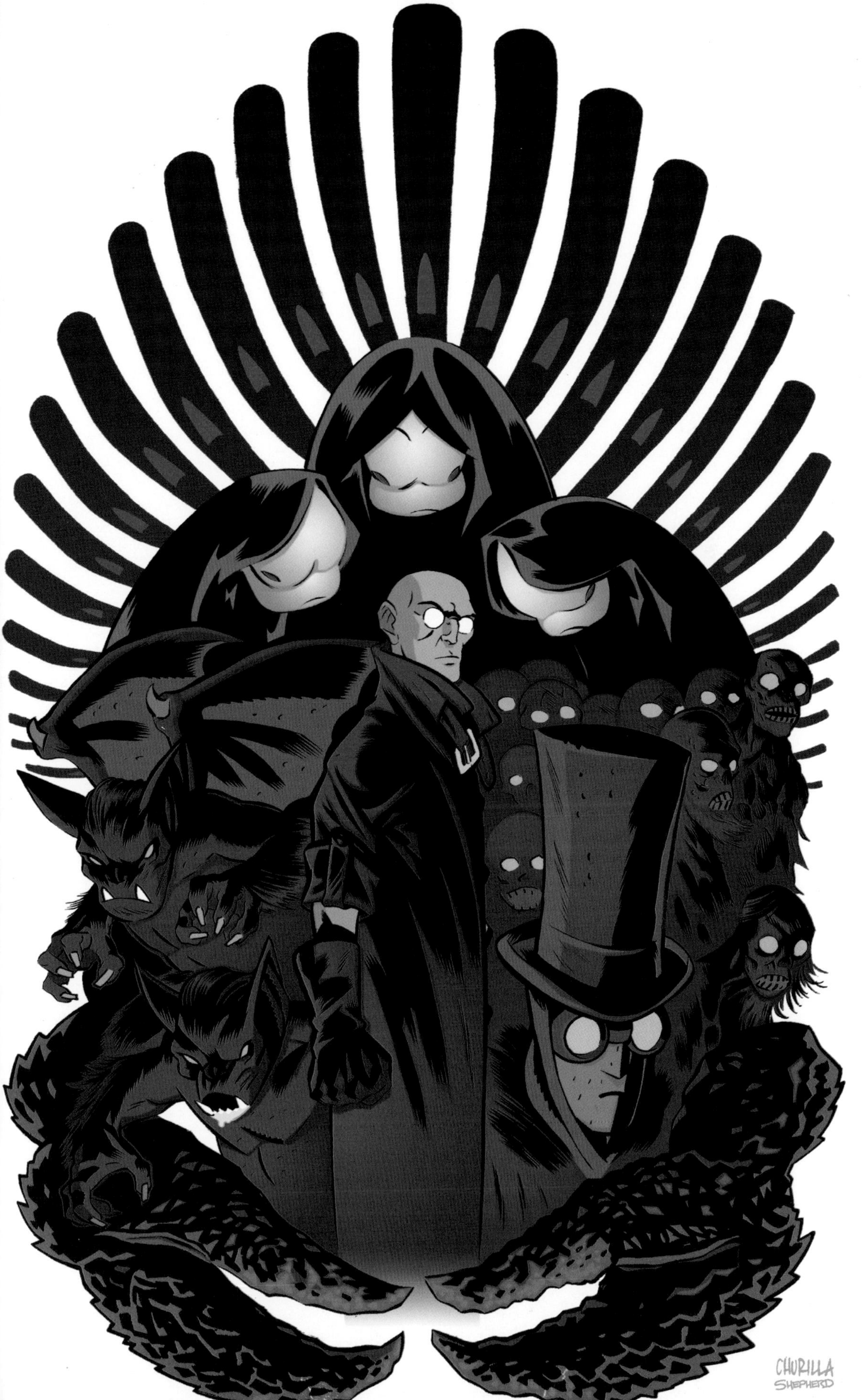
CHURILLA
SHEPHERD

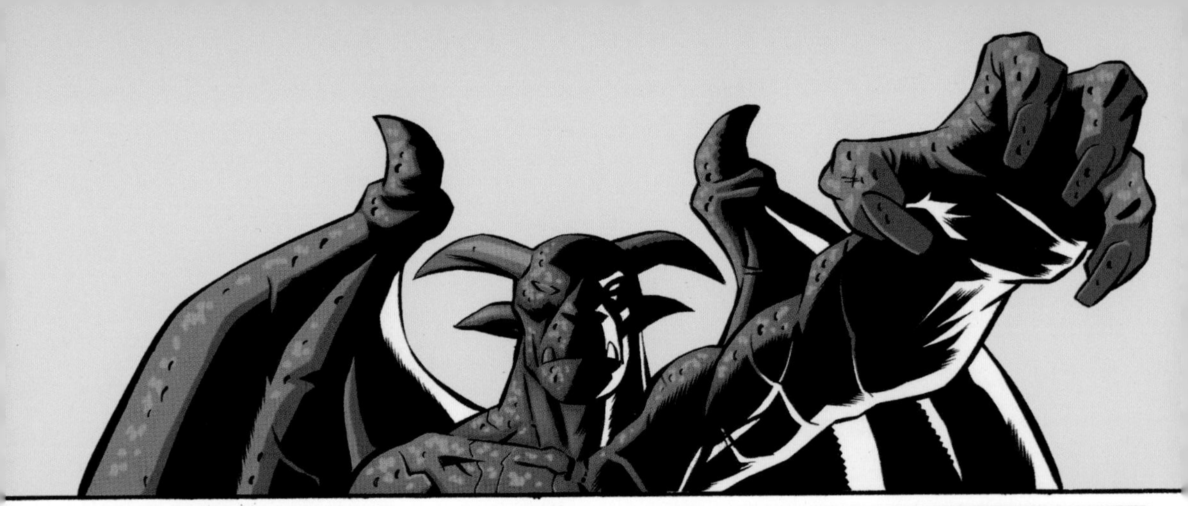

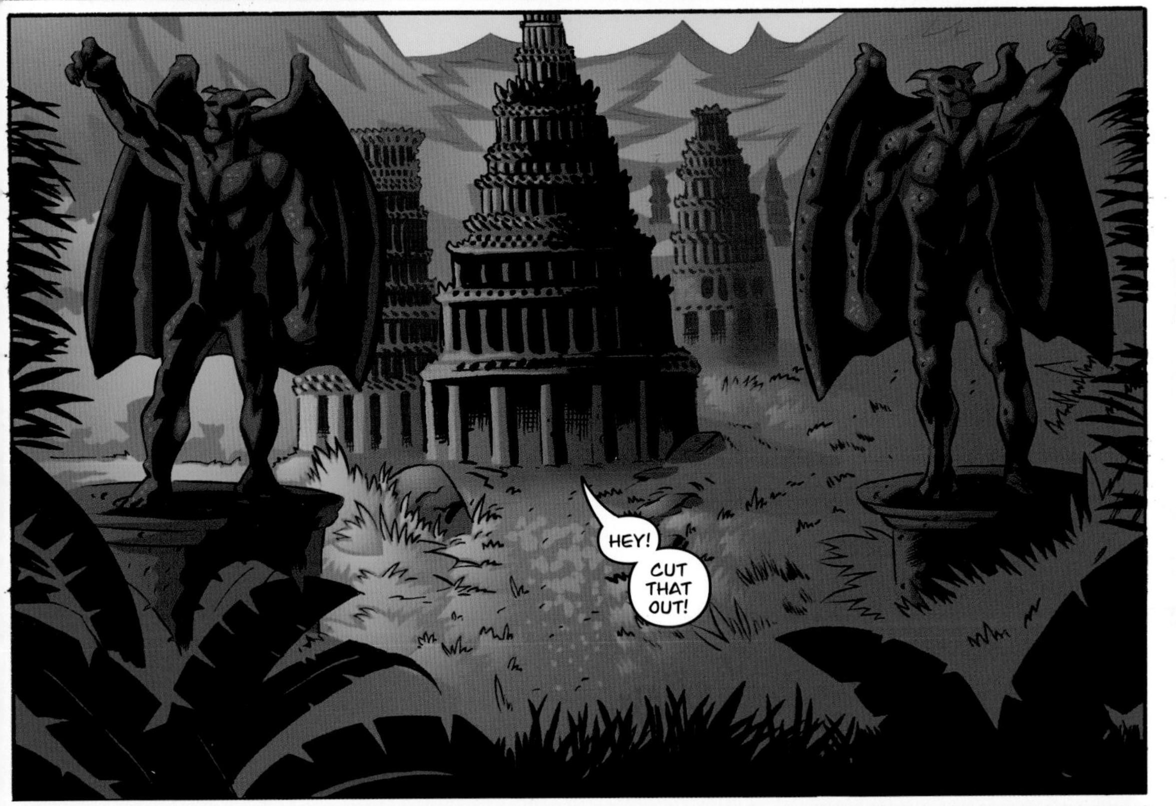
HEY!
CUT THAT OUT!

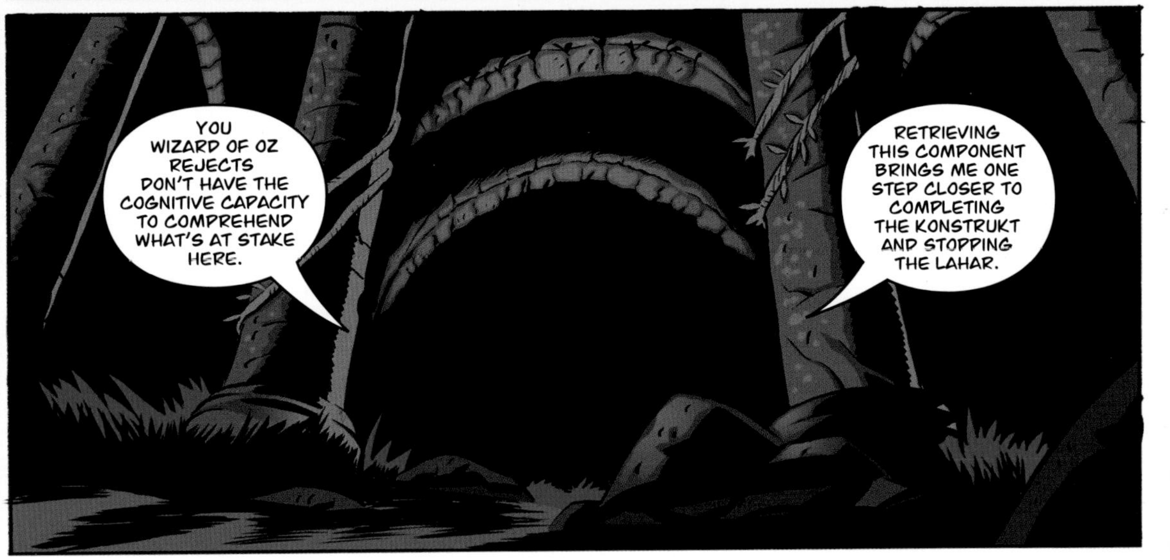
YOU WIZARD OF OZ REJECTS DON'T HAVE THE COGNITIVE CAPACITY TO COMPREHEND WHAT'S AT STAKE HERE.
RETRIEVING THIS COMPONENT BRINGS ME ONE STEP CLOSER TO COMPLETING THE KONSTRUKT AND STOPPING THE LAHAR.

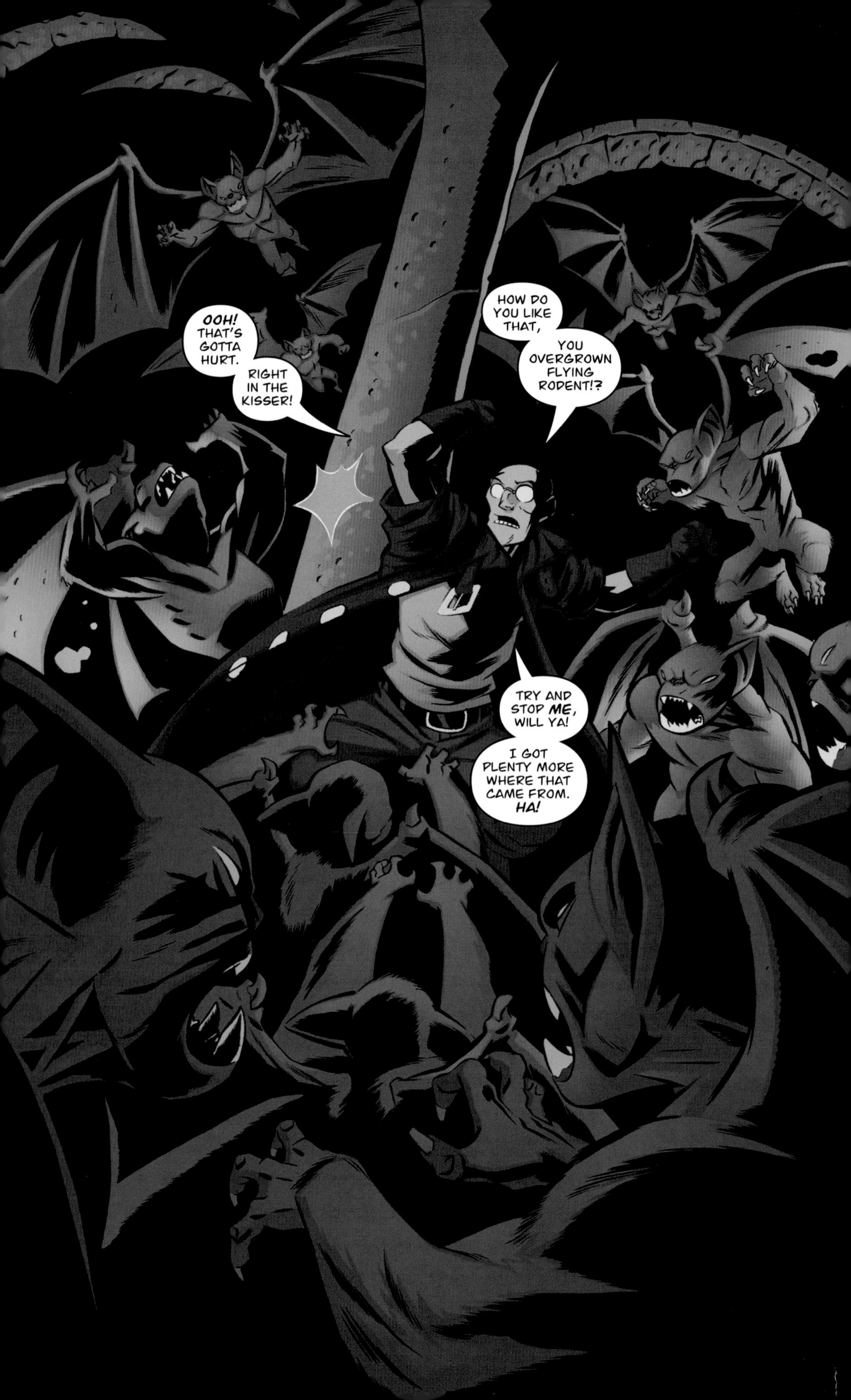
OOH! THAT'S GOTTA HURT.
RIGHT IN THE KISSER!
HOW DO YOU LIKE THAT,
YOU OVERGROWN FLYING RODENT!?
TRY AND STOP ME, WILL YA!
I GOT PLENTY MORE WHERE THAT CAME FROM. HA!

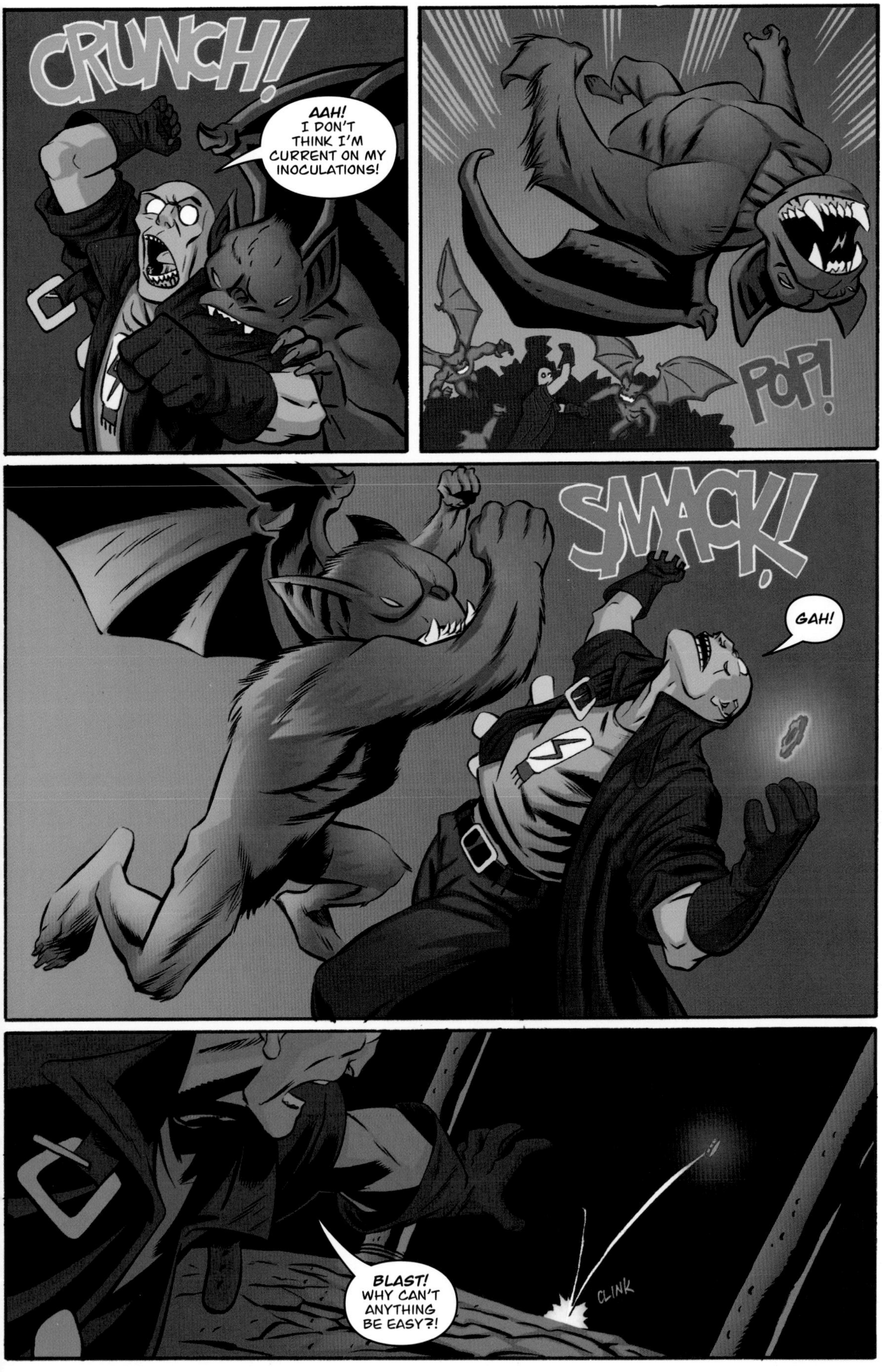
CRUNCH!
AAH! I DON'T THINK I'M CURRENT ON MY INOCULATIONS!
POP!
SMACK!
GAH!
BLAST! WHY CAN'T ANYTHING BE EASY?!
CLINK

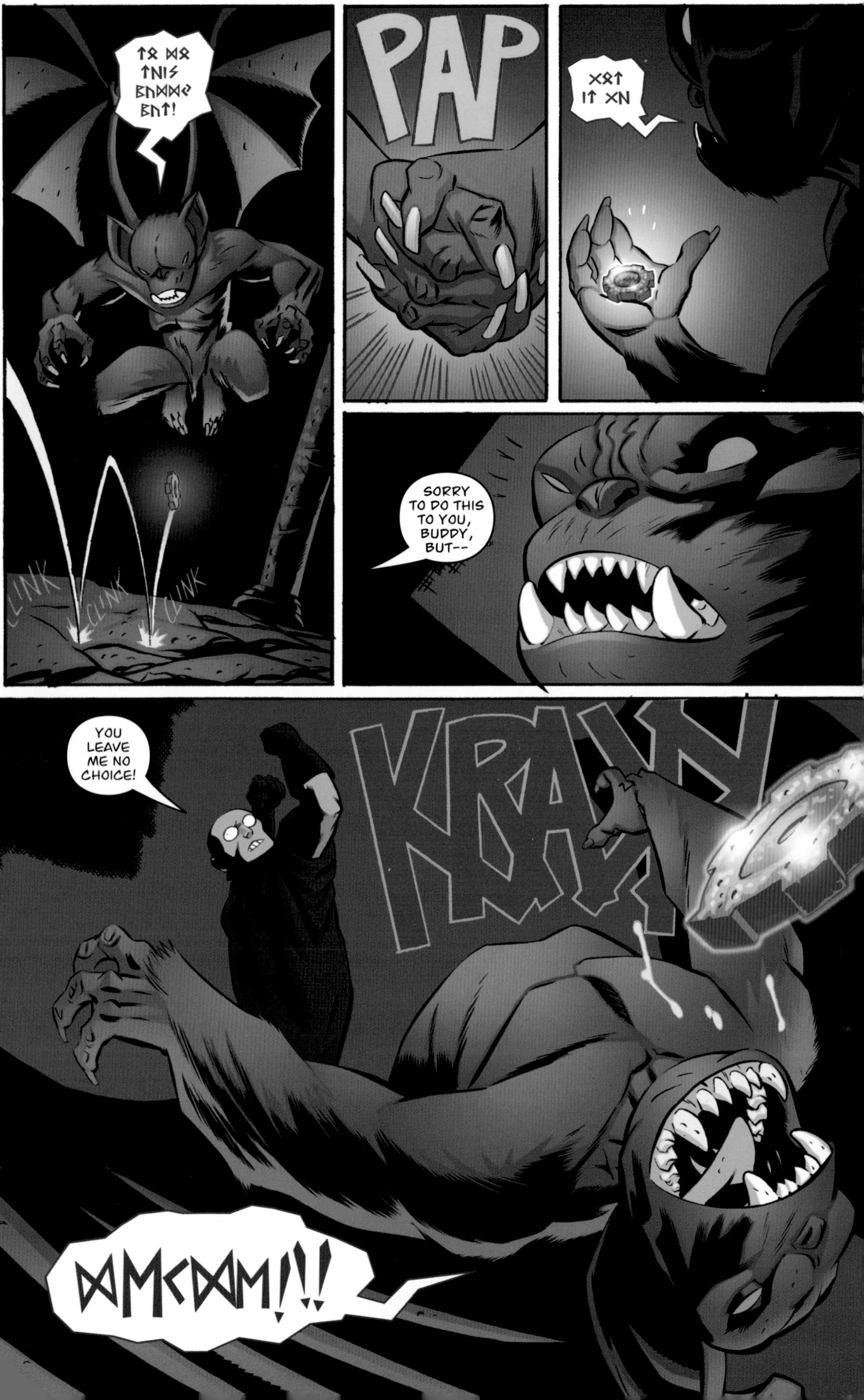
CLINK
CLINK
CLINK
PAP
SORRY TO DO THIS TO YOU, BUDDY, BUT--
YOU LEAVE ME NO CHOICE!

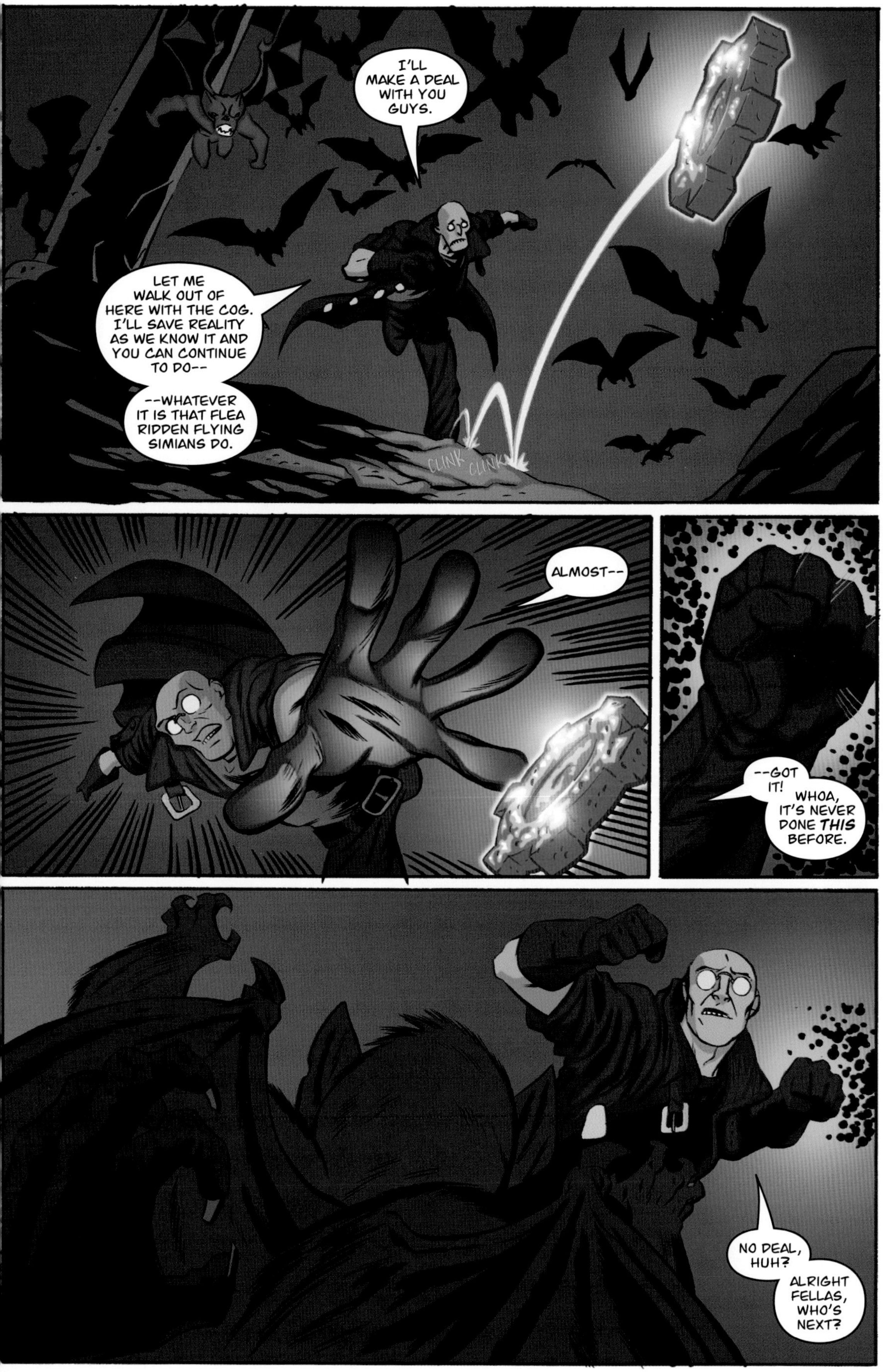
I'LL MAKE A DEAL WITH YOU GUYS.
LET ME WALK OUT OF HERE WITH THE COG. I'LL SAVE REALITY AS WE KNOW IT AND YOU CAN CONTINUE TO DO--
--WHATEVER IT IS THAT FLEA RIDDEN FLYING SIMIANS DO.
CLINK
CLINK
ALMOST--
--GOT IT!
WHOA, IT'S NEVER DONE **THIS** BEFORE.
NO DEAL, HUH?
ALRIGHT FELLAS, WHO'S NEXT?

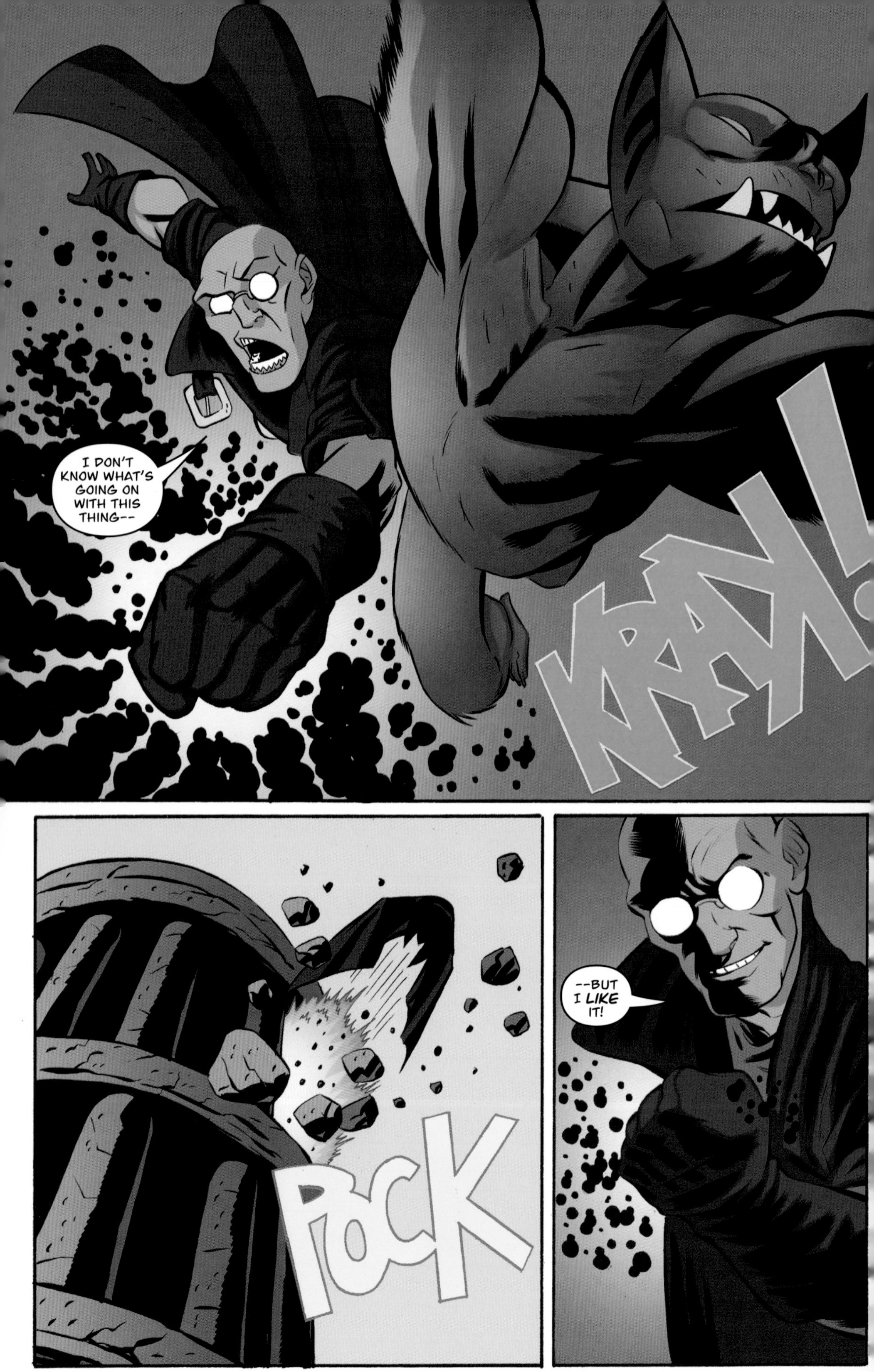
I DON'T KNOW WHAT'S GOING ON WITH THIS THING--
KRAK!
POCK
--BUT I **LIKE** IT!

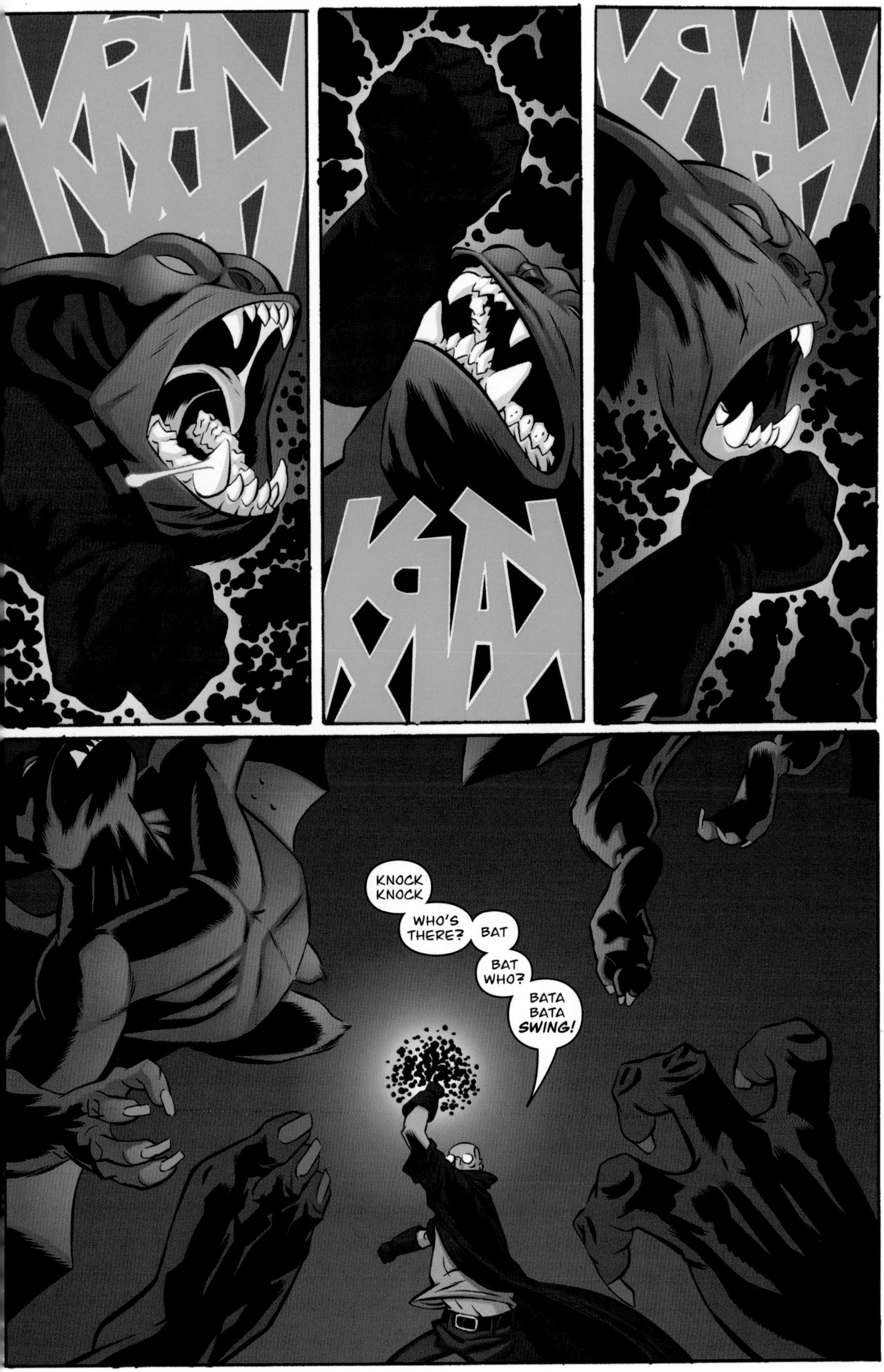
KNOCK KNOCK
WHO'S THERE?
BAT
BAT WHO?
BATA BATA **SWING!**

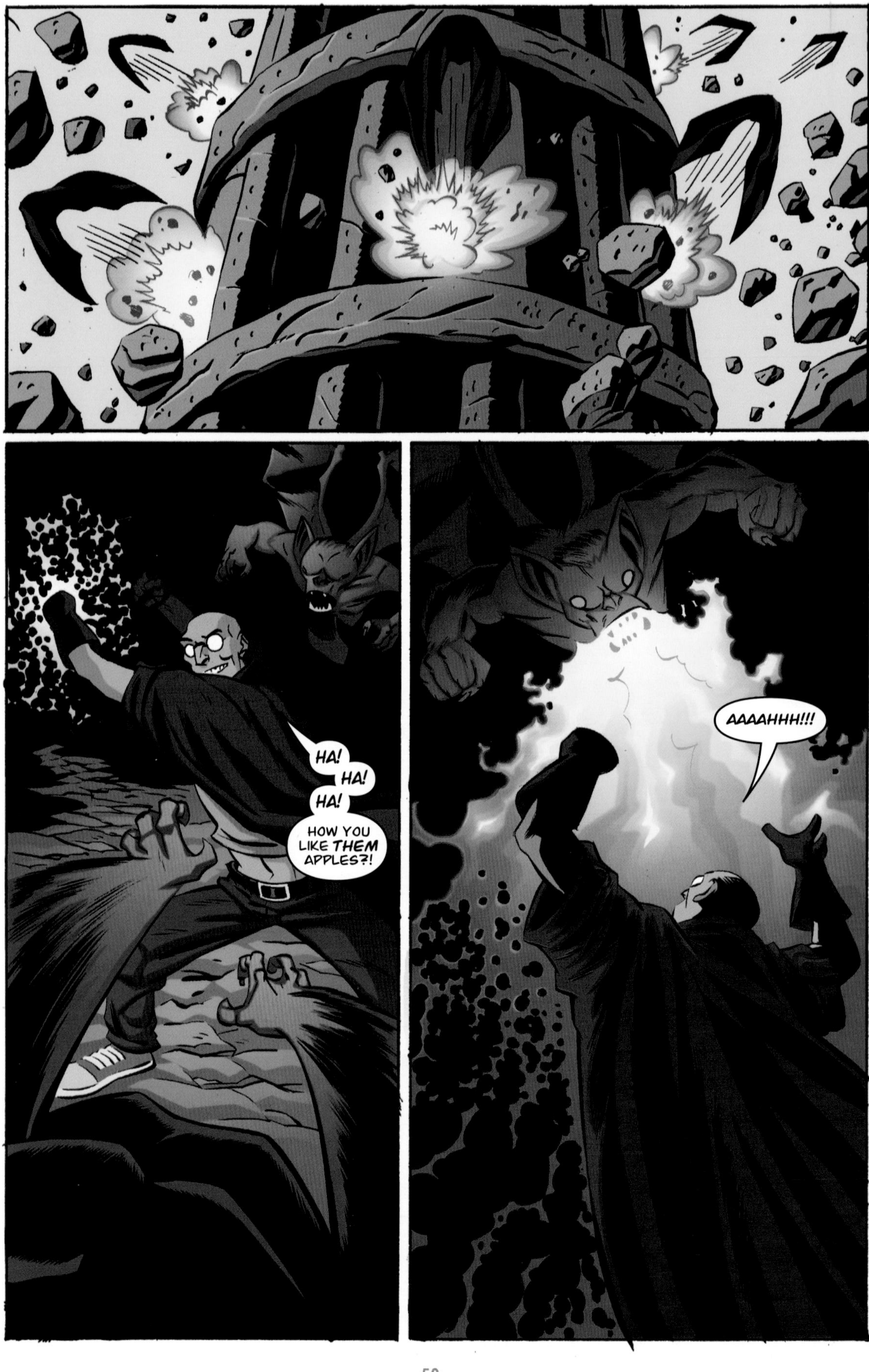
HA!
HA!
HA!
HOW YOU LIKE THEM APPLES?!
AAAAHHH!!!

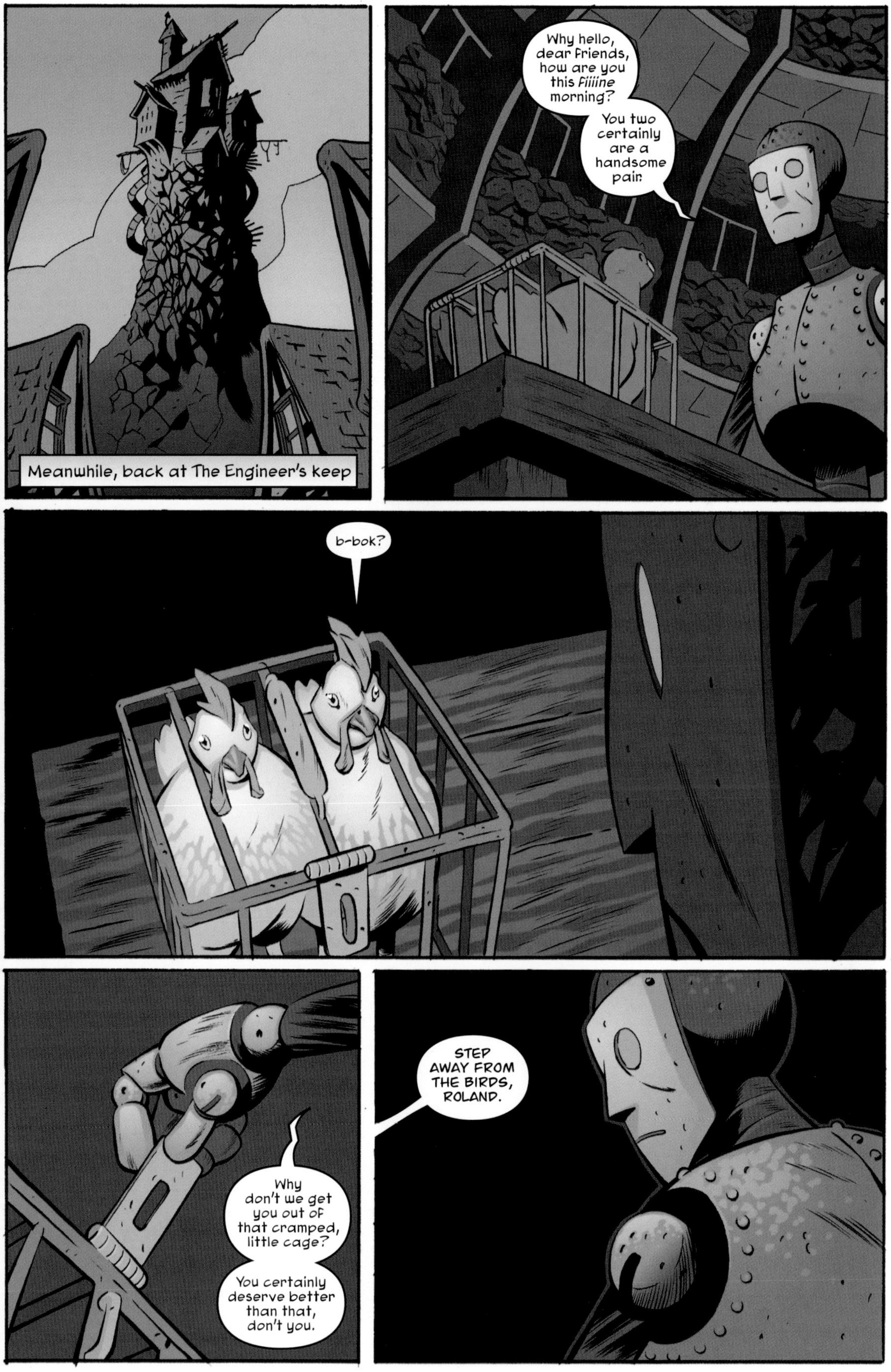

Meanwhile, back at The Engineer's keep
Why hello, dear friends, how are you this *fiiiine* morning?
You two certainly are a handsome pair.
b-bok?
Why don't we get you out of that cramped, little cage?
You certainly deserve better than that, don't you.
STEP AWAY FROM THE BIRDS, ROLAND.

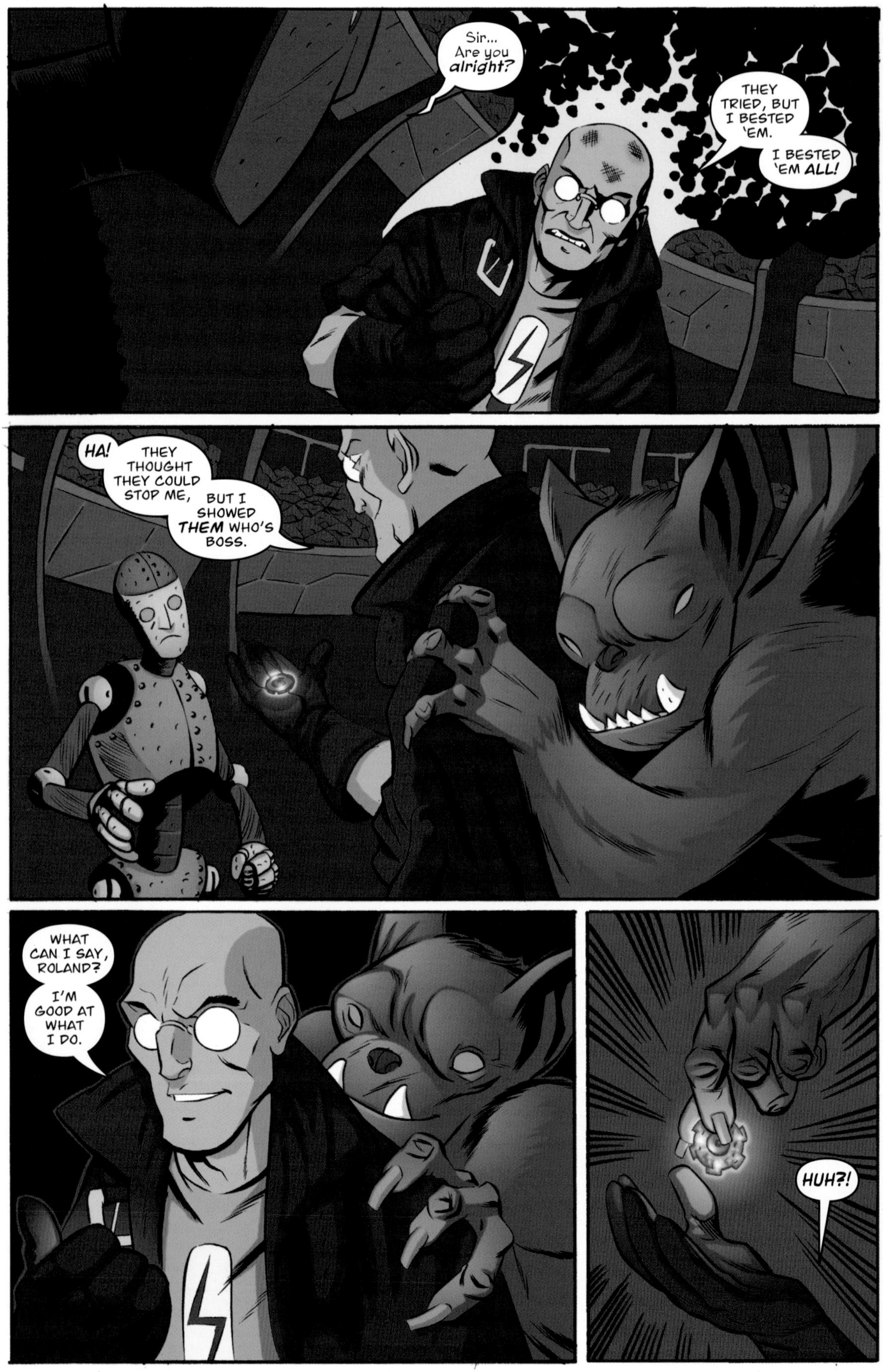

Sir... Are you alright?
THEY TRIED, BUT I BESTED 'EM.
I BESTED 'EM ALL!
HA!
THEY THOUGHT THEY COULD STOP ME,
BUT I SHOWED THEM WHO'S BOSS.
WHAT CAN I SAY, ROLAND?
I'M GOOD AT WHAT I DO.
HUH?!

LISTEN, YOU UGLY BAT-MONKEY.

GET BACK HERE WITH THAT OR I'LL-- I'LL--

WELL, I DON'T KNOW WHAT I'M GONNA' DO TO YA', BUT REST ASSURED, IT'LL BE NASTY.

I'M A GENERALLY VINDICTIVE SORT OF PERSON, SO JUST USE YOUR IMAGINATION.

ᚠᚾᚲᚲ ᛖᛊᚾ!

OH NO YOU'RE NOT!--

HLP!

GET BACK HERE, YOU WINGED MONKEY! I NEED TO LEARN YOU SOME MANNERS --

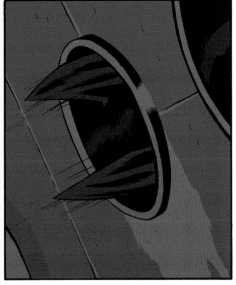

53

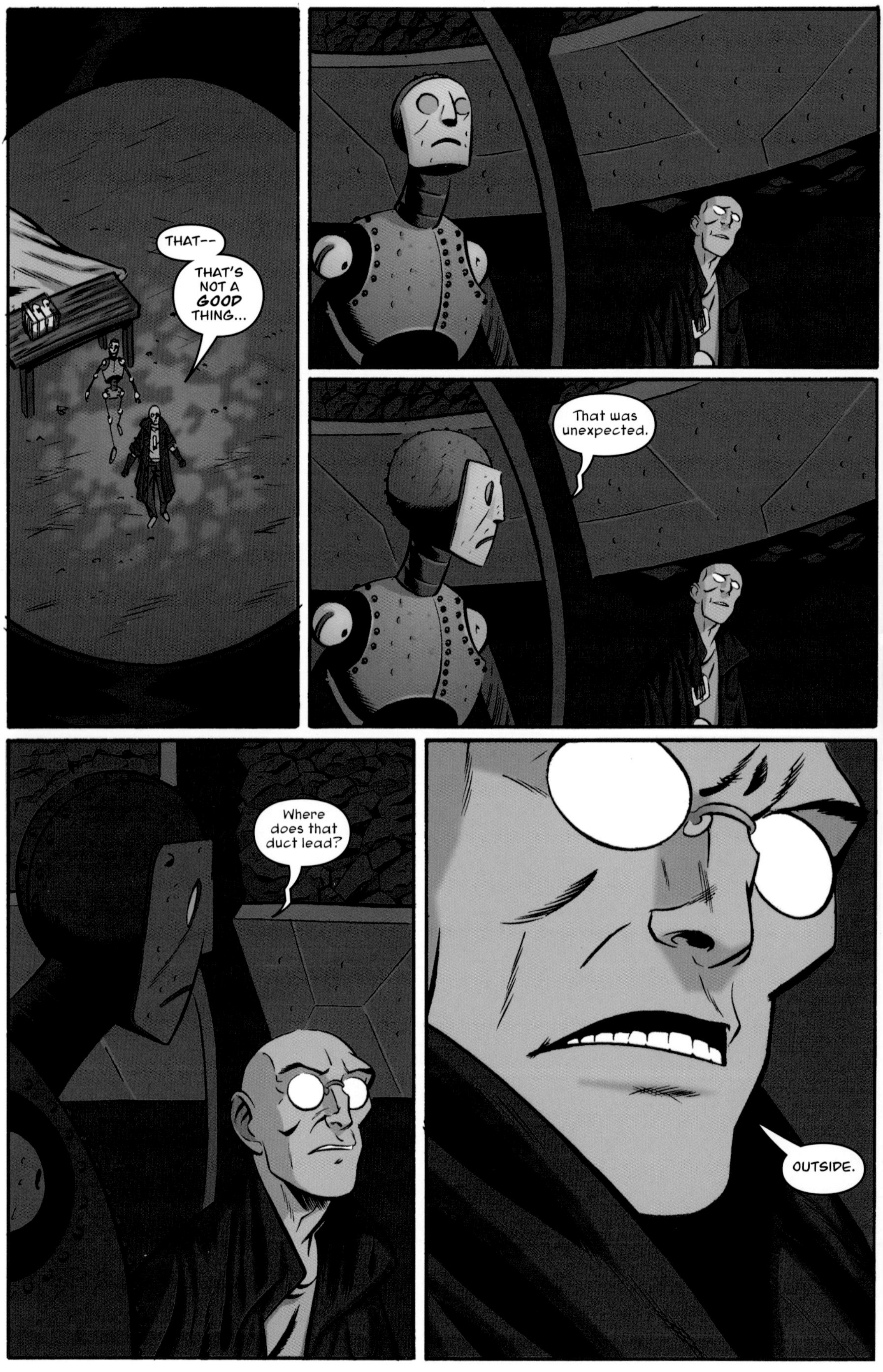
THAT--
THAT'S NOT A GOOD THING...
That was unexpected.
Where does that duct lead?
OUTSIDE.

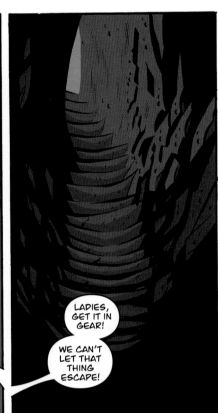

C'MON! GET A MOVE ON, ROLAND.

LOOK LIVELY! HUSTLE. GET THOSE CLUNKY CLOD HOPPERS OF YOURS MOVING!

LADIES, GET IT IN GEAR!

WE CAN'T LET THAT THING ESCAPE!

WHAT "THING"?

YOU CANNOT BE TRUSTED TO DO THINGS ON YOUR OWN.

--THIS IS WHY WE MUST ACCOMPANY YOU ON YOUR EXCURSIONS.

PLEASE! MY SCREW-UPS DON'T END UP IN GENOCIDES, LIKE WITH YOU LADIES.

WHOA!

THAT'S ONE BIG--

-- WHATEVER THE HECK IT IS.

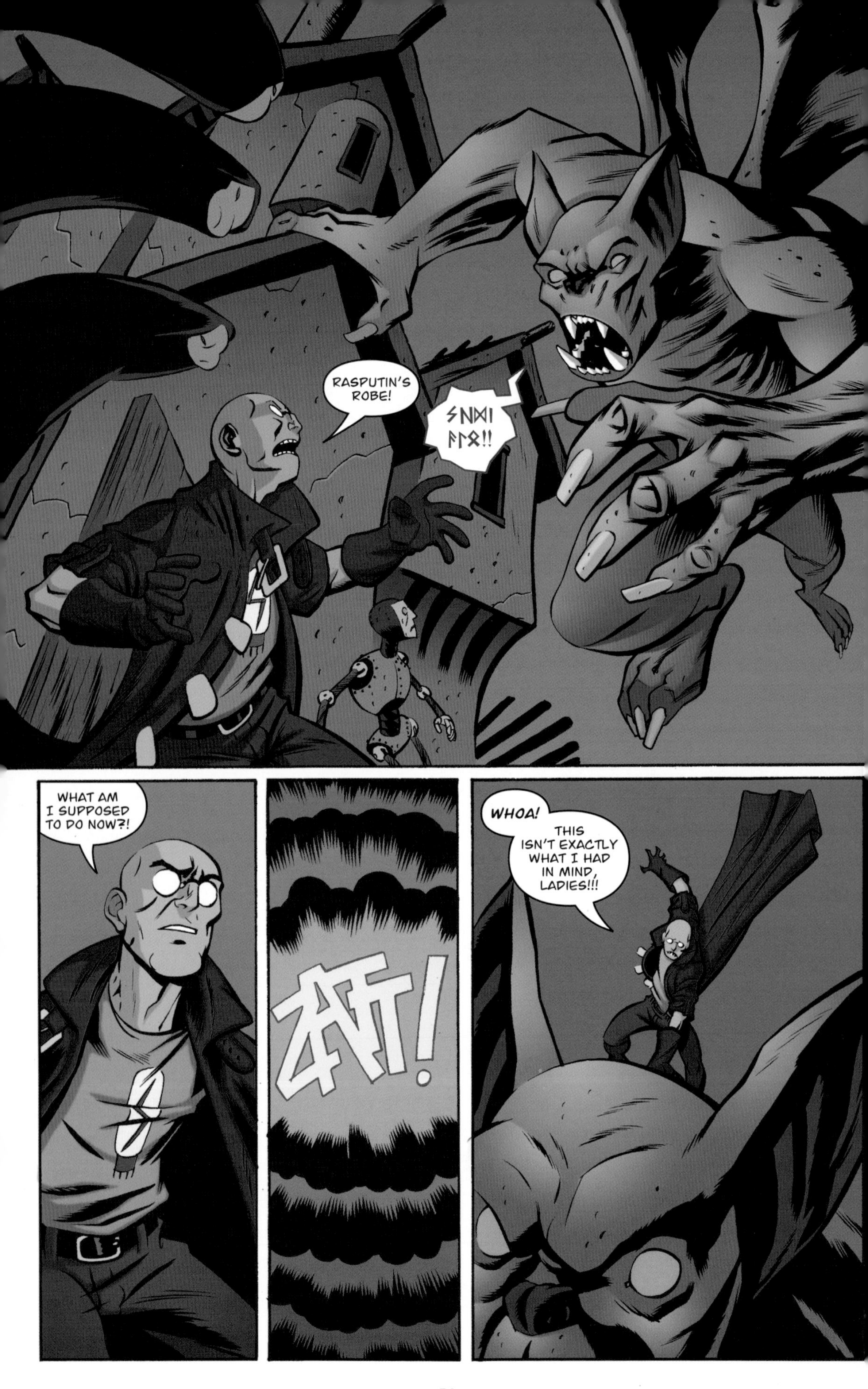
RASPUTIN'S ROBE!
WHAT AM I SUPPOSED TO DO NOW?!
ZAFT!
WHOA!
THIS ISN'T EXACTLY WHAT I HAD IN MIND, LADIES!!!

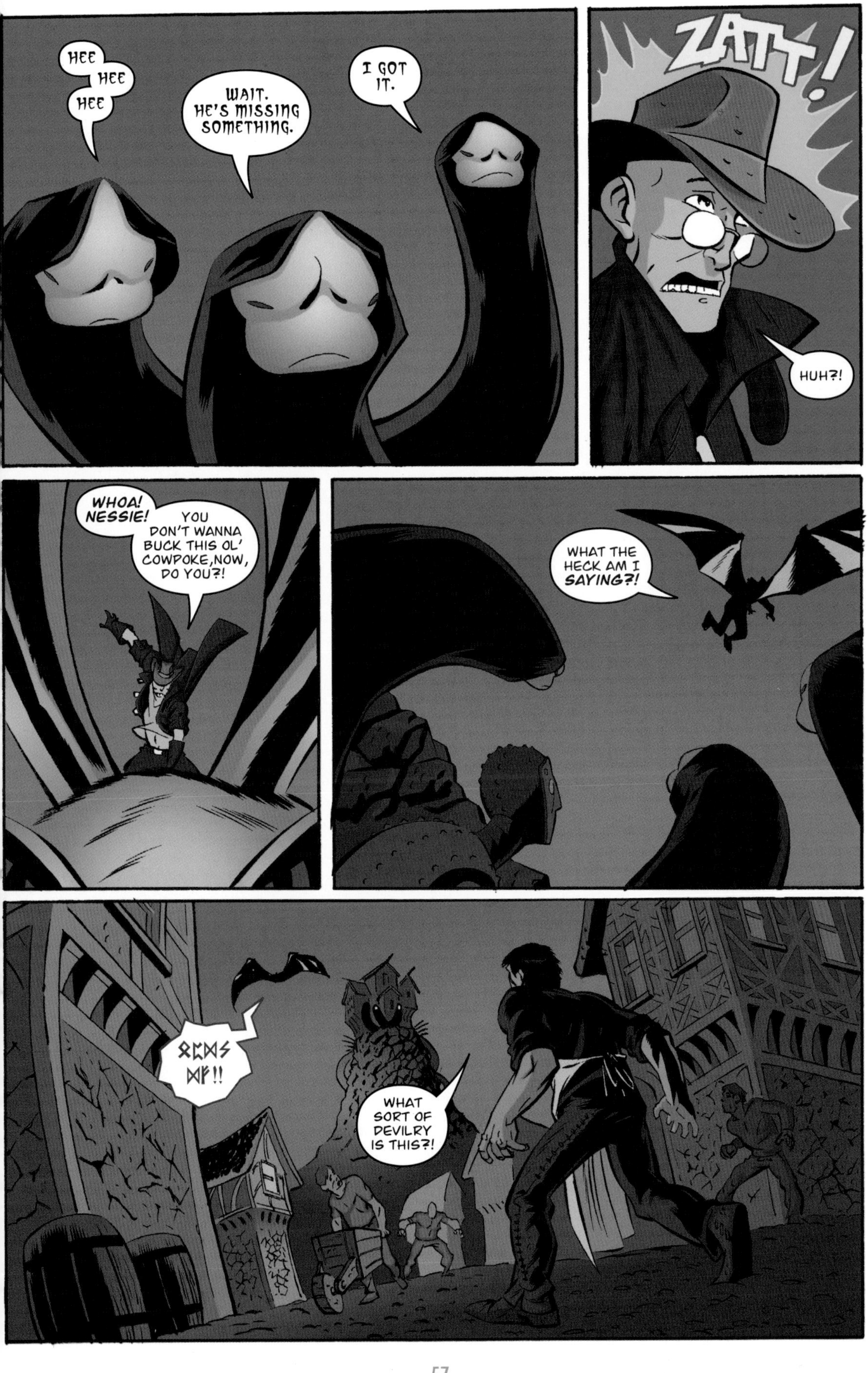
HEE HEE HEE
WAIT. HE'S MISSING SOMETHING.
I GOT IT.
ZATT!
HUH?!
WHOA! NESSIE!
YOU DON'T WANNA BUCK THIS OL' COWPOKE, NOW, DO YOU?!
WHAT THE HECK AM I SAYING?!
WHAT SORT OF DEVILRY IS THIS?!

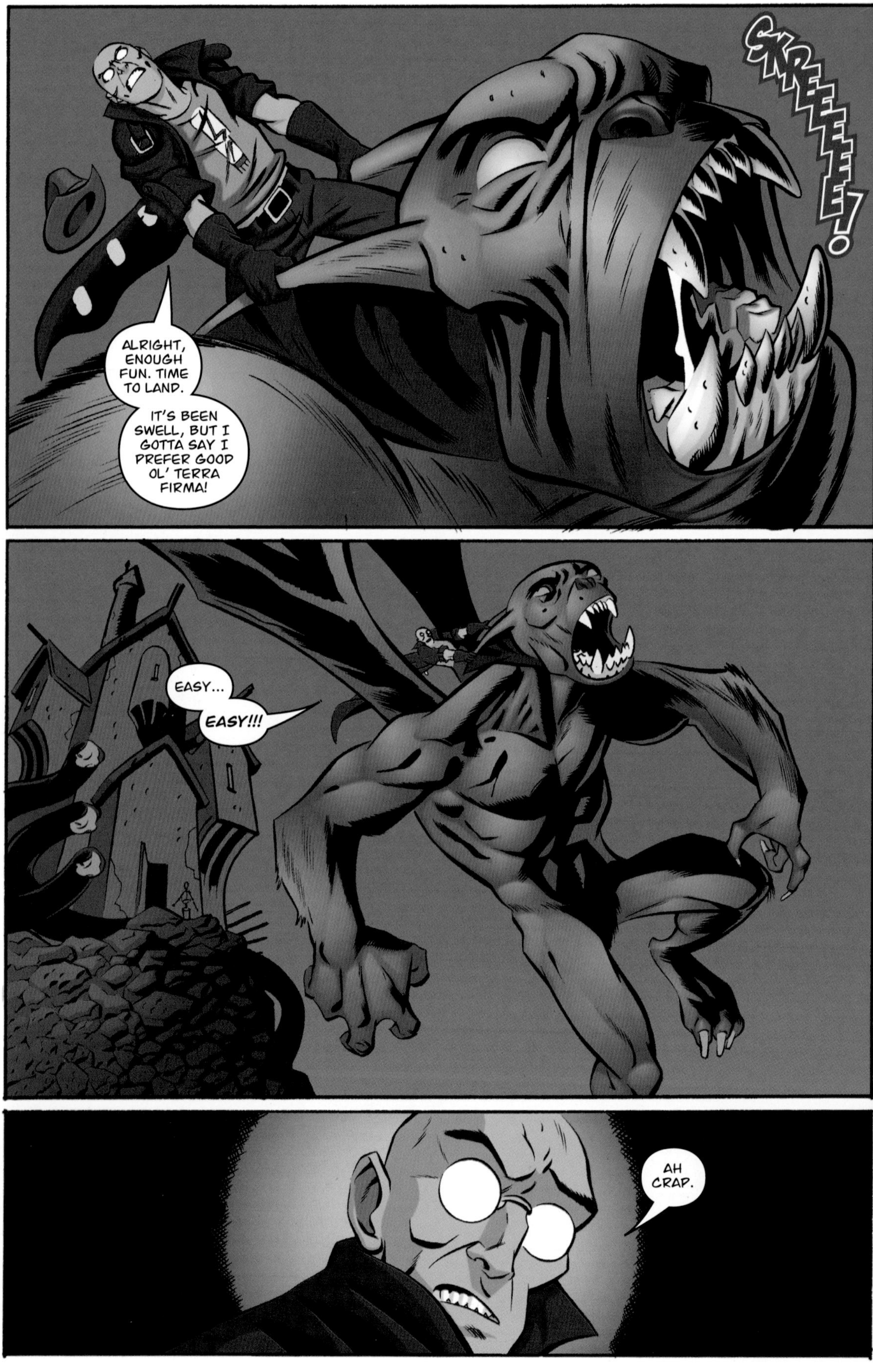
SKREEEEE!
ALRIGHT, ENOUGH FUN. TIME TO LAND.
IT'S BEEN SWELL, BUT I GOTTA SAY I PREFER GOOD OL' TERRA FIRMA!
EASY...
EASY!!!
AH CRAP.

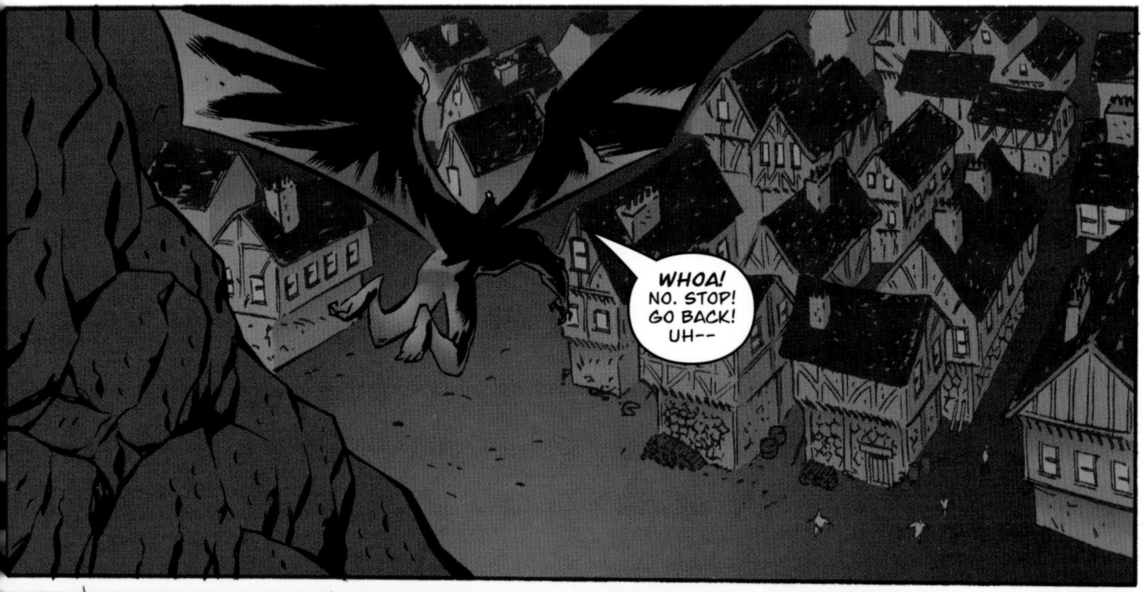
WHOA! NO. STOP! GO BACK! UH--
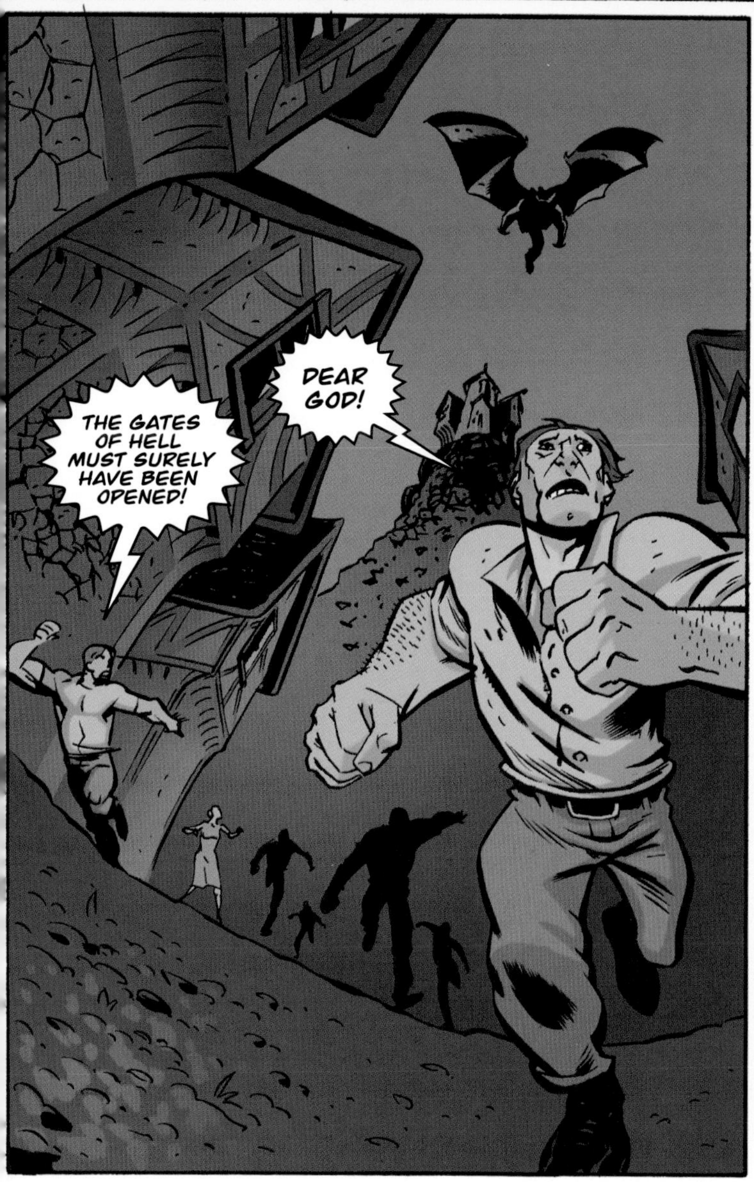
THE GATES OF HELL MUST SURELY HAVE BEEN OPENED!
DEAR GOD!
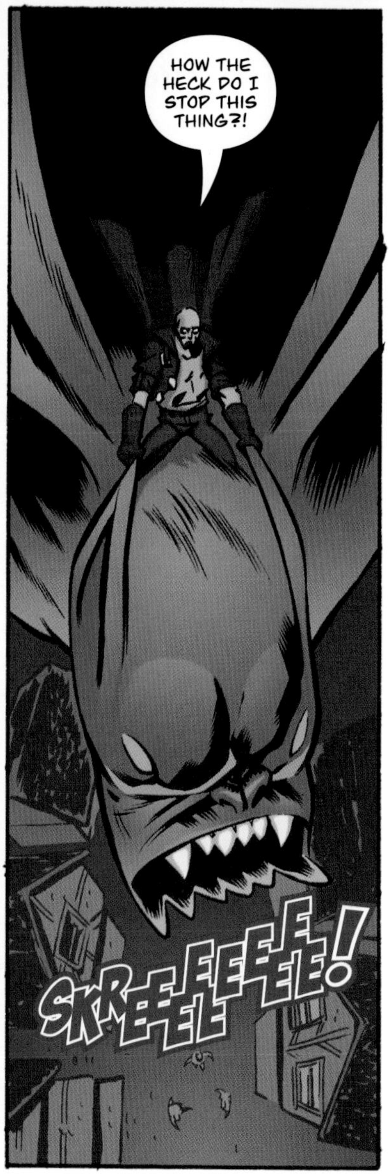
HOW THE HECK DO I STOP THIS THING?!
SKREEEEEEEEEEE!

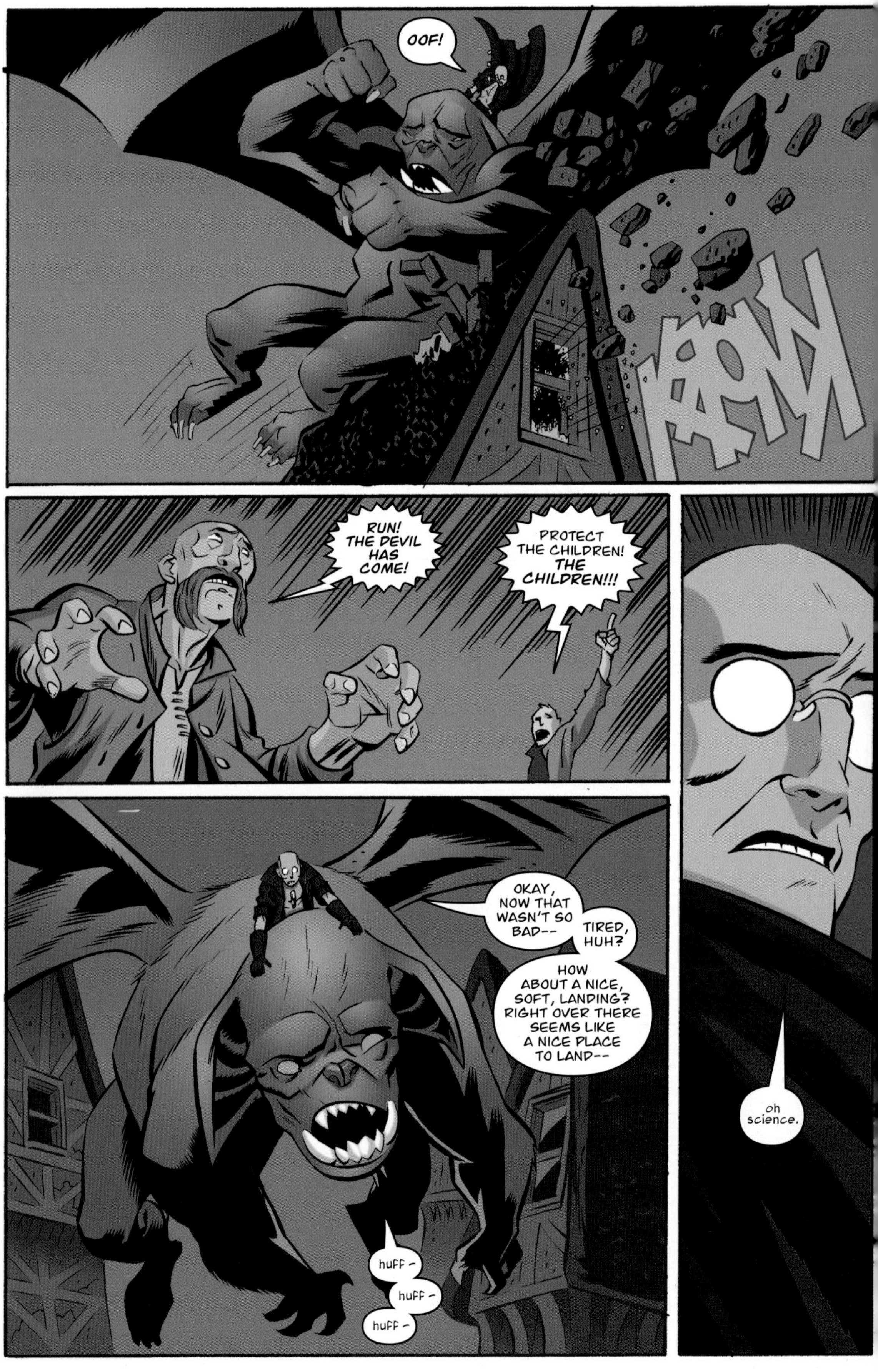
OOF!
RUN! THE DEVIL HAS COME!
PROTECT THE CHILDREN! THE CHILDREN!!!
OKAY, NOW THAT WASN'T SO BAD--
TIRED, HUH?
HOW ABOUT A NICE, SOFT, LANDING? RIGHT OVER THERE SEEMS LIKE A NICE PLACE TO LAND--
huff -
huff -
huff -
oh science.

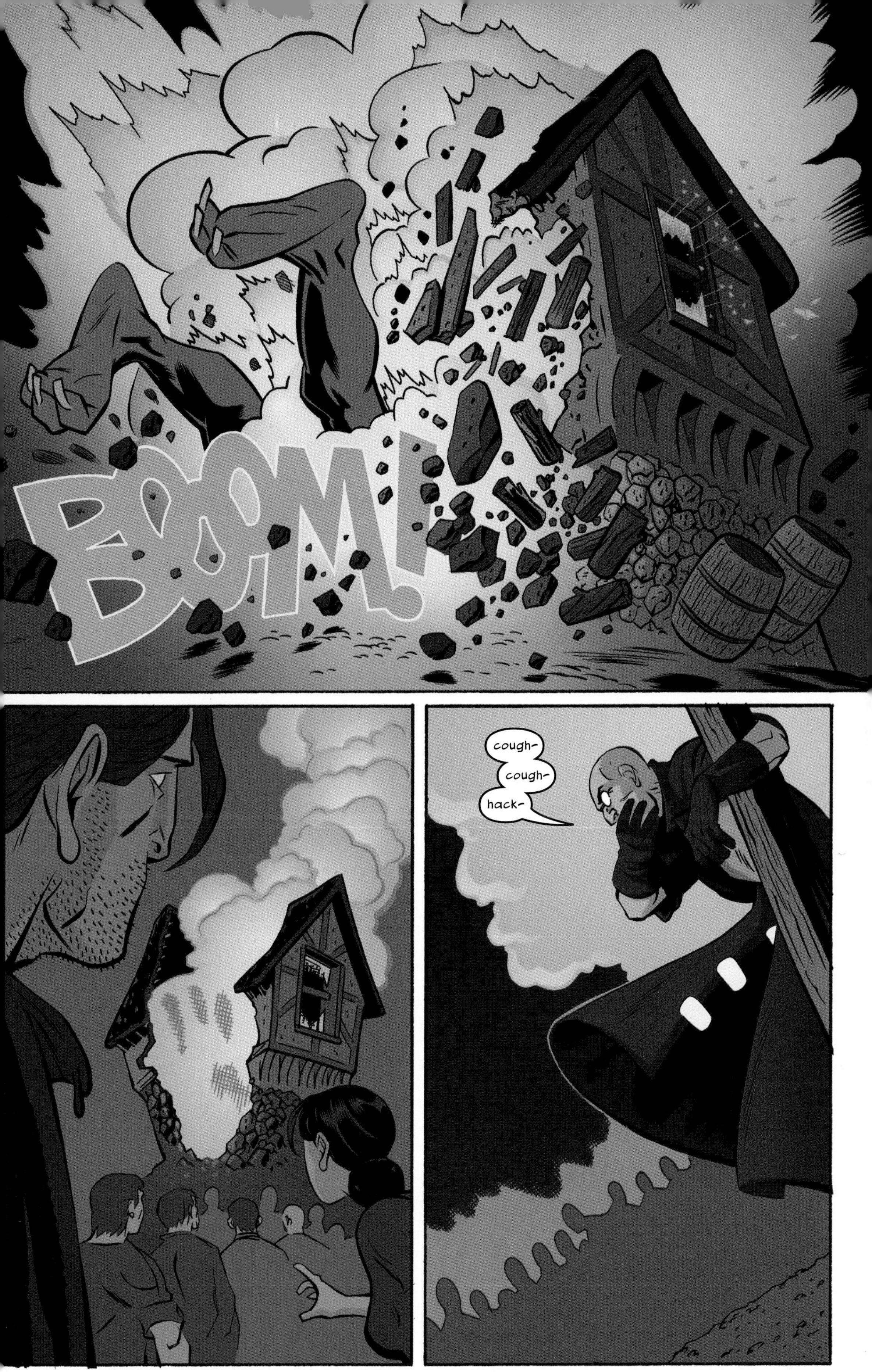
BOOM!
cough-
cough-
hack-

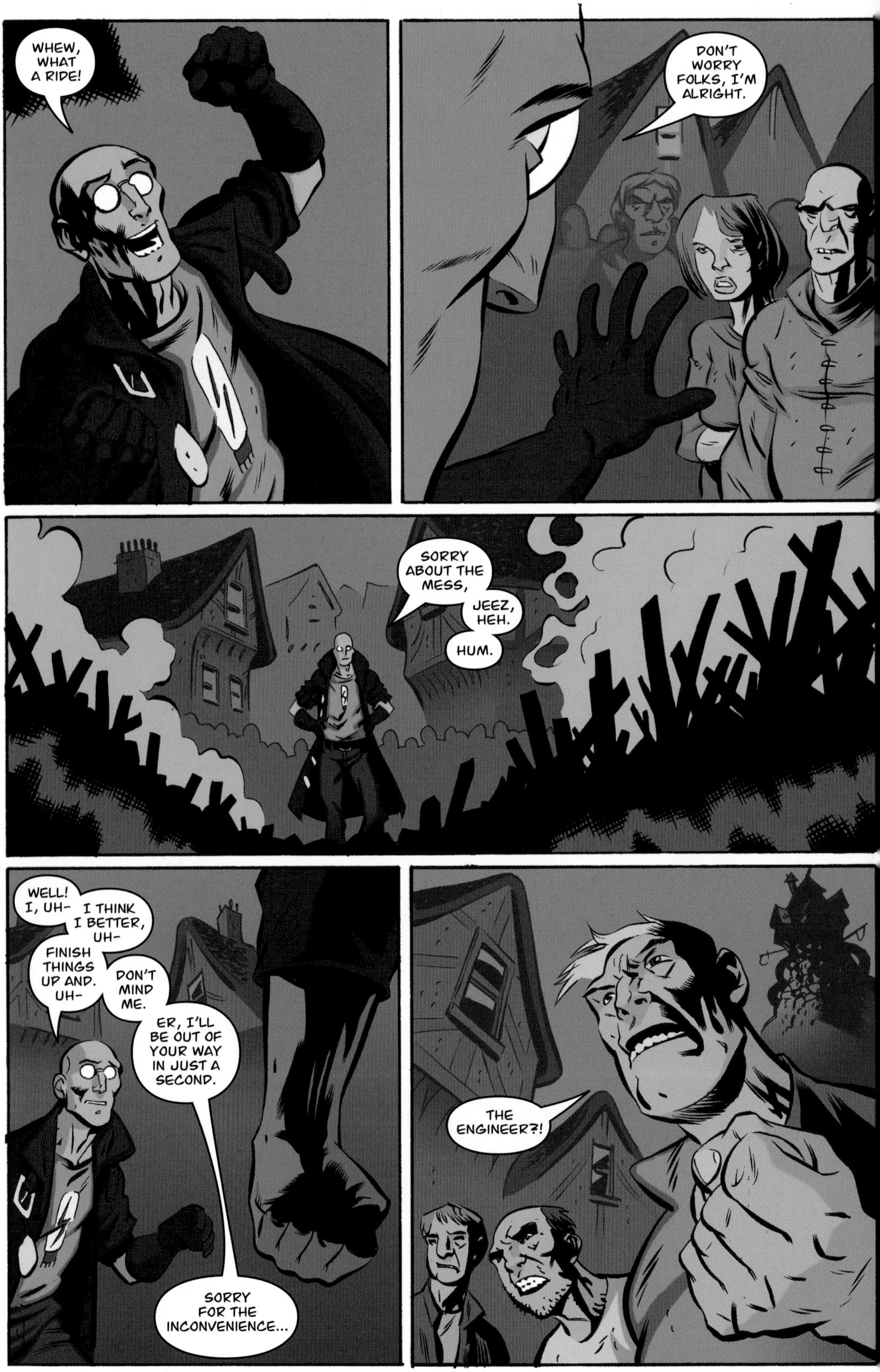
WHEW, WHAT A RIDE!
DON'T WORRY FOLKS, I'M ALRIGHT.
SORRY ABOUT THE MESS,
JEEZ, HEH.
HUM.
WELL! I, UH-
I THINK I BETTER, UH-
FINISH THINGS UP AND. UH-
DON'T MIND ME.
ER, I'LL BE OUT OF YOUR WAY IN JUST A SECOND.
SORRY FOR THE INCONVENIENCE...
THE ENGINEER?!

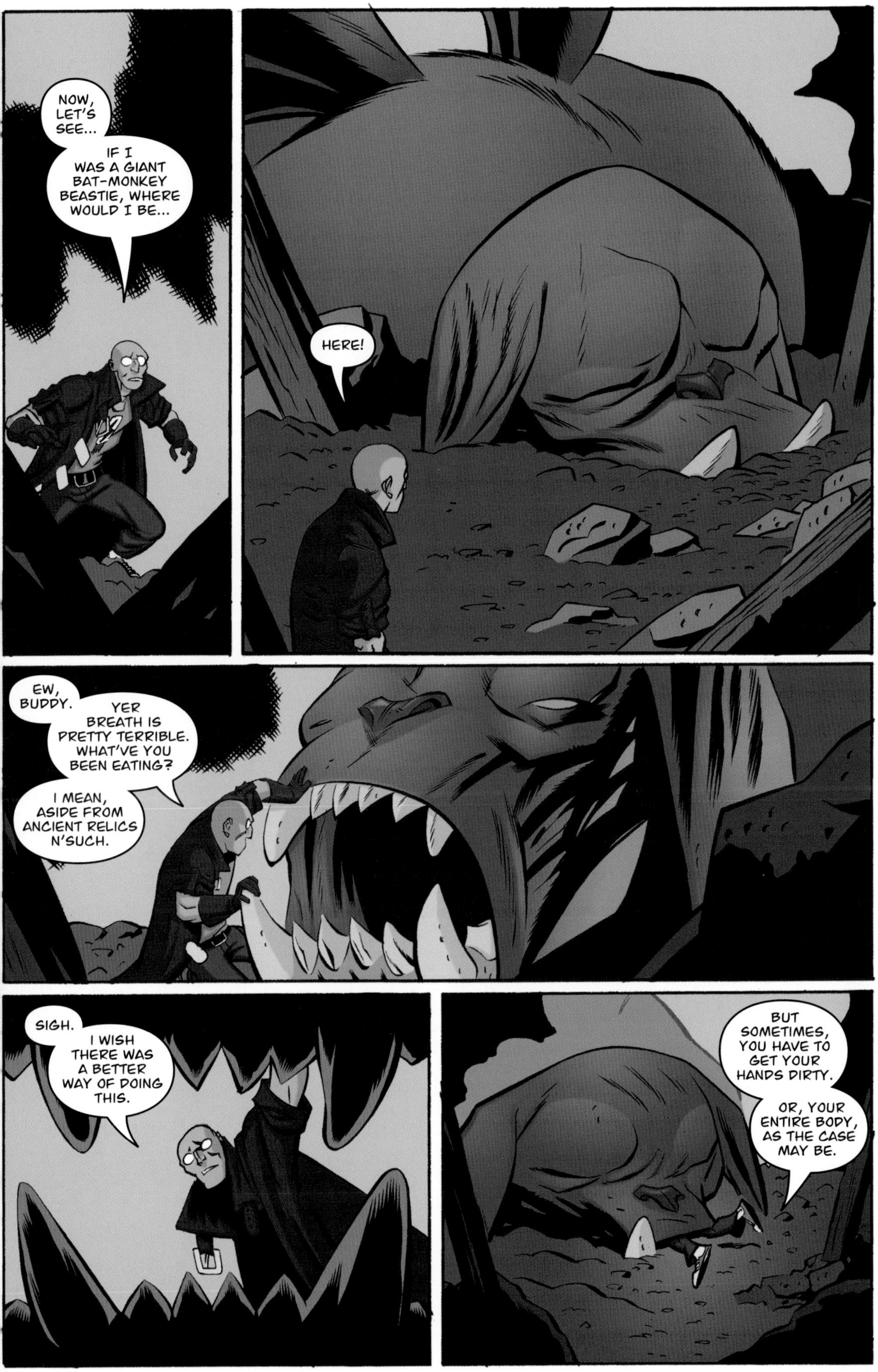
NOW, LET'S SEE...
IF I WAS A GIANT BAT-MONKEY BEASTIE, WHERE WOULD I BE...
HERE!
EW, BUDDY.
YER BREATH IS PRETTY TERRIBLE. WHAT'VE YOU BEEN EATING?
I MEAN, ASIDE FROM ANCIENT RELICS N'SUCH.
SIGH.
I WISH THERE WAS A BETTER WAY OF DOING THIS.
BUT SOMETIMES, YOU HAVE TO GET YOUR HANDS DIRTY.
OR, YOUR ENTIRE BODY, AS THE CASE MAY BE.

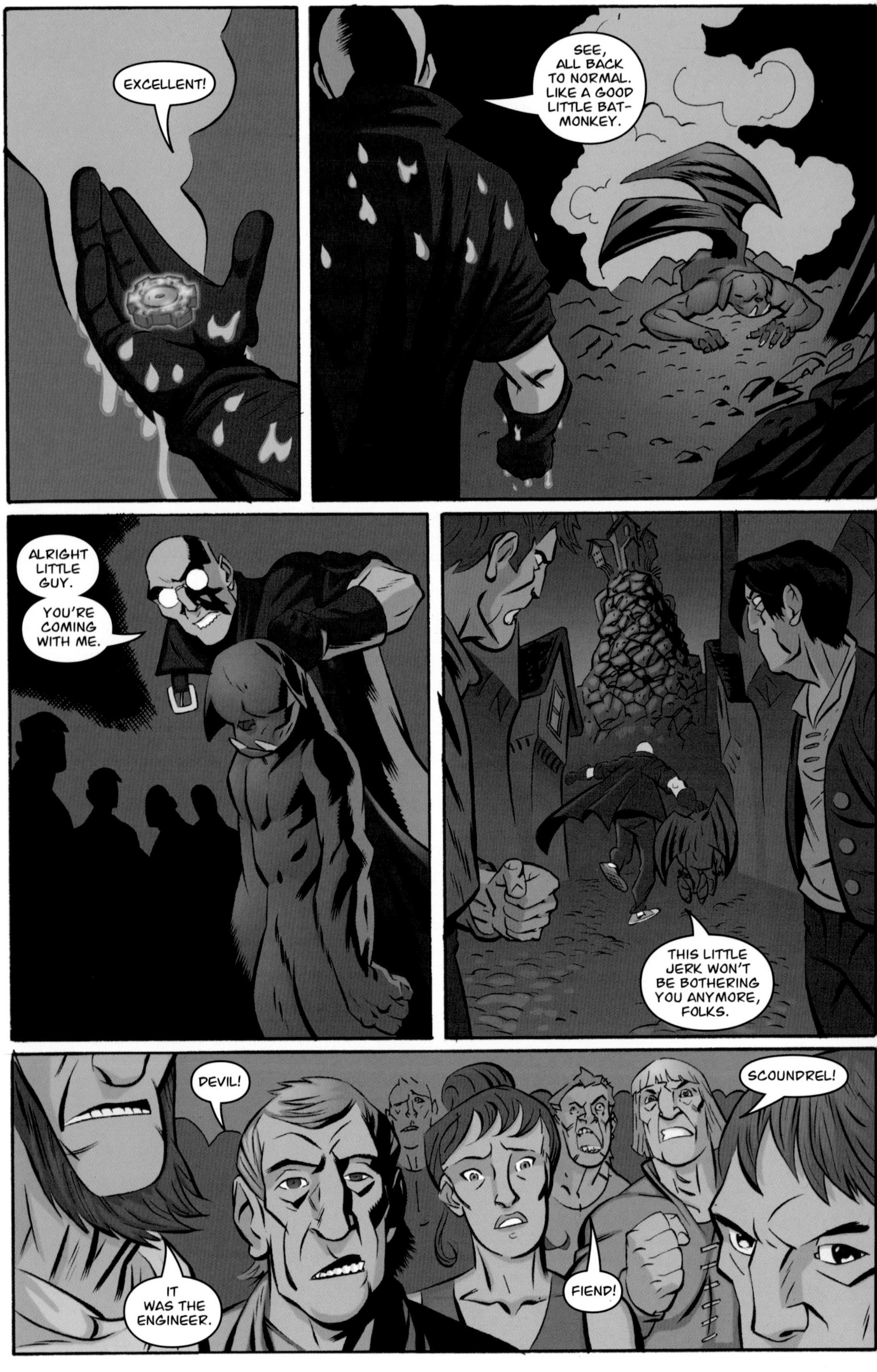
EXCELLENT!
SEE, ALL BACK TO NORMAL. LIKE A GOOD LITTLE BAT-MONKEY.
ALRIGHT LITTLE GUY.
YOU'RE COMING WITH ME.
THIS LITTLE JERK WON'T BE BOTHERING YOU ANYMORE, FOLKS.
DEVIL!
IT WAS THE ENGINEER.
FIEND!
SCOUNDREL!

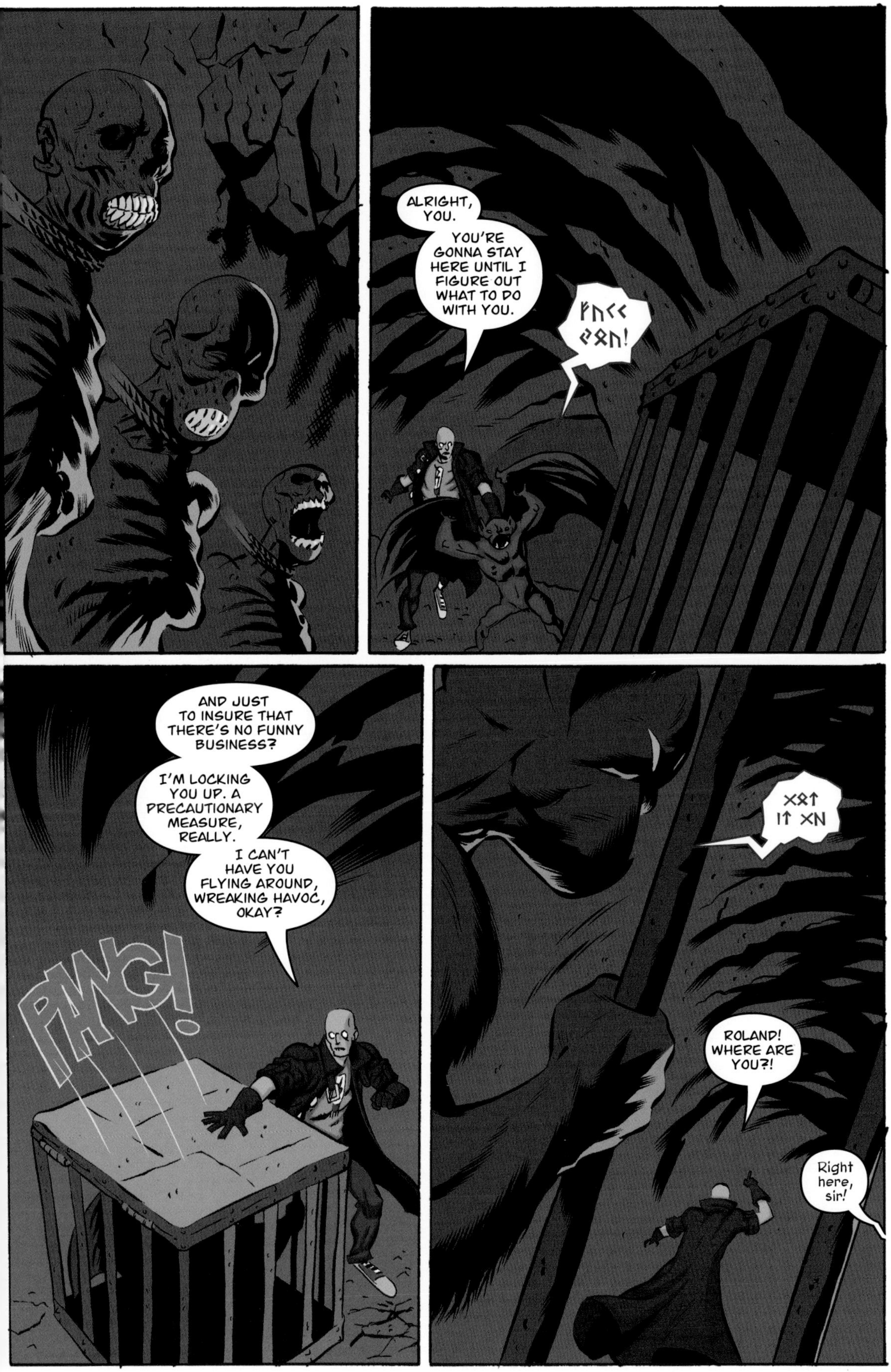

ALRIGHT, YOU.
YOU'RE GONNA STAY HERE UNTIL I FIGURE OUT WHAT TO DO WITH YOU.
AND JUST TO INSURE THAT THERE'S NO FUNNY BUSINESS?
I'M LOCKING YOU UP. A PRECAUTIONARY MEASURE, REALLY.
I CAN'T HAVE YOU FLYING AROUND, WREAKING HAVOC, OKAY?
PING!
ROLAND! WHERE ARE YOU?!
Right here, sir!

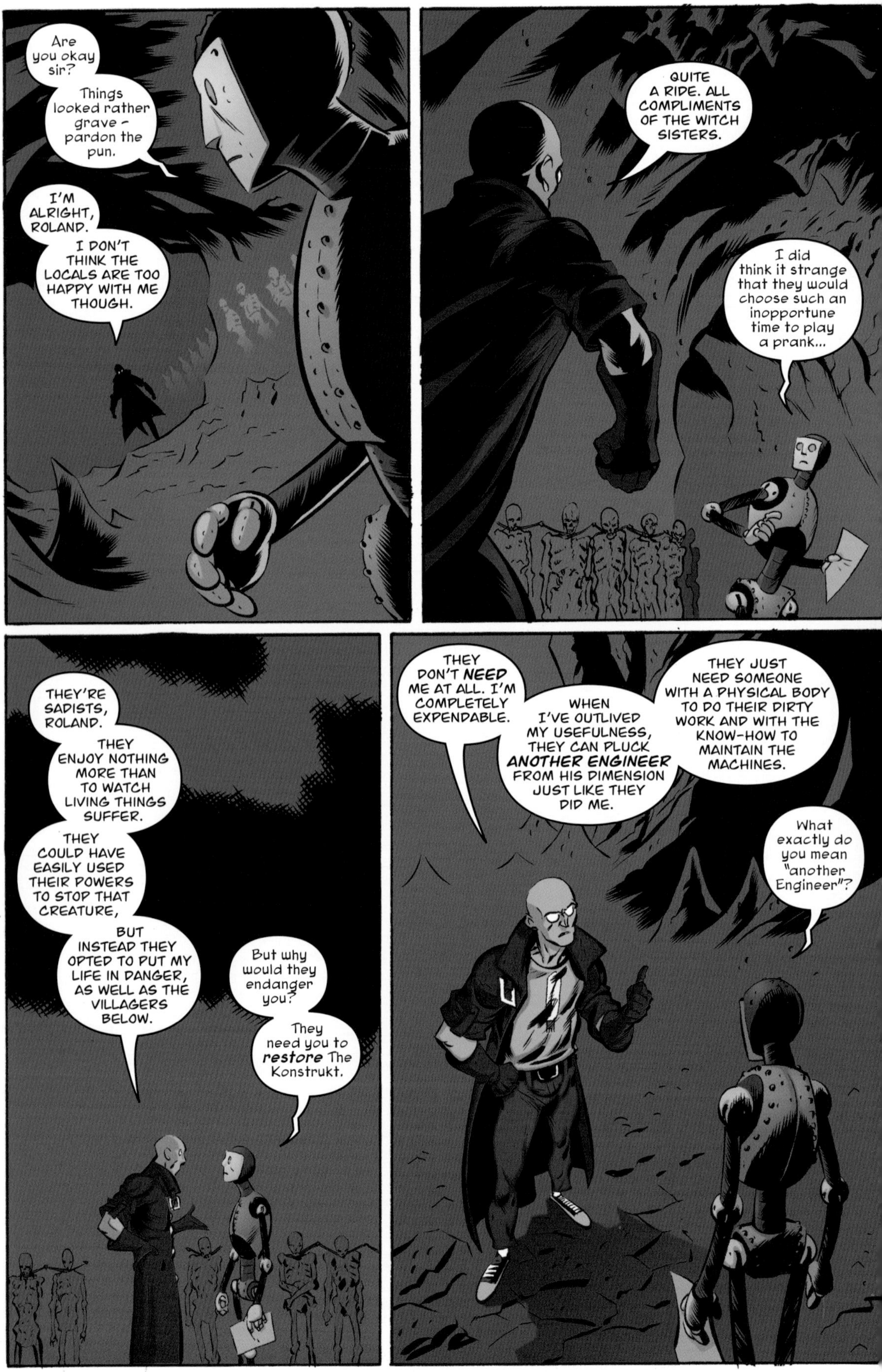
Are you okay sir?
Things looked rather grave - pardon the pun.
I'M ALRIGHT, ROLAND.
I DON'T THINK THE LOCALS ARE TOO HAPPY WITH ME THOUGH.
QUITE A RIDE. ALL COMPLIMENTS OF THE WITCH SISTERS.
I did think it strange that they would choose such an inopportune time to play a prank...
THEY'RE SADISTS, ROLAND.
THEY ENJOY NOTHING MORE THAN TO WATCH LIVING THINGS SUFFER.
THEY COULD HAVE EASILY USED THEIR POWERS TO STOP THAT CREATURE,
BUT INSTEAD THEY OPTED TO PUT MY LIFE IN DANGER, AS WELL AS THE VILLAGERS BELOW.
But why would they endanger you?
They need you to ***restore*** The Konstrukt.
THEY DON'T **NEED** ME AT ALL. I'M COMPLETELY EXPENDABLE.
WHEN I'VE OUTLIVED MY USEFULNESS, THEY CAN PLUCK ***ANOTHER ENGINEER*** FROM HIS DIMENSION JUST LIKE THEY DID ME.
THEY JUST NEED SOMEONE WITH A PHYSICAL BODY TO DO THEIR DIRTY WORK AND WITH THE KNOW-HOW TO MAINTAIN THE MACHINES.
What exactly do you mean "another Engineer"?

LOOK AROUND.

THESE CATACOMBS ARE LINED WITH THE REMAINS OF MY PREDECESSORS.

DOPPLEGANGERS -- EVERY ONE OF THEM. THEY EITHER OUTLIVED THEIR USEFULNESS --

OR SOMEHOW SUMMONED THE INTESTINAL FORTITUDE TO STAND UP TO THOSE WITCHES, AND WERE DESTROYED.

IT IS MERELY A MATTER OF TIME BEFORE I JOIN THEIR RANKS.

Oh dear.

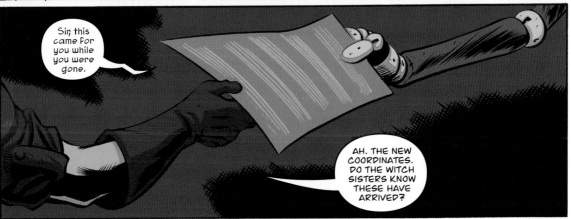

Sir, this came for you while you were gone.

AH. THE NEW COORDINATES. DO THE WITCH SISTERS KNOW THESE HAVE ARRIVED?

No. I mean, I don't think so, no.

Shall I prepare Atlas?

YES, DO.

COME, ROLAND. LET'S PLAY SOME MUSIC.

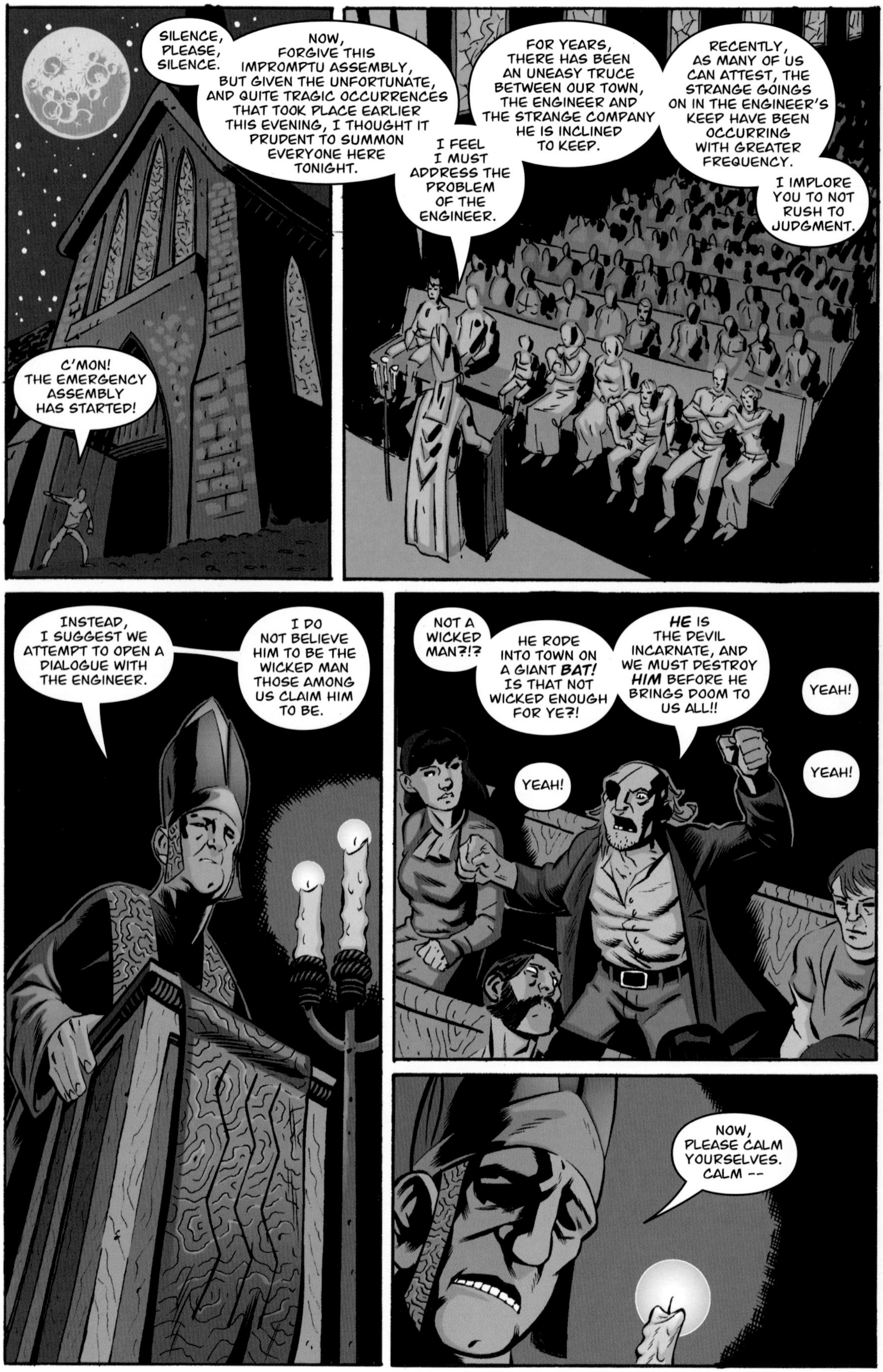
SILENCE, PLEASE, SILENCE.
C'MON! THE EMERGENCY ASSEMBLY HAS STARTED!
NOW, FORGIVE THIS IMPROMPTU ASSEMBLY, BUT GIVEN THE UNFORTUNATE, AND QUITE TRAGIC OCCURRENCES THAT TOOK PLACE EARLIER THIS EVENING, I THOUGHT IT PRUDENT TO SUMMON EVERYONE HERE TONIGHT.
I FEEL I MUST ADDRESS THE PROBLEM OF THE ENGINEER.
FOR YEARS, THERE HAS BEEN AN UNEASY TRUCE BETWEEN OUR TOWN, THE ENGINEER AND THE STRANGE COMPANY HE IS INCLINED TO KEEP.
RECENTLY, AS MANY OF US CAN ATTEST, THE STRANGE GOINGS ON IN THE ENGINEER'S KEEP HAVE BEEN OCCURRING WITH GREATER FREQUENCY.
I IMPLORE YOU TO NOT RUSH TO JUDGMENT.
INSTEAD, I SUGGEST WE ATTEMPT TO OPEN A DIALOGUE WITH THE ENGINEER.
I DO NOT BELIEVE HIM TO BE THE WICKED MAN THOSE AMONG US CLAIM HIM TO BE.
NOT A WICKED MAN?!?
HE RODE INTO TOWN ON A GIANT BAT! IS THAT NOT WICKED ENOUGH FOR YE?!
HE IS THE DEVIL INCARNATE, AND WE MUST DESTROY HIM BEFORE HE BRINGS DOOM TO US ALL!!
YEAH!
YEAH!
YEAH!
NOW, PLEASE CALM YOURSELVES. CALM --

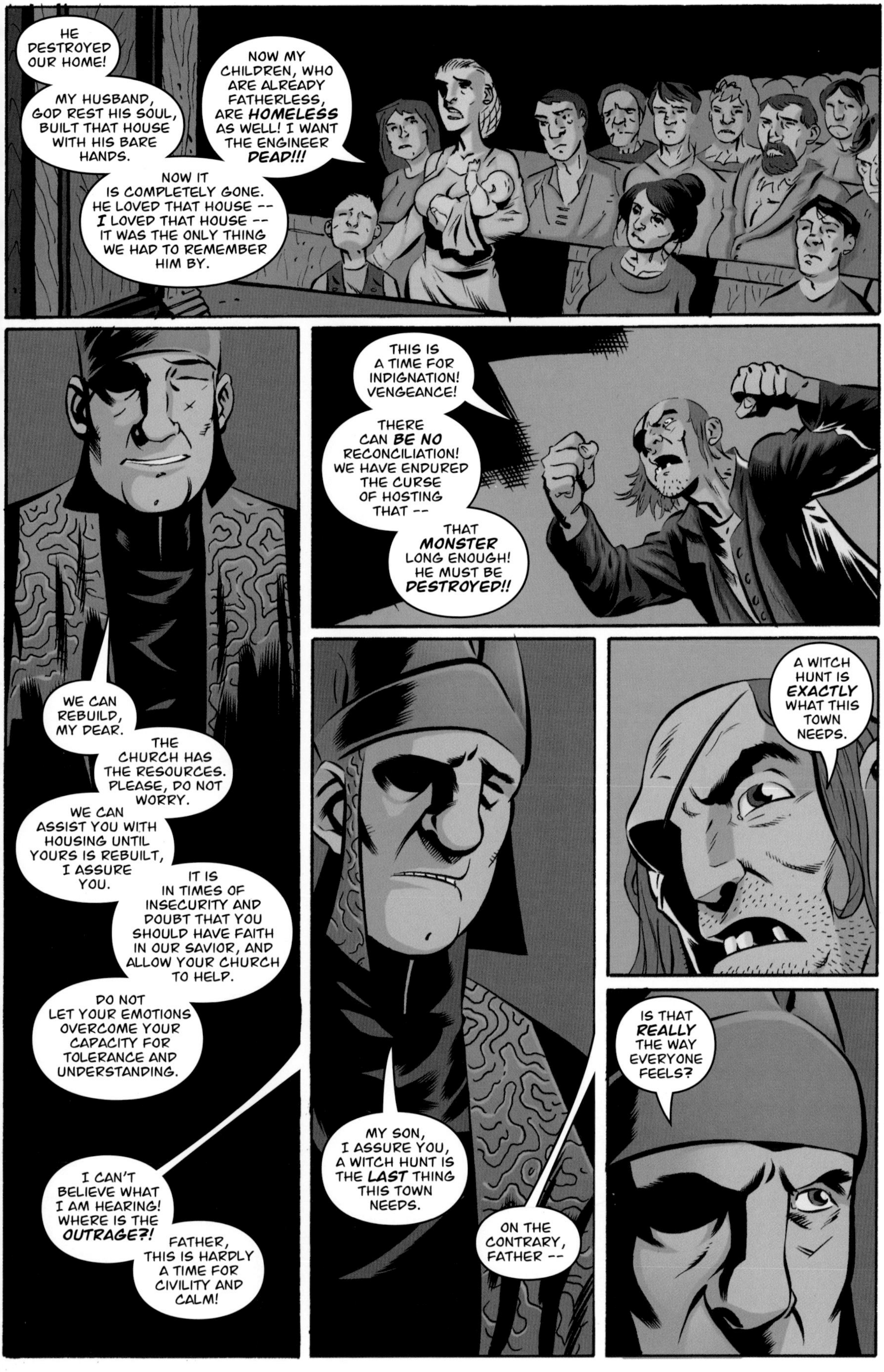

HE DESTROYED OUR HOME!
MY HUSBAND, GOD REST HIS SOUL, BUILT THAT HOUSE WITH HIS BARE HANDS.
NOW IT IS COMPLETELY GONE. HE LOVED THAT HOUSE -- I LOVED THAT HOUSE -- IT WAS THE ONLY THING WE HAD TO REMEMBER HIM BY.
NOW MY CHILDREN, WHO ARE ALREADY FATHERLESS, ARE HOMELESS AS WELL! I WANT THE ENGINEER DEAD!!!
WE CAN REBUILD, MY DEAR.
THE CHURCH HAS THE RESOURCES. PLEASE, DO NOT WORRY.
WE CAN ASSIST YOU WITH HOUSING UNTIL YOURS IS REBUILT, I ASSURE YOU.
IT IS IN TIMES OF INSECURITY AND DOUBT THAT YOU SHOULD HAVE FAITH IN OUR SAVIOR, AND ALLOW YOUR CHURCH TO HELP.
DO NOT LET YOUR EMOTIONS OVERCOME YOUR CAPACITY FOR TOLERANCE AND UNDERSTANDING.
I CAN'T BELIEVE WHAT I AM HEARING! WHERE IS THE OUTRAGE?!
FATHER, THIS IS HARDLY A TIME FOR CIVILITY AND CALM!
THIS IS A TIME FOR INDIGNATION! VENGEANCE!
THERE CAN BE NO RECONCILIATION! WE HAVE ENDURED THE CURSE OF HOSTING THAT --
THAT MONSTER LONG ENOUGH! HE MUST BE DESTROYED!!
MY SON, I ASSURE YOU, A WITCH HUNT IS THE LAST THING THIS TOWN NEEDS.
A WITCH HUNT IS EXACTLY WHAT THIS TOWN NEEDS.
ON THE CONTRARY, FATHER --
IS THAT REALLY THE WAY EVERYONE FEELS?

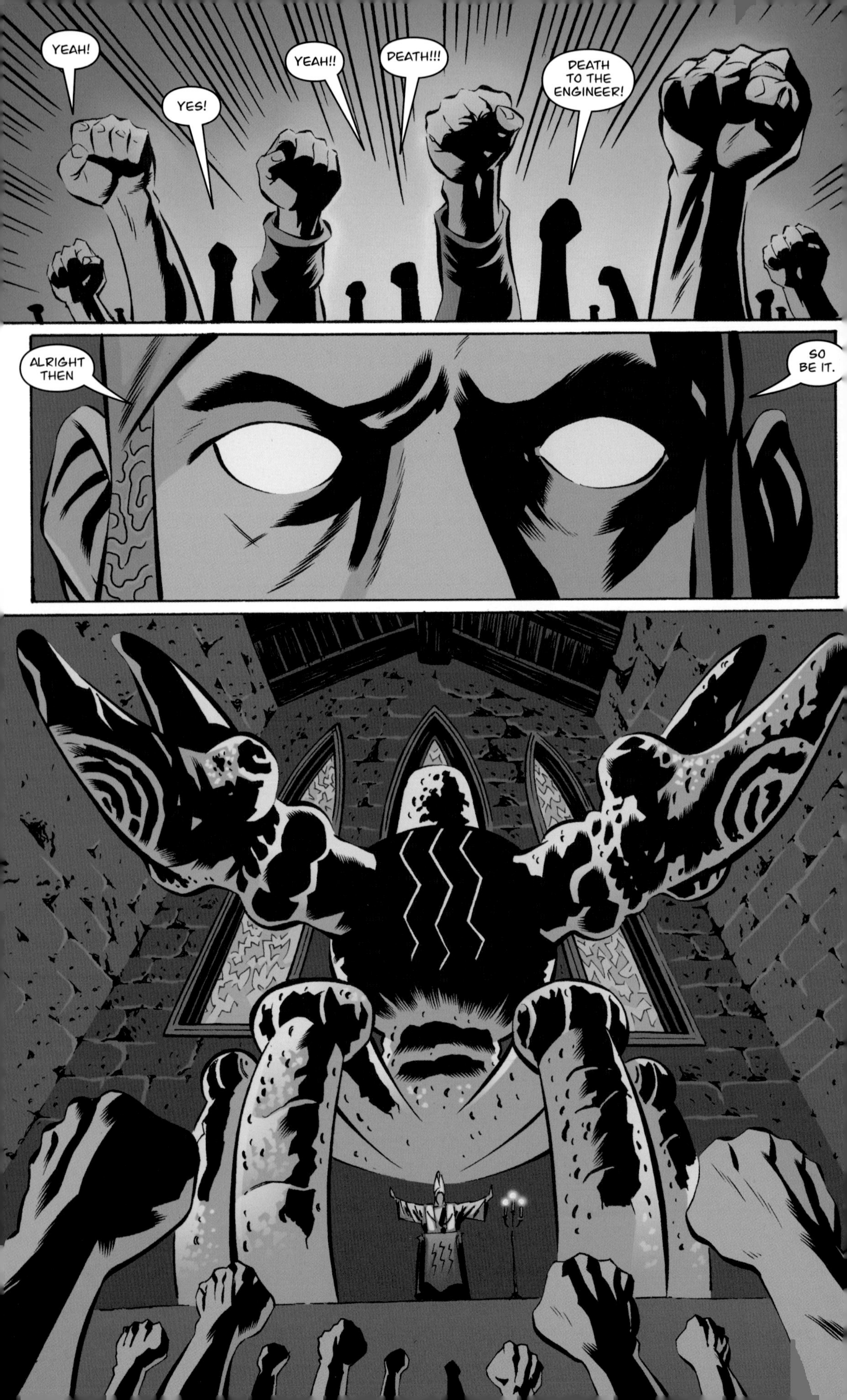
YEAH!
YES!
YEAH!!
DEATH!!!
DEATH TO THE ENGINEER!
ALRIGHT THEN
SO BE IT.

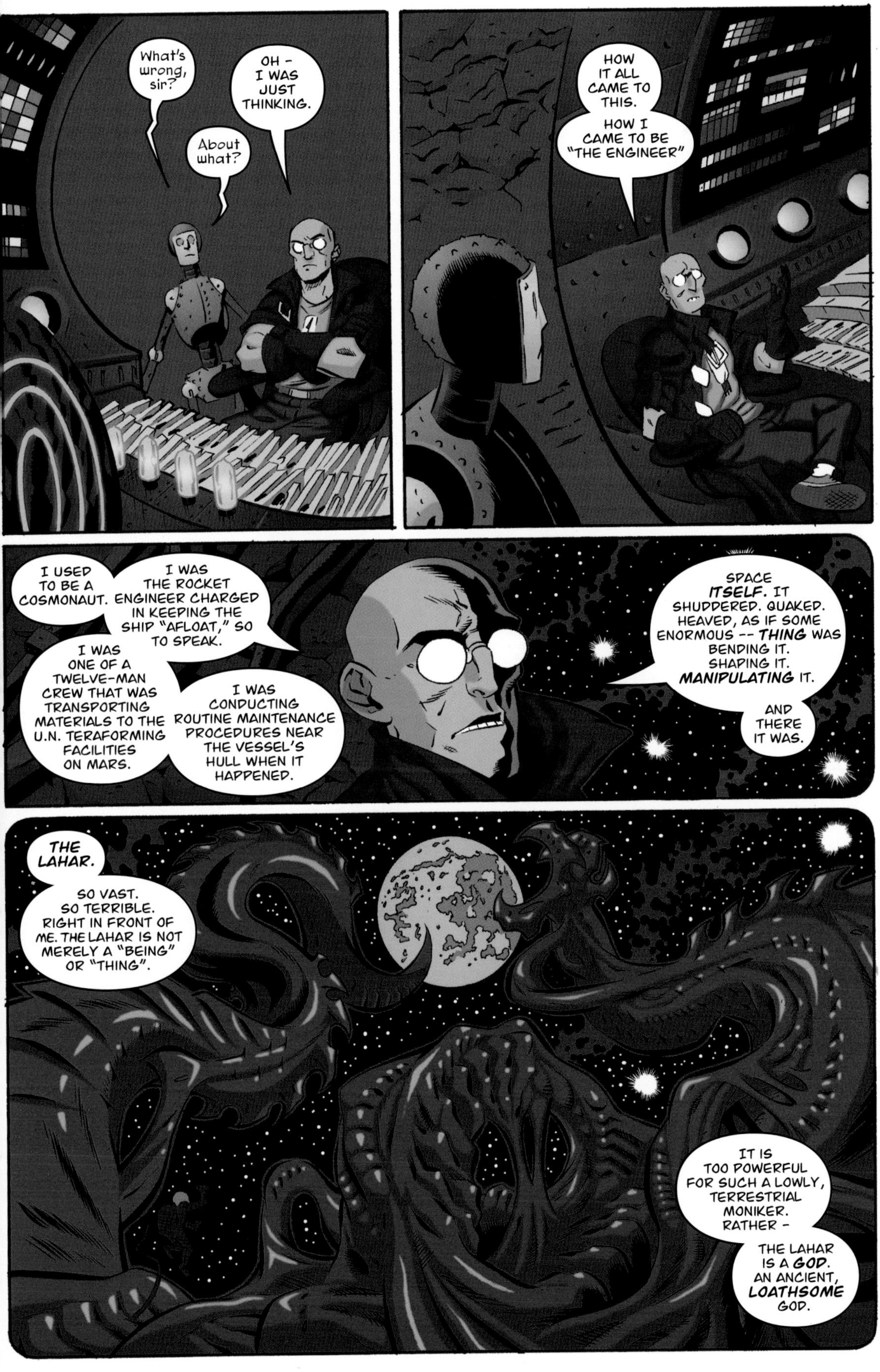
What's wrong, sir?
OH - I WAS JUST THINKING.
About what?
HOW IT ALL CAME TO THIS.
HOW I CAME TO BE "THE ENGINEER"
I USED TO BE A COSMONAUT.
I WAS THE ROCKET ENGINEER CHARGED IN KEEPING THE SHIP "AFLOAT," SO TO SPEAK.
I WAS ONE OF A TWELVE-MAN CREW THAT WAS TRANSPORTING MATERIALS TO THE U.N. TERAFORMING FACILITIES ON MARS.
I WAS CONDUCTING ROUTINE MAINTENANCE PROCEDURES NEAR THE VESSEL'S HULL WHEN IT HAPPENED.
SPACE ITSELF. IT SHUDDERED. QUAKED. HEAVED, AS IF SOME ENORMOUS -- THING WAS BENDING IT. SHAPING IT. MANIPULATING IT.
AND THERE IT WAS.
THE LAHAR.
SO VAST. SO TERRIBLE. RIGHT IN FRONT OF ME. THE LAHAR IS NOT MERELY A "BEING" OR "THING".
IT IS TOO POWERFUL FOR SUCH A LOWLY, TERRESTRIAL MONIKER. RATHER -
THE LAHAR IS A GOD. AN ANCIENT, LOATHSOME GOD.

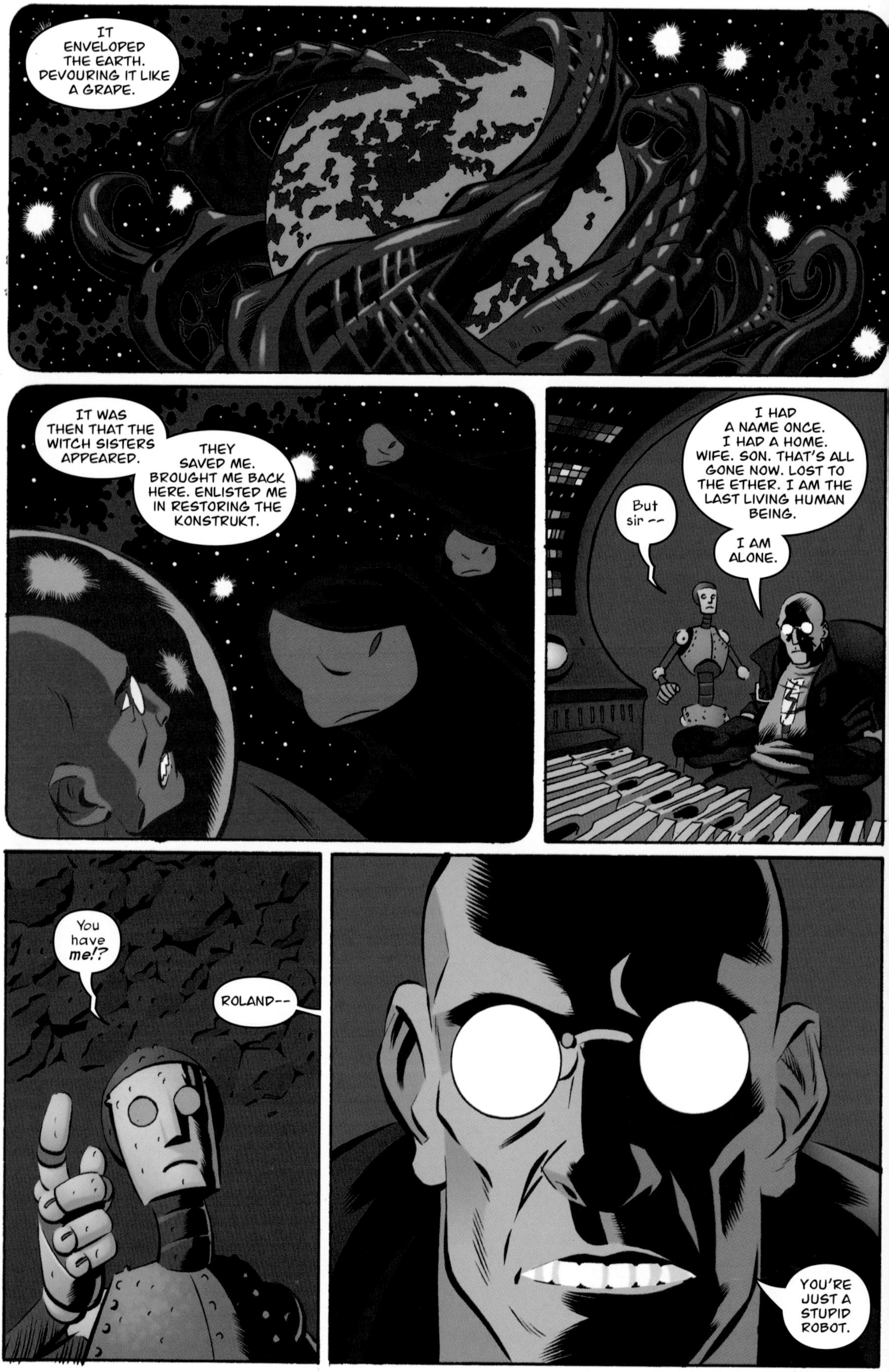
IT ENVELOPED THE EARTH. DEVOURING IT LIKE A GRAPE.
IT WAS THEN THAT THE WITCH SISTERS APPEARED.
THEY SAVED ME. BROUGHT ME BACK HERE. ENLISTED ME IN RESTORING THE KONSTRUKT.
I HAD A NAME ONCE. I HAD A HOME. WIFE. SON. THAT'S ALL GONE NOW. LOST TO THE ETHER. I AM THE LAST LIVING HUMAN BEING.
But sir --
I AM ALONE.
You have me!?
ROLAND--
YOU'RE JUST A STUPID ROBOT.

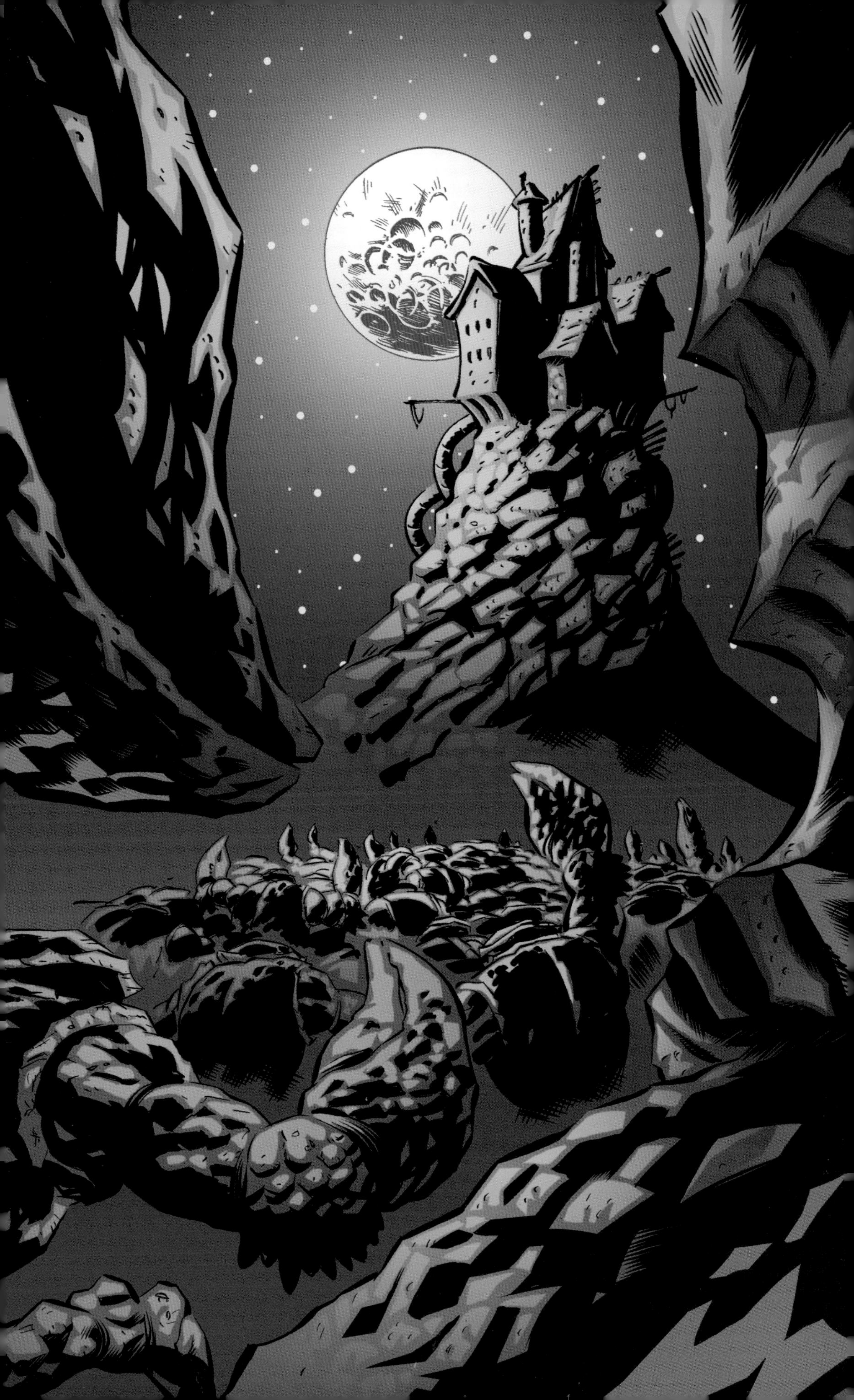

Oh dear.

What *are* they?

CRABS.

A CRUDE, *LOWLY* CREATURE.

PRIMITIVE BOTTOM FEEDERS... INELEGANT.

Why are they coming here?

LONG AGO, THE TOWNSFOLK WERE CURSED WITH TRANSMOGRIFICATION.

Transmogri-who?

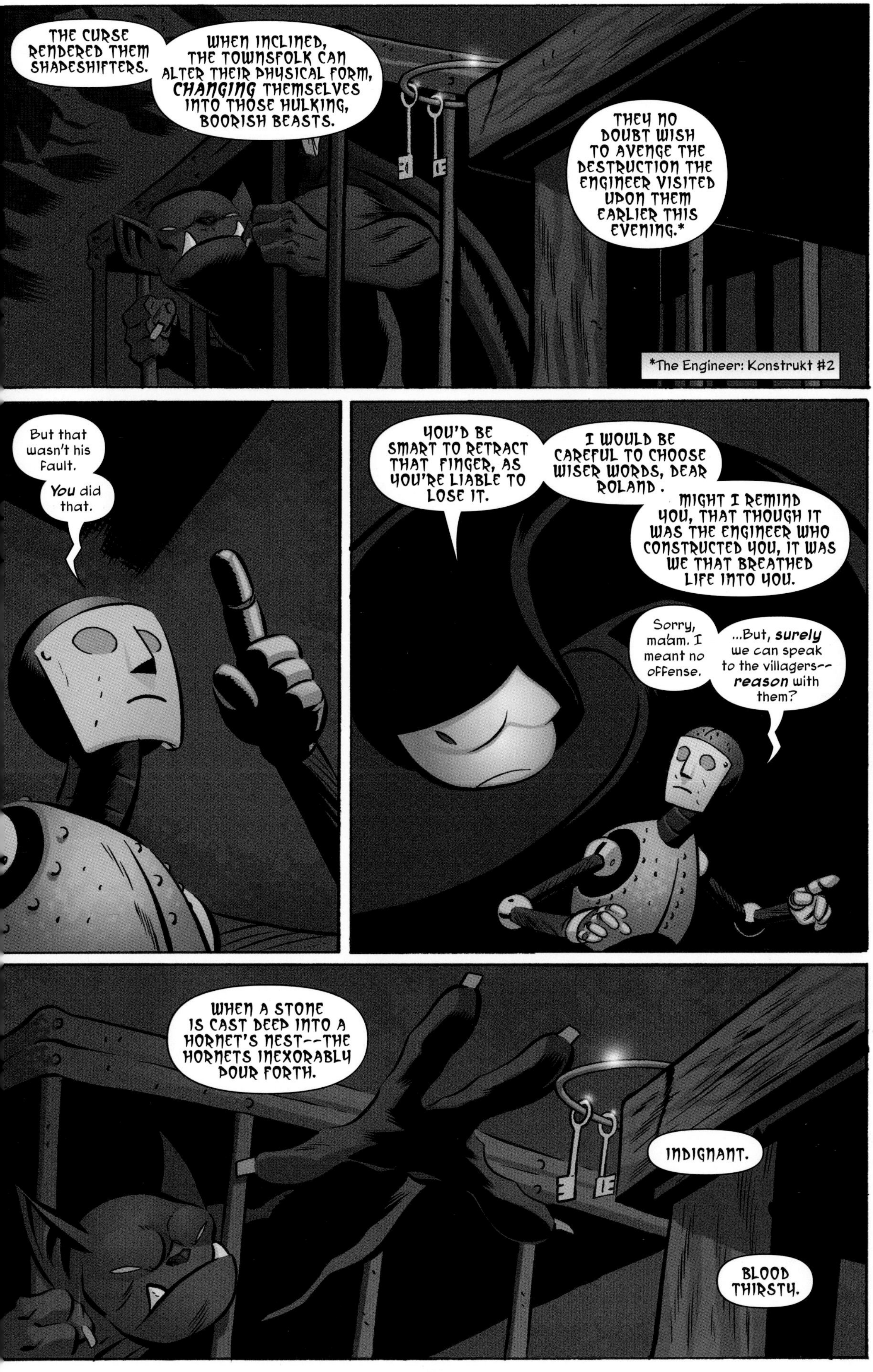
THE CURSE RENDERED THEM SHAPESHIFTERS.
WHEN INCLINED, THE TOWNSFOLK CAN ALTER THEIR PHYSICAL FORM, CHANGING THEMSELVES INTO THOSE HULKING, BOORISH BEASTS.
THEY NO DOUBT WISH TO AVENGE THE DESTRUCTION THE ENGINEER VISITED UPON THEM EARLIER THIS EVENING.*
*The Engineer: Konstrukt #2
But that wasn't his fault.
You did that.
YOU'D BE SMART TO RETRACT THAT FINGER, AS YOU'RE LIABLE TO LOSE IT.
I WOULD BE CAREFUL TO CHOOSE WISER WORDS, DEAR ROLAND.
MIGHT I REMIND YOU, THAT THOUGH IT WAS THE ENGINEER WHO CONSTRUCTED YOU, IT WAS WE THAT BREATHED LIFE INTO YOU.
Sorry, ma'am. I meant no offense.
...But, surely we can speak to the villagers--reason with them?
WHEN A STONE IS CAST DEEP INTO A HORNET'S NEST--THE HORNETS INEXORABLY POUR FORTH.
INDIGNANT.
BLOOD THIRSTY.

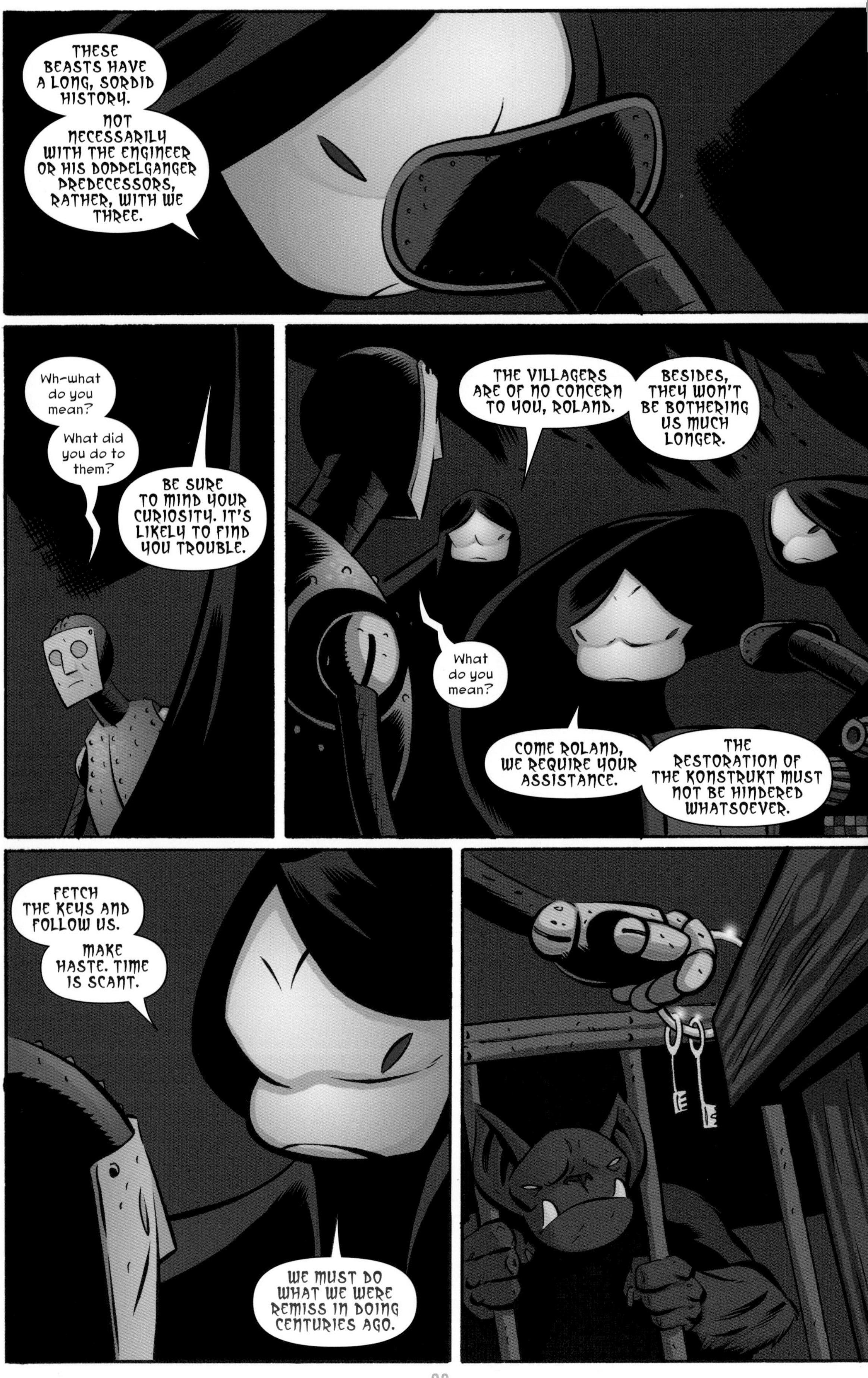
THESE BEASTS HAVE A LONG, SORDID HISTORY.
NOT NECESSARILY WITH THE ENGINEER OR HIS DOPPELGANGER PREDECESSORS, RATHER, WITH WE THREE.
Wh-what do you mean?
What did you do to them?
BE SURE TO MIND YOUR CURIOSITY. IT'S LIKELY TO FIND YOU TROUBLE.
THE VILLAGERS ARE OF NO CONCERN TO YOU, ROLAND.
BESIDES, THEY WON'T BE BOTHERING US MUCH LONGER.
What do you mean?
COME ROLAND, WE REQUIRE YOUR ASSISTANCE.
THE RESTORATION OF THE KONSTRUKT MUST NOT BE HINDERED WHATSOEVER.
FETCH THE KEYS AND FOLLOW US.
MAKE HASTE. TIME IS SCANT.
WE MUST DO WHAT WE WERE REMISS IN DOING CENTURIES AGO.

Elsewhere...

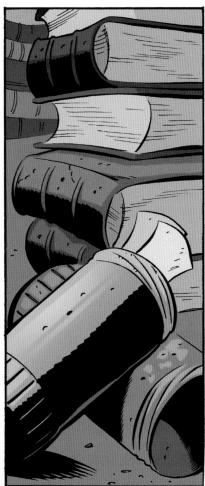

81

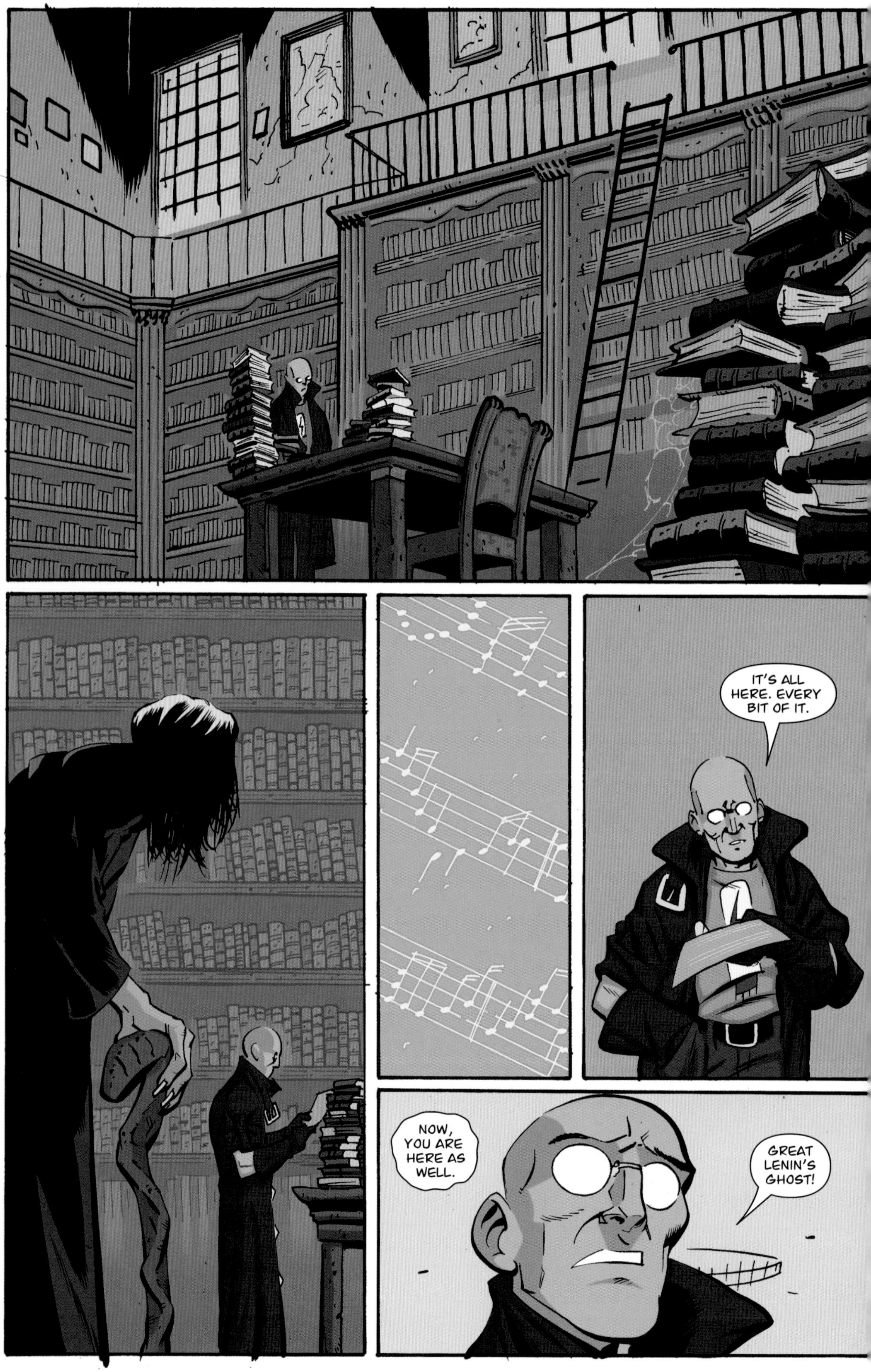
IT'S ALL HERE. EVERY BIT OF IT.
NOW, YOU ARE HERE AS WELL.
GREAT LENIN'S GHOST!

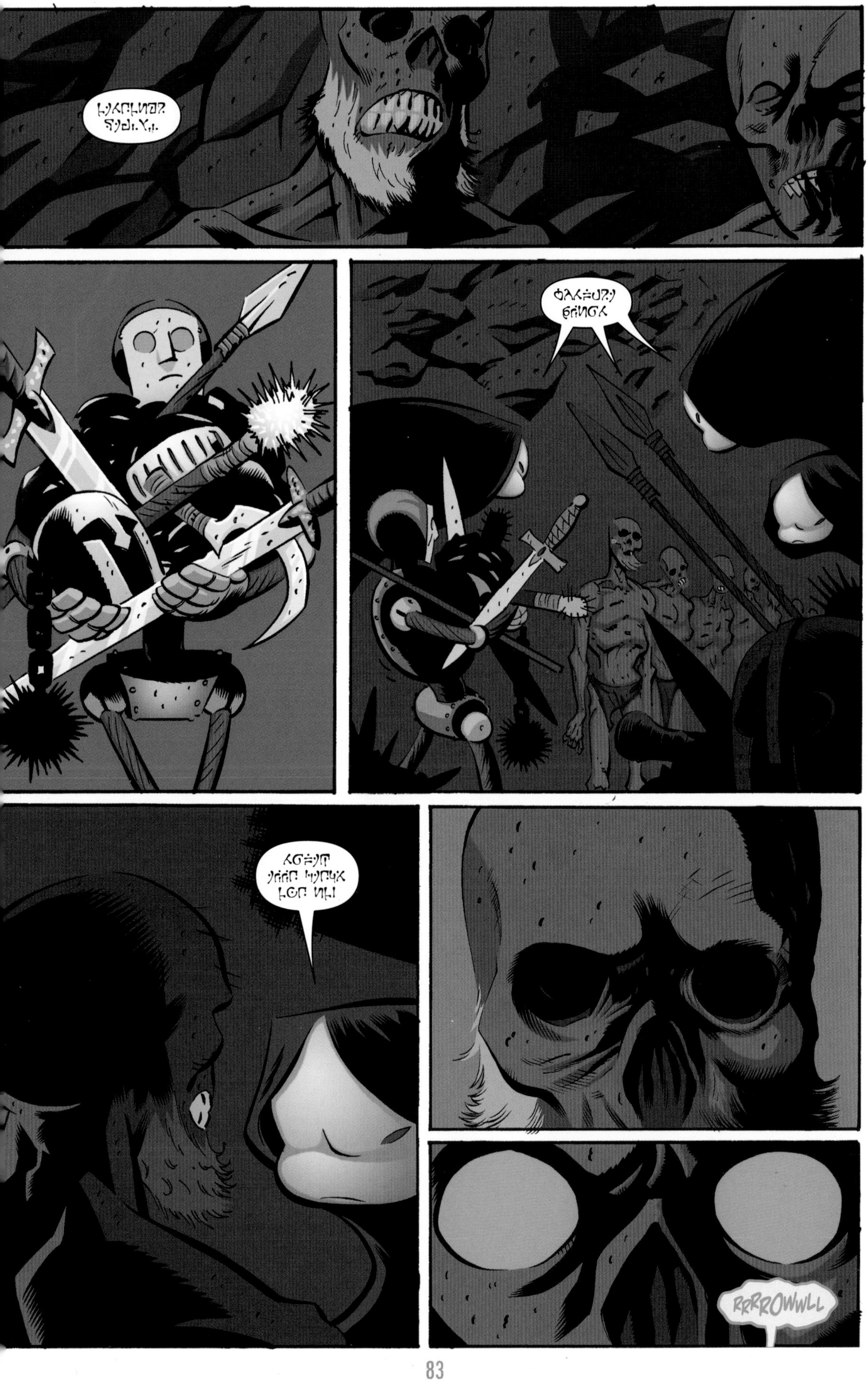
RRRROWWLL

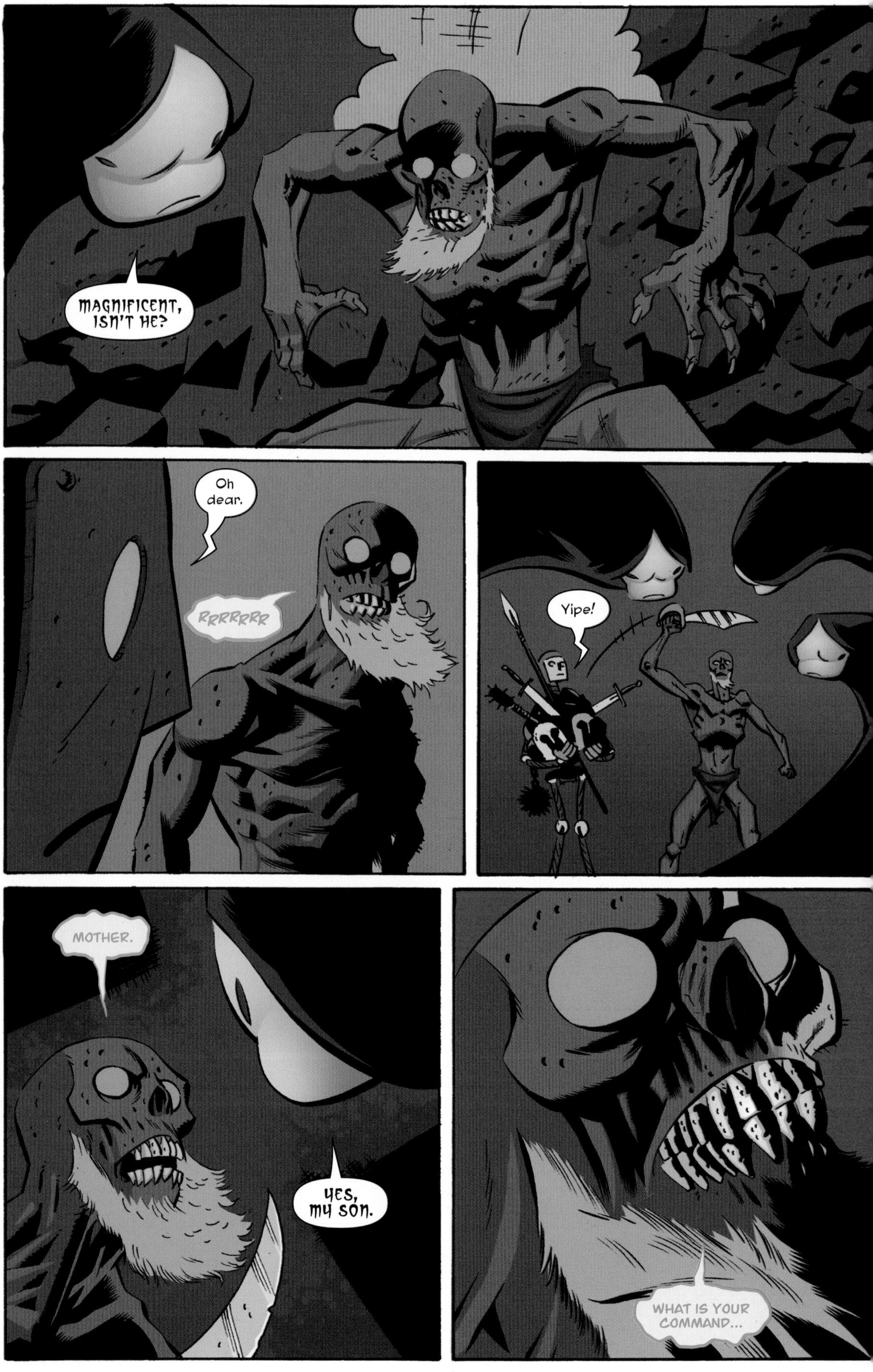
MAGNIFICENT, ISN'T HE?
Oh dear.
RRRRRRR
Yipe!
MOTHER.
YES, MY SON.
WHAT IS YOUR COMMAND...

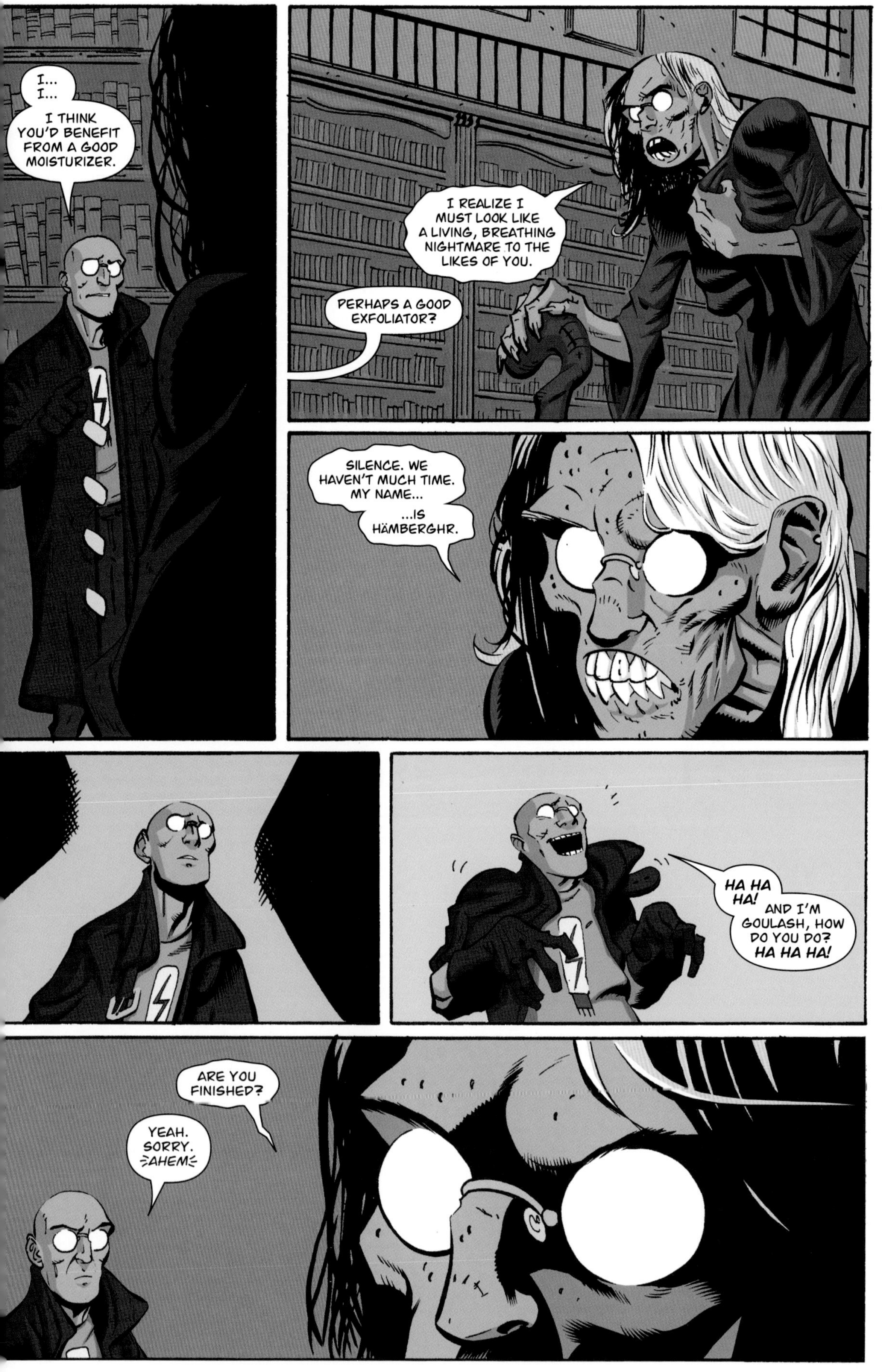
I...
I...
I THINK YOU'D BENEFIT FROM A GOOD MOISTURIZER.
I REALIZE I MUST LOOK LIKE A LIVING, BREATHING NIGHTMARE TO THE LIKES OF YOU.
PERHAPS A GOOD EXFOLIATOR?
SILENCE. WE HAVEN'T MUCH TIME. MY NAME...
...IS HÄMBERGHR.
HA HA HA! AND I'M GOULASH, HOW DO YOU DO? HA HA HA!
ARE YOU FINISHED?
YEAH. SORRY. AHEM

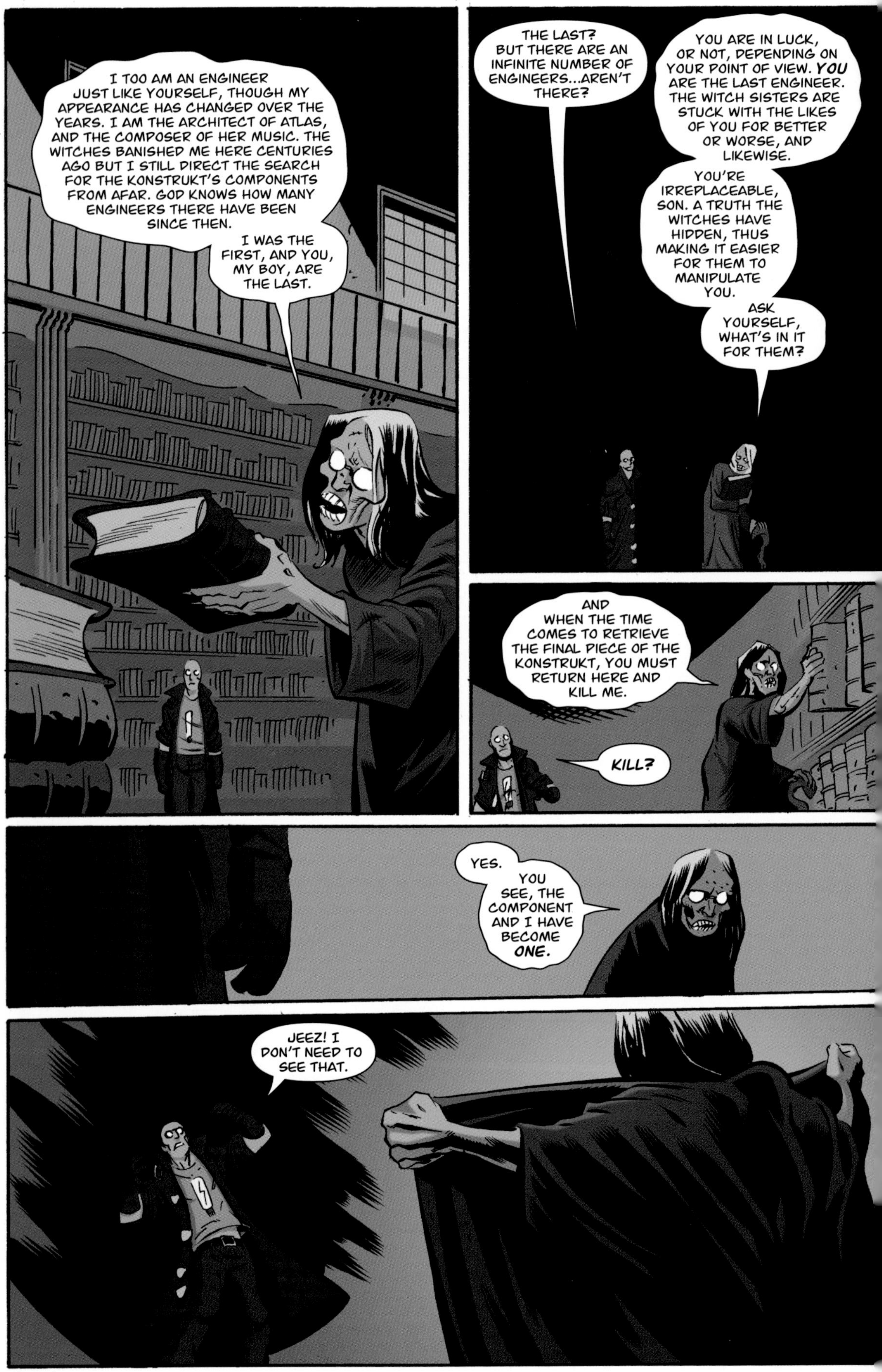
I TOO AM AN ENGINEER JUST LIKE YOURSELF, THOUGH MY APPEARANCE HAS CHANGED OVER THE YEARS. I AM THE ARCHITECT OF ATLAS, AND THE COMPOSER OF HER MUSIC. THE WITCHES BANISHED ME HERE CENTURIES AGO BUT I STILL DIRECT THE SEARCH FOR THE KONSTRUKT'S COMPONENTS FROM AFAR. GOD KNOWS HOW MANY ENGINEERS THERE HAVE BEEN SINCE THEN.
I WAS THE FIRST, AND YOU, MY BOY, ARE THE LAST.
THE LAST? BUT THERE ARE AN INFINITE NUMBER OF ENGINEERS...AREN'T THERE?
YOU ARE IN LUCK, OR NOT, DEPENDING ON YOUR POINT OF VIEW. ***YOU*** ARE THE LAST ENGINEER. THE WITCH SISTERS ARE STUCK WITH THE LIKES OF YOU FOR BETTER OR WORSE, AND LIKEWISE.
YOU'RE IRREPLACEABLE, SON. A TRUTH THE WITCHES HAVE HIDDEN, THUS MAKING IT EASIER FOR THEM TO MANIPULATE YOU.
ASK YOURSELF, WHAT'S IN IT FOR THEM?
AND WHEN THE TIME COMES TO RETRIEVE THE FINAL PIECE OF THE KONSTRUKT, YOU MUST RETURN HERE AND KILL ME.
KILL?
YES.
YOU SEE, THE COMPONENT AND I HAVE BECOME ***ONE.***
JEEZ! I DON'T NEED TO SEE THAT.

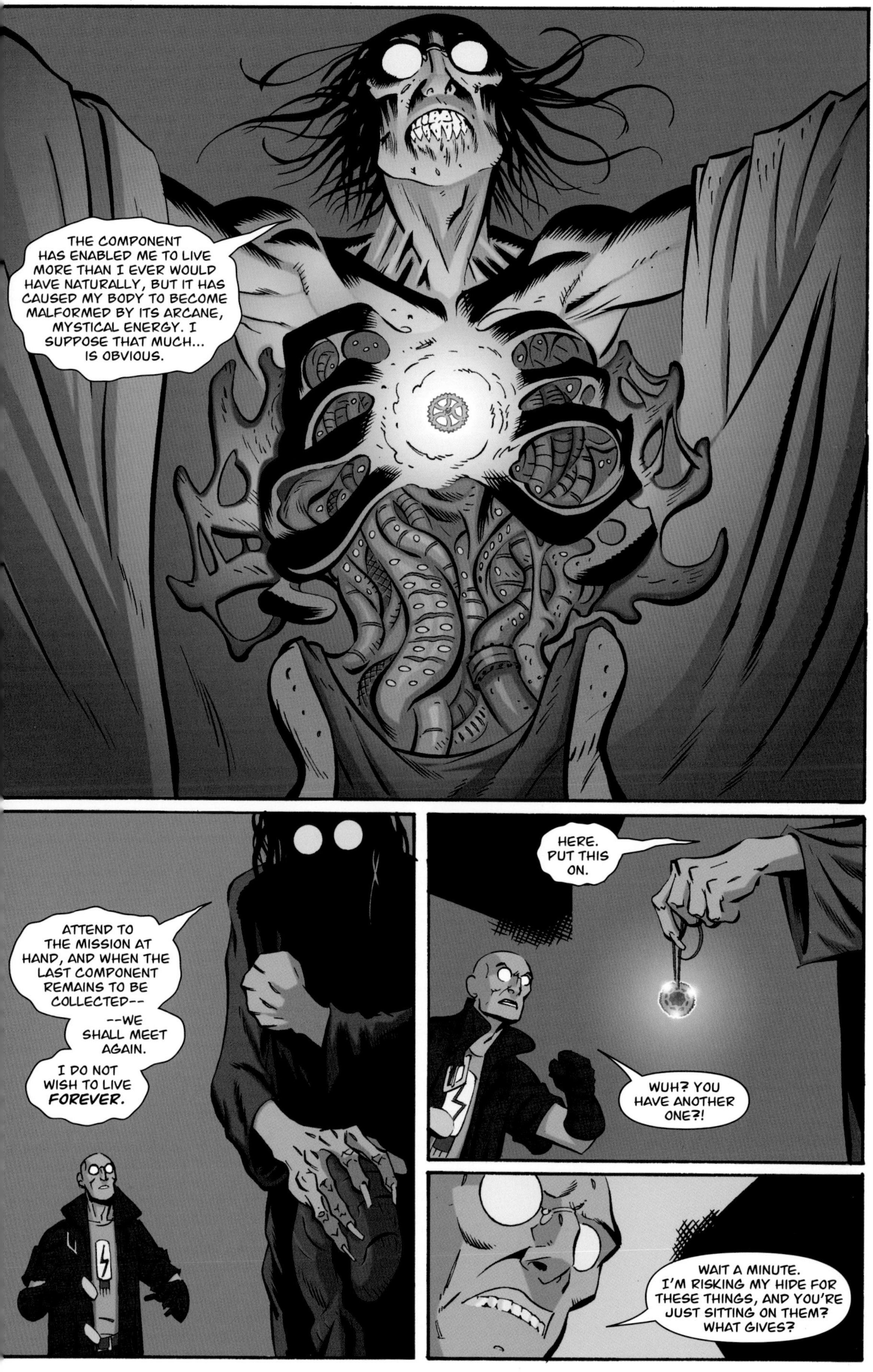
THE COMPONENT HAS ENABLED ME TO LIVE MORE THAN I EVER WOULD HAVE NATURALLY, BUT IT HAS CAUSED MY BODY TO BECOME MALFORMED BY ITS ARCANE, MYSTICAL ENERGY. I SUPPOSE THAT MUCH... IS OBVIOUS.
ATTEND TO THE MISSION AT HAND, AND WHEN THE LAST COMPONENT REMAINS TO BE COLLECTED--
--WE SHALL MEET AGAIN.
I DO NOT WISH TO LIVE **FOREVER.**
HERE. PUT THIS ON.
WUH? YOU HAVE ANOTHER ONE?!
WAIT A MINUTE. I'M RISKING MY HIDE FOR THESE THINGS, AND YOU'RE JUST SITTING ON THEM? WHAT GIVES?

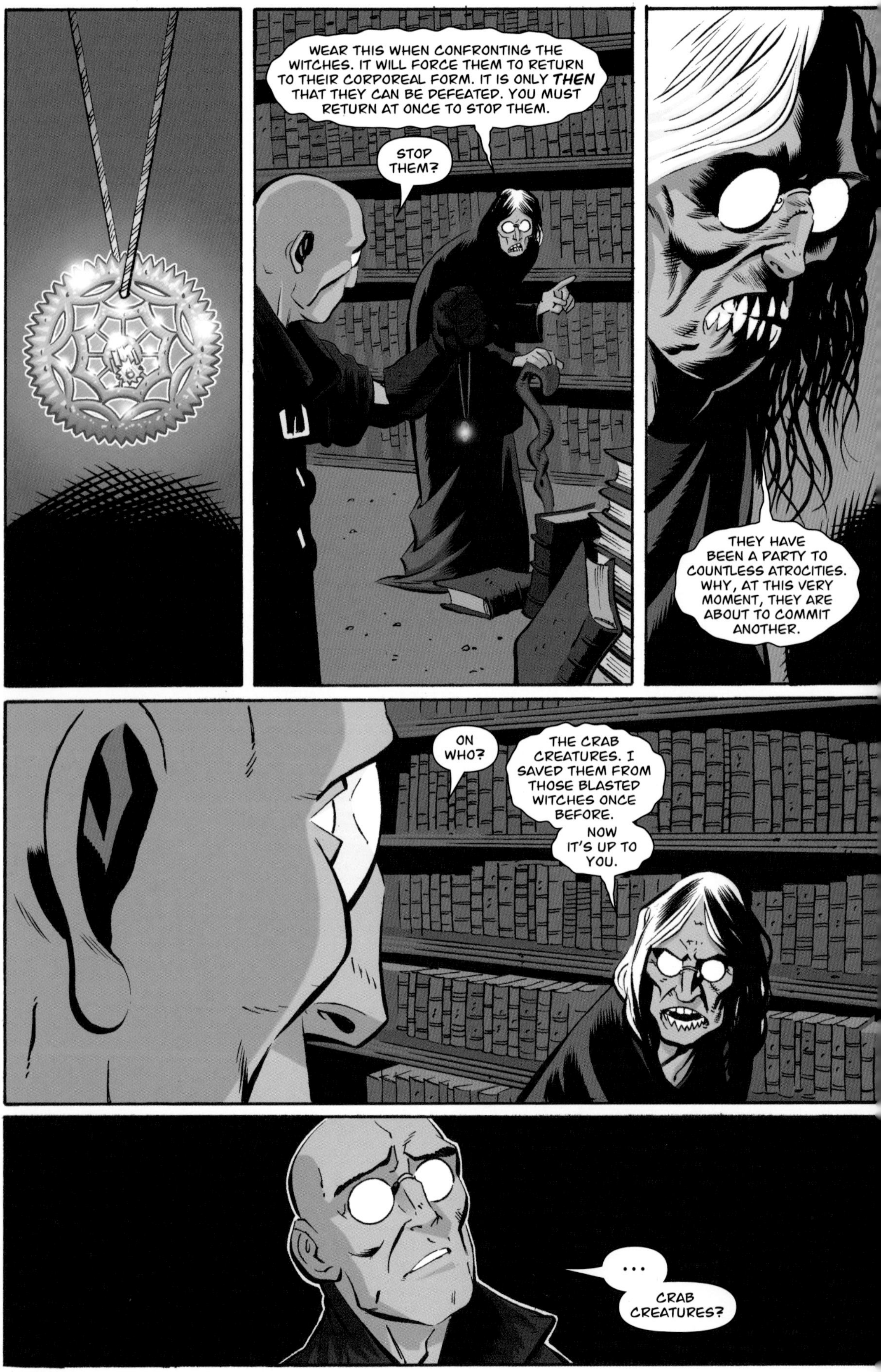
WEAR THIS WHEN CONFRONTING THE WITCHES. IT WILL FORCE THEM TO RETURN TO THEIR CORPOREAL FORM. IT IS ONLY **THEN** THAT THEY CAN BE DEFEATED. YOU MUST RETURN AT ONCE TO STOP THEM.
STOP THEM?
THEY HAVE BEEN A PARTY TO COUNTLESS ATROCITIES. WHY, AT THIS VERY MOMENT, THEY ARE ABOUT TO COMMIT ANOTHER.
ON WHO?
THE CRAB CREATURES. I SAVED THEM FROM THOSE BLASTED WITCHES ONCE BEFORE.
NOW IT'S UP TO YOU.
...
CRAB CREATURES?

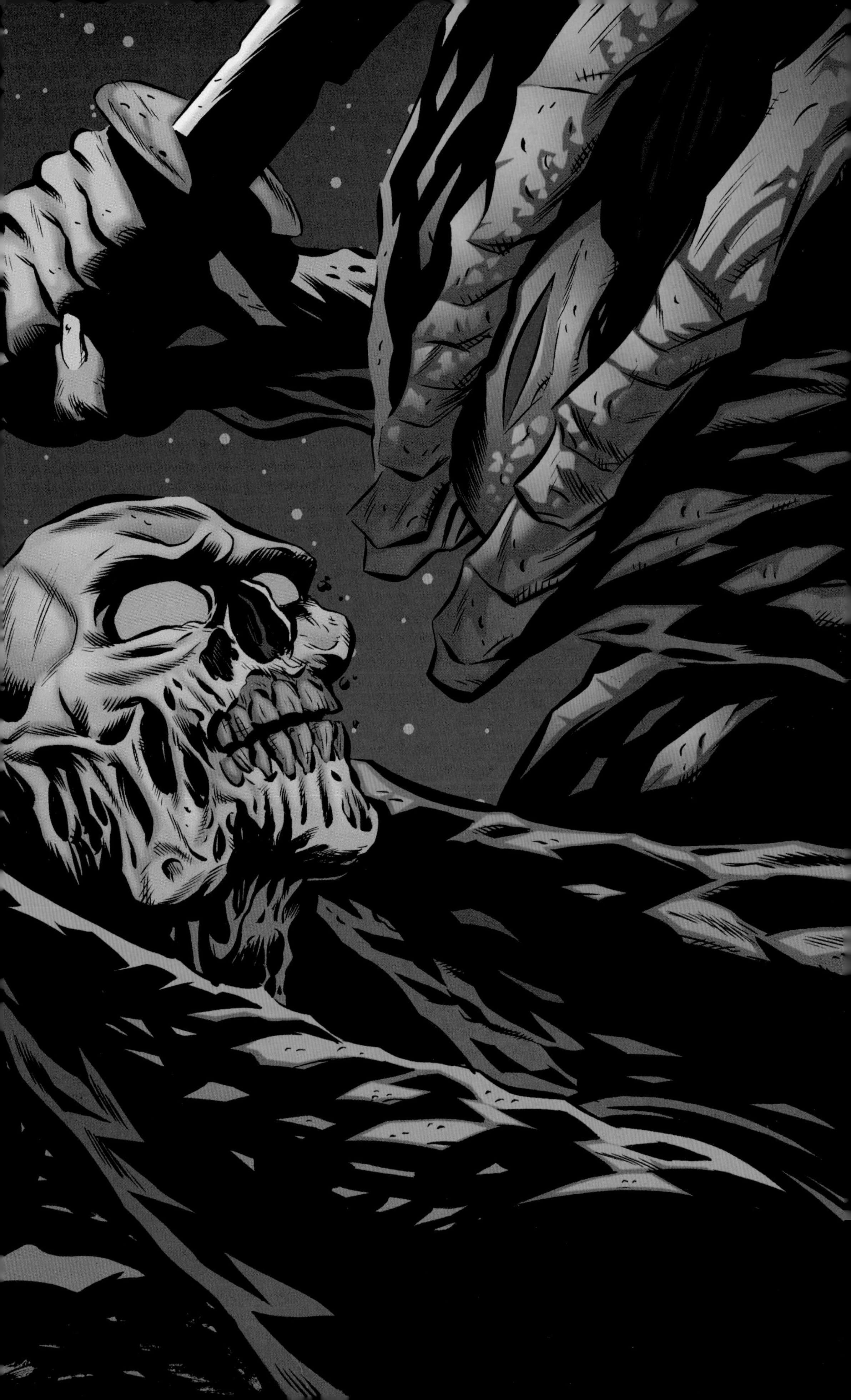

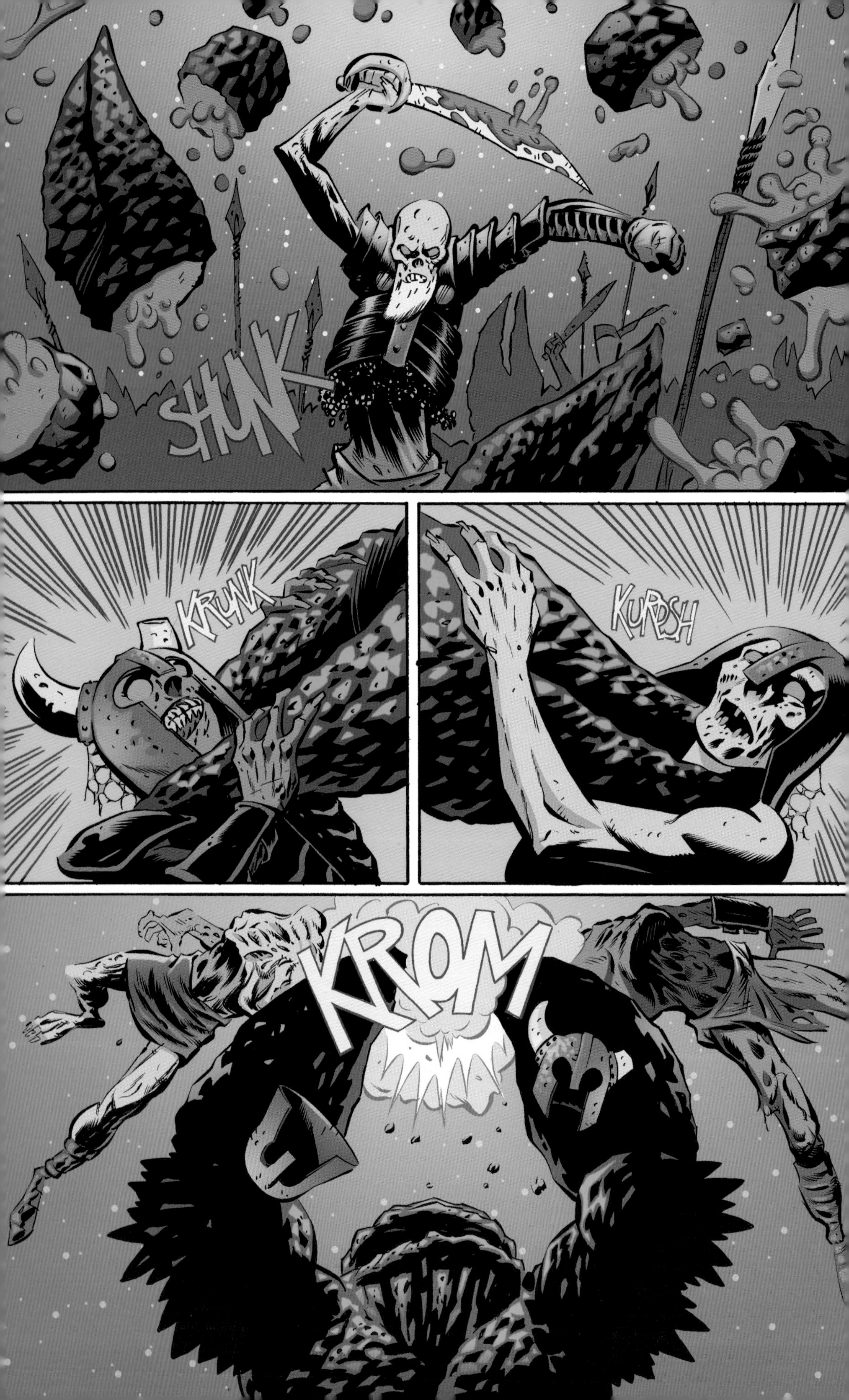
SHUNK
KRUNK
KURDSH
KROM

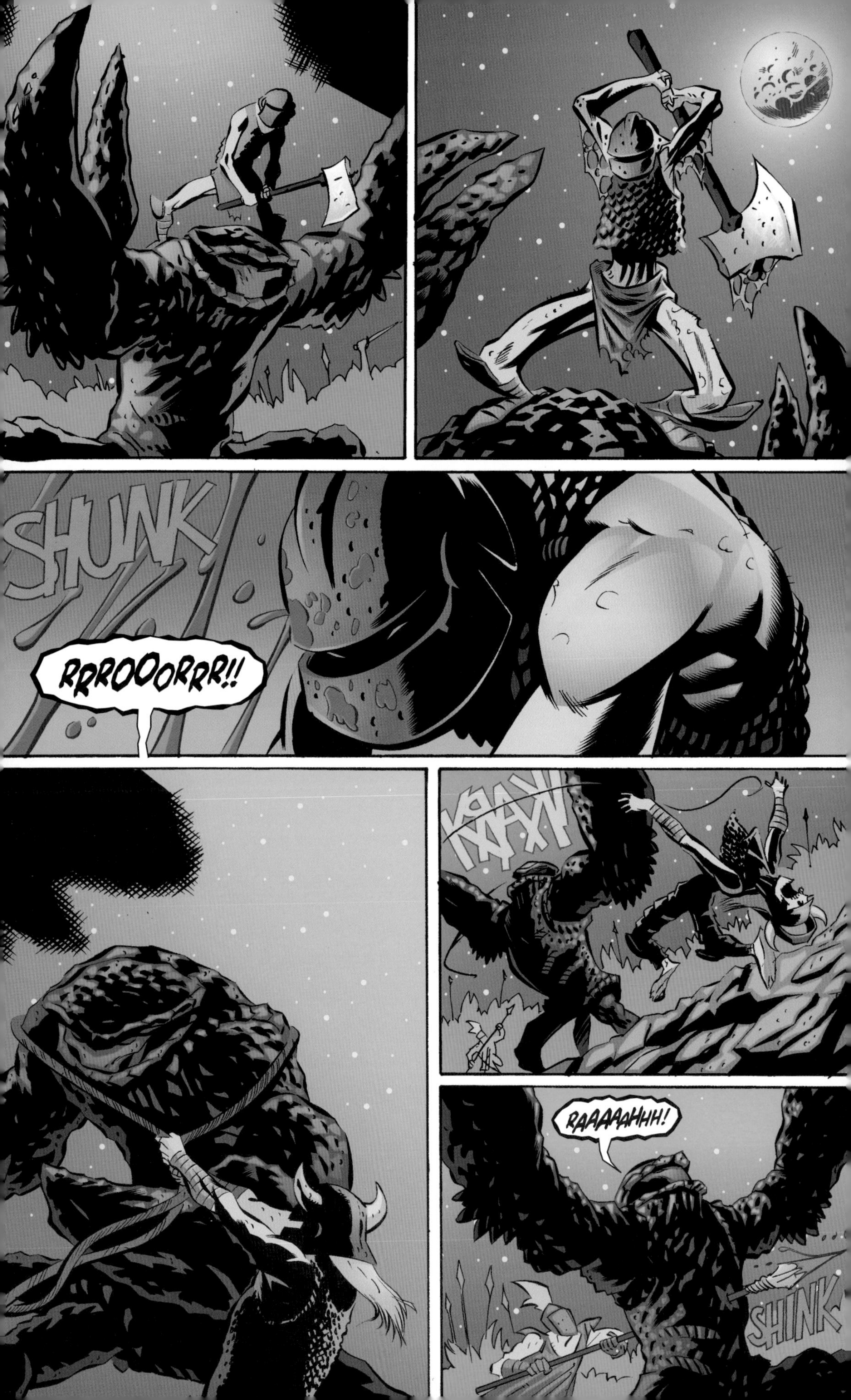
SHUNK
RRROOORRR!!
RAAAAAHHH!
SHINK

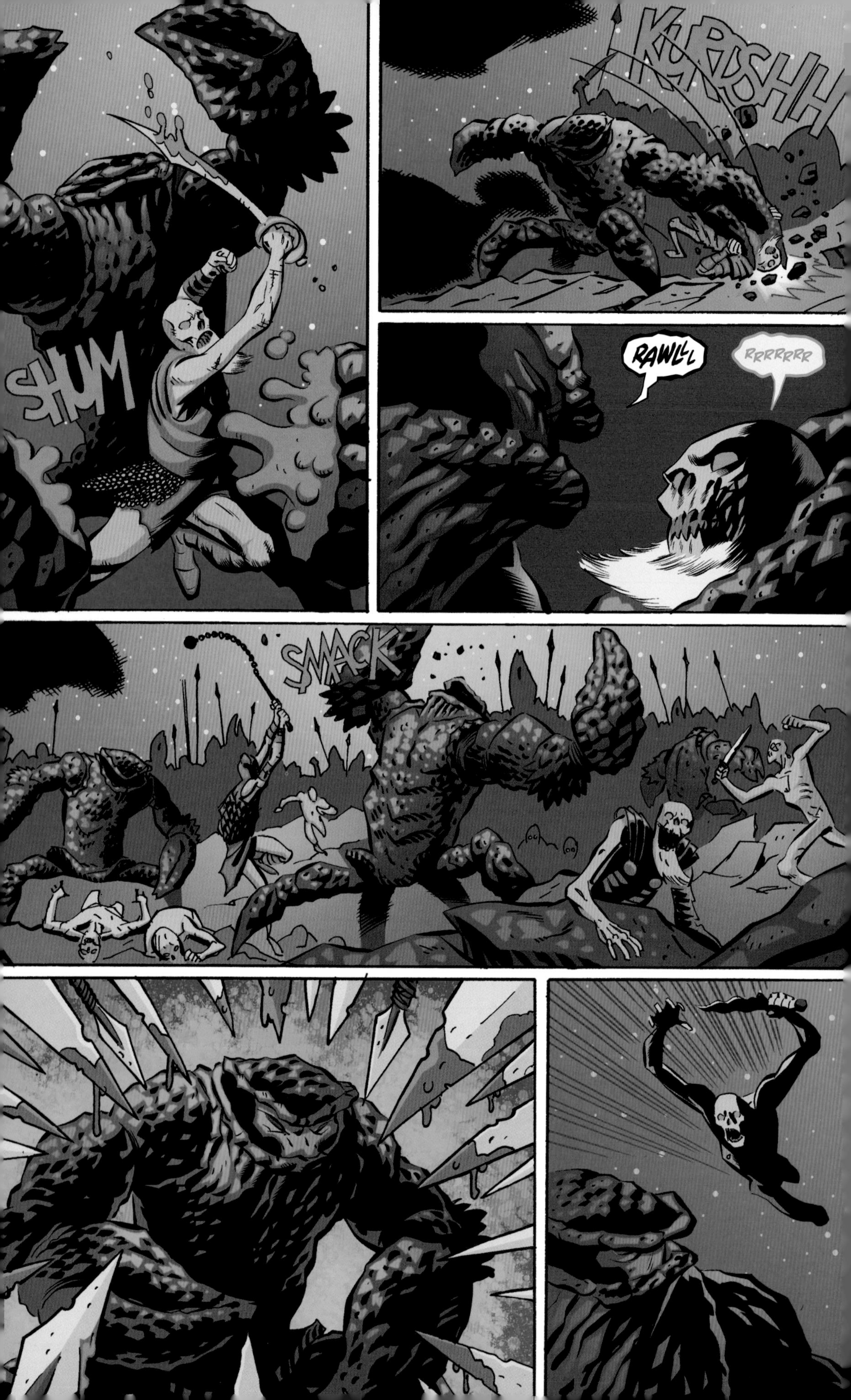
SHUM
KYRUSHH
RAWLLL
RRRRRRR
SMACK

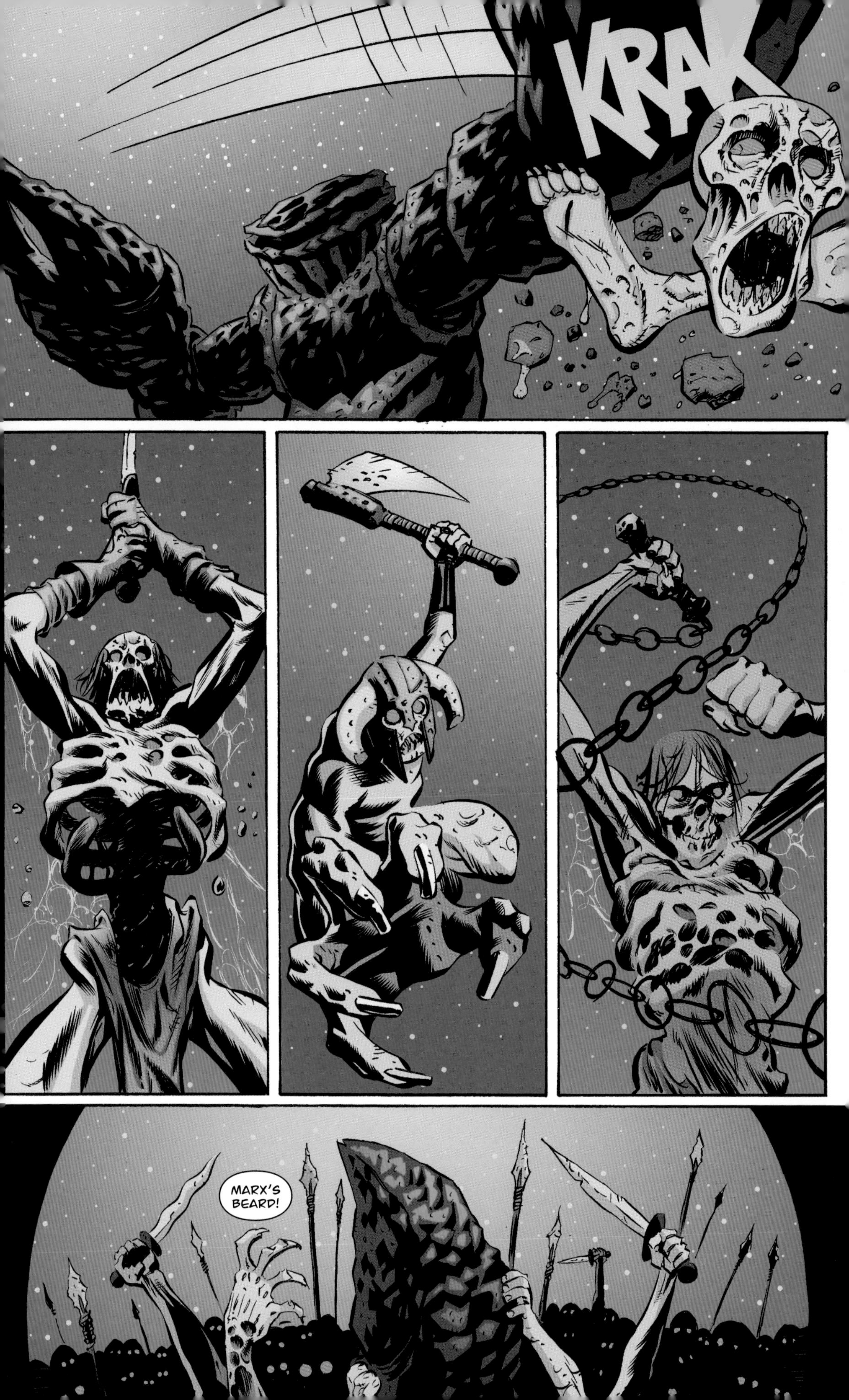
KRAK
MARX'S BEARD!

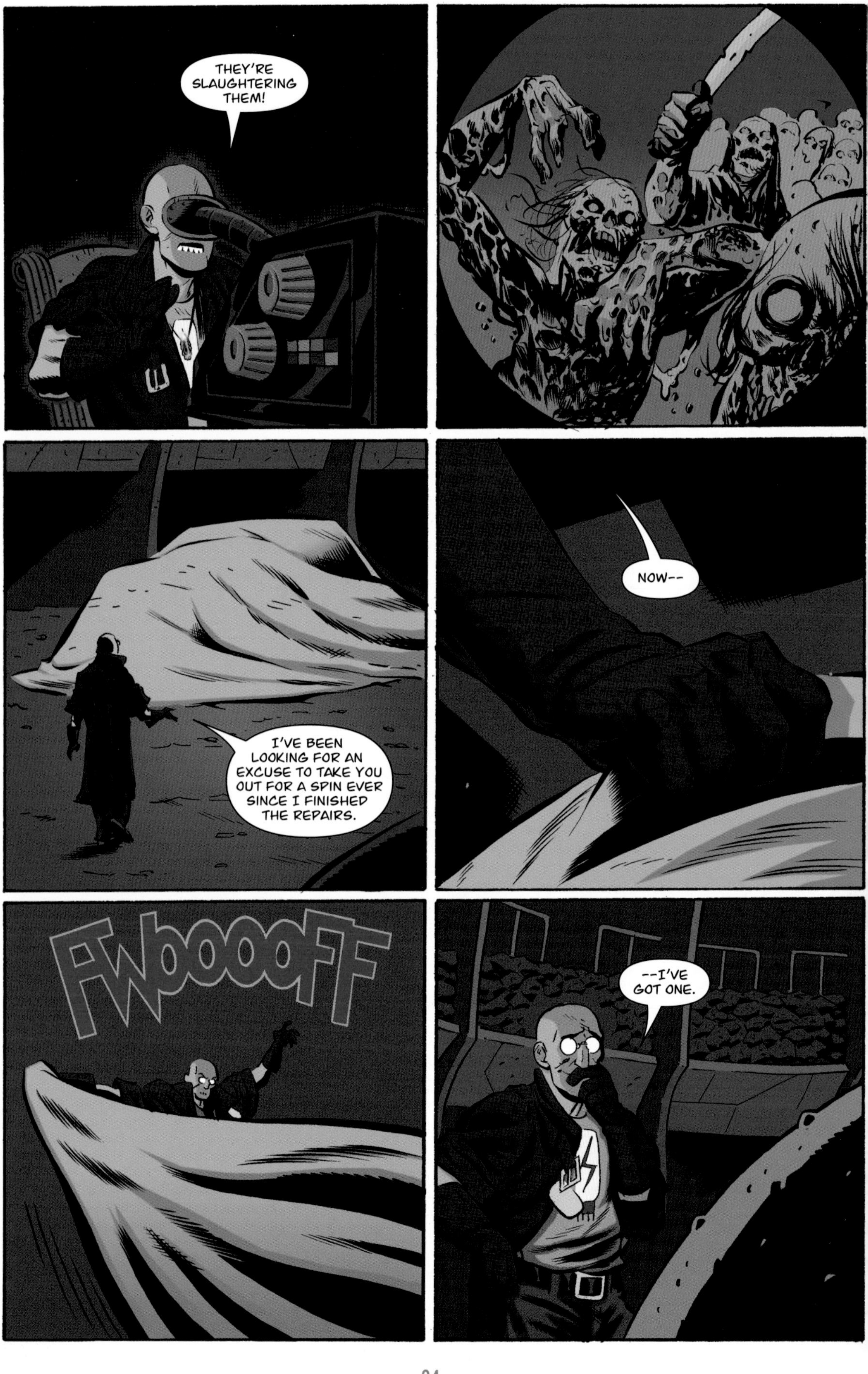
THEY'RE SLAUGHTERING THEM!
I'VE BEEN LOOKING FOR AN EXCUSE TO TAKE YOU OUT FOR A SPIN EVER SINCE I FINISHED THE REPAIRS.
NOW--
FWOOOFF
--I'VE GOT ONE.

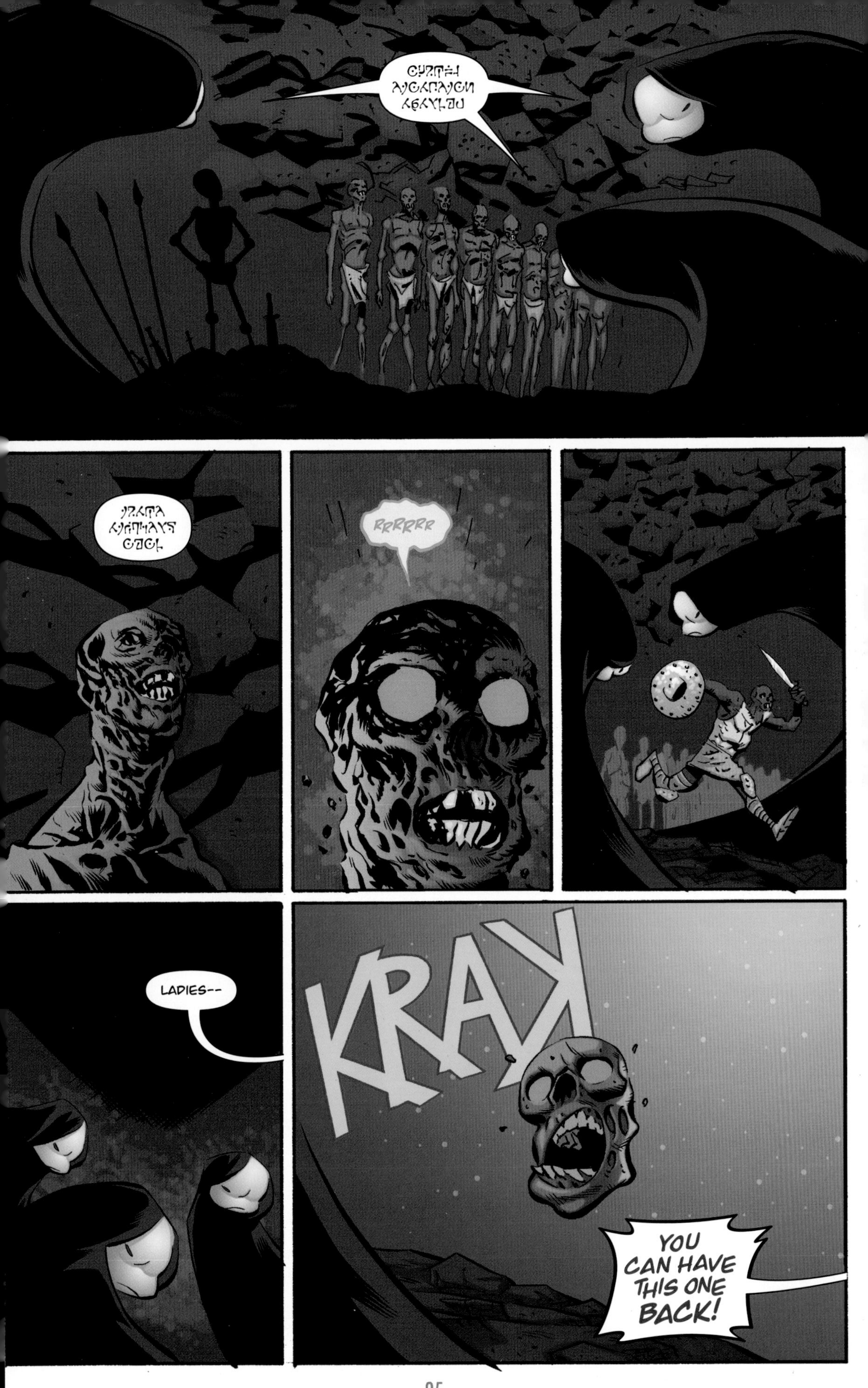
RRRRRR
LADIES--
KRAK
YOU CAN HAVE THIS ONE BACK!

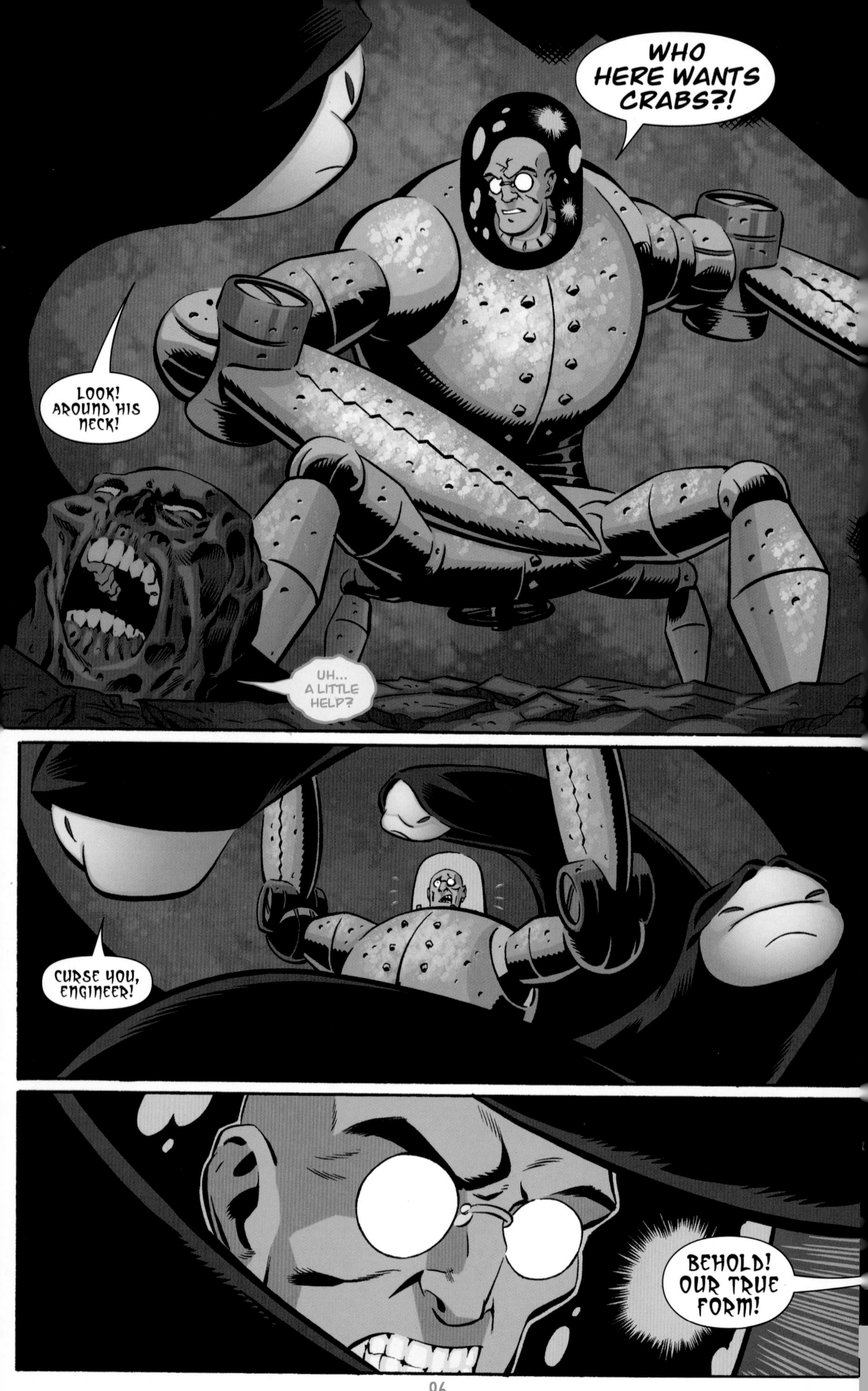
WHO HERE WANTS CRABS?!
LOOK! AROUND HIS NECK!
UH... A LITTLE HELP?
CURSE YOU, ENGINEER!
BEHOLD! OUR TRUE FORM!

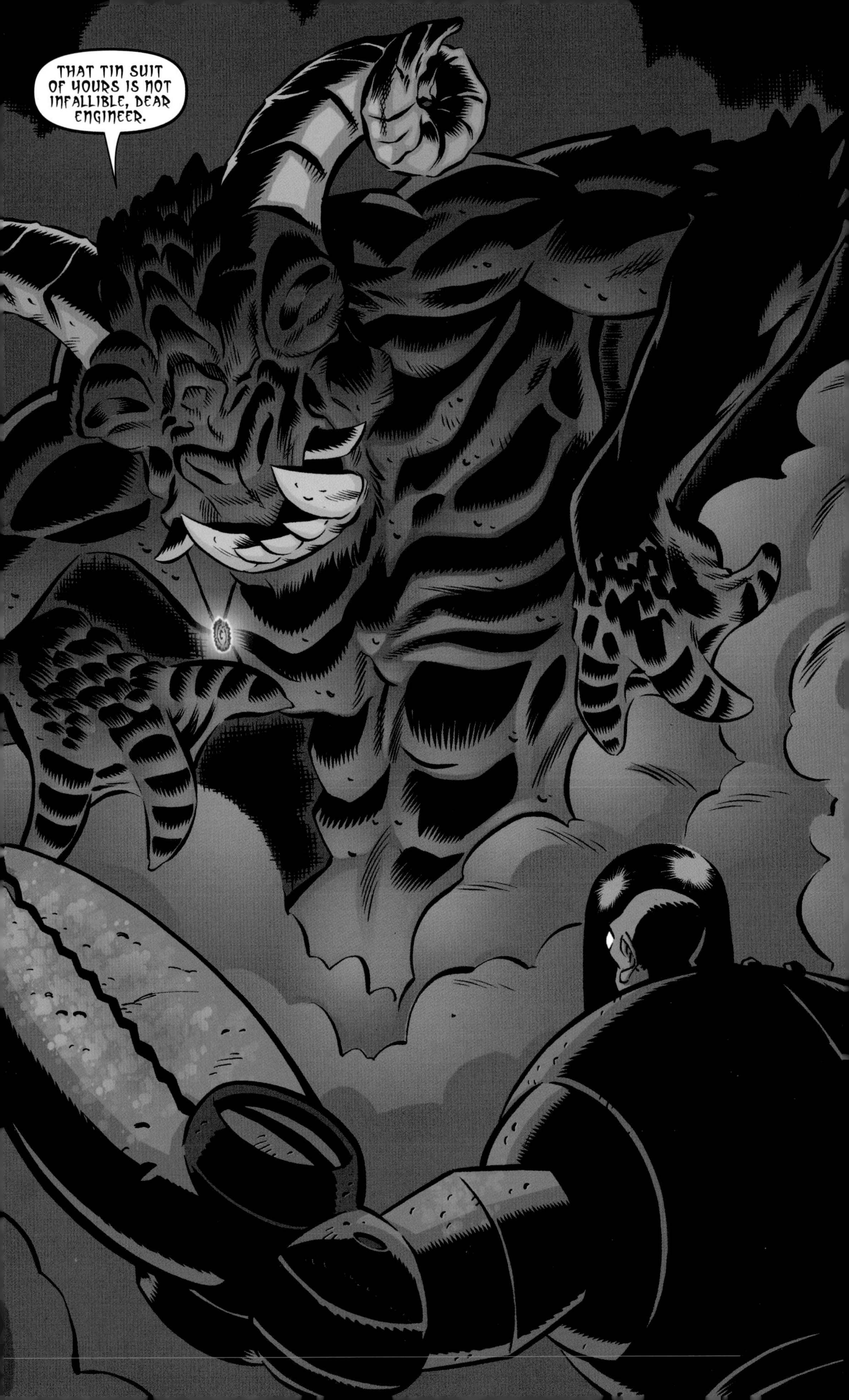
THAT TIN SUIT OF YOURS IS NOT INFALLIBLE, DEAR ENGINEER.

IT WILL BE YOUR TOMB.

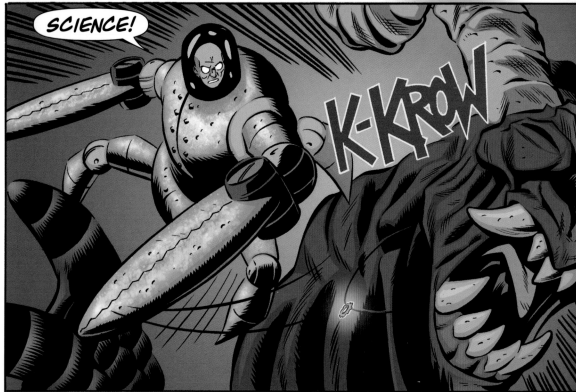

SCIENCE!

K-KROW

Actually, more like mysticism really, because the inherent properties of the Konstrukt component around your neck--

SHUT UP, ROLAND.

Shutting.

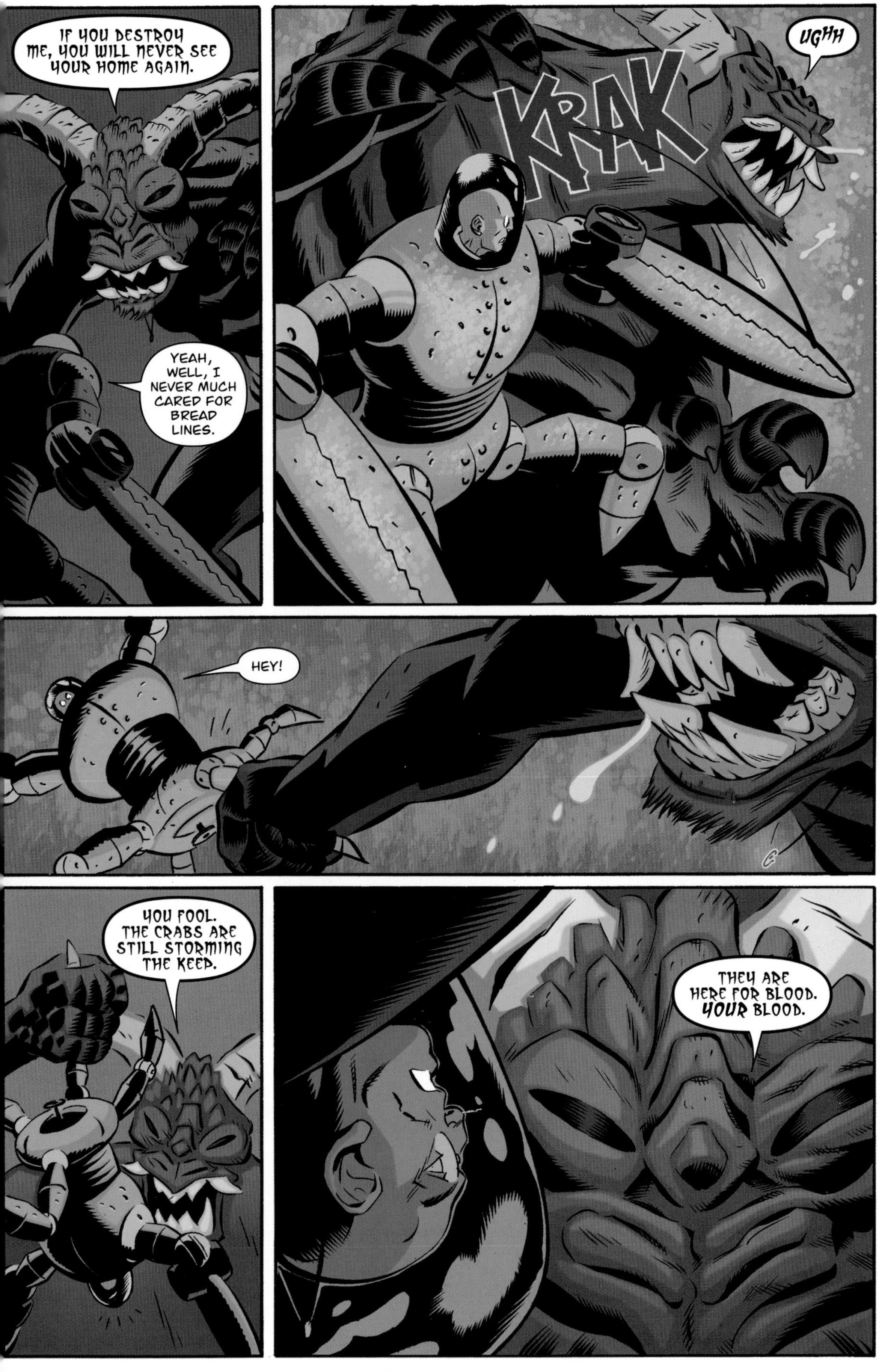
IF YOU DESTROY ME, YOU WILL NEVER SEE YOUR HOME AGAIN.
YEAH, WELL, I NEVER MUCH CARED FOR BREAD LINES.
KRAK
UGHH
HEY!
YOU FOOL. THE CRABS ARE STILL STORMING THE KEEP.
THEY ARE HERE FOR BLOOD. YOUR BLOOD.

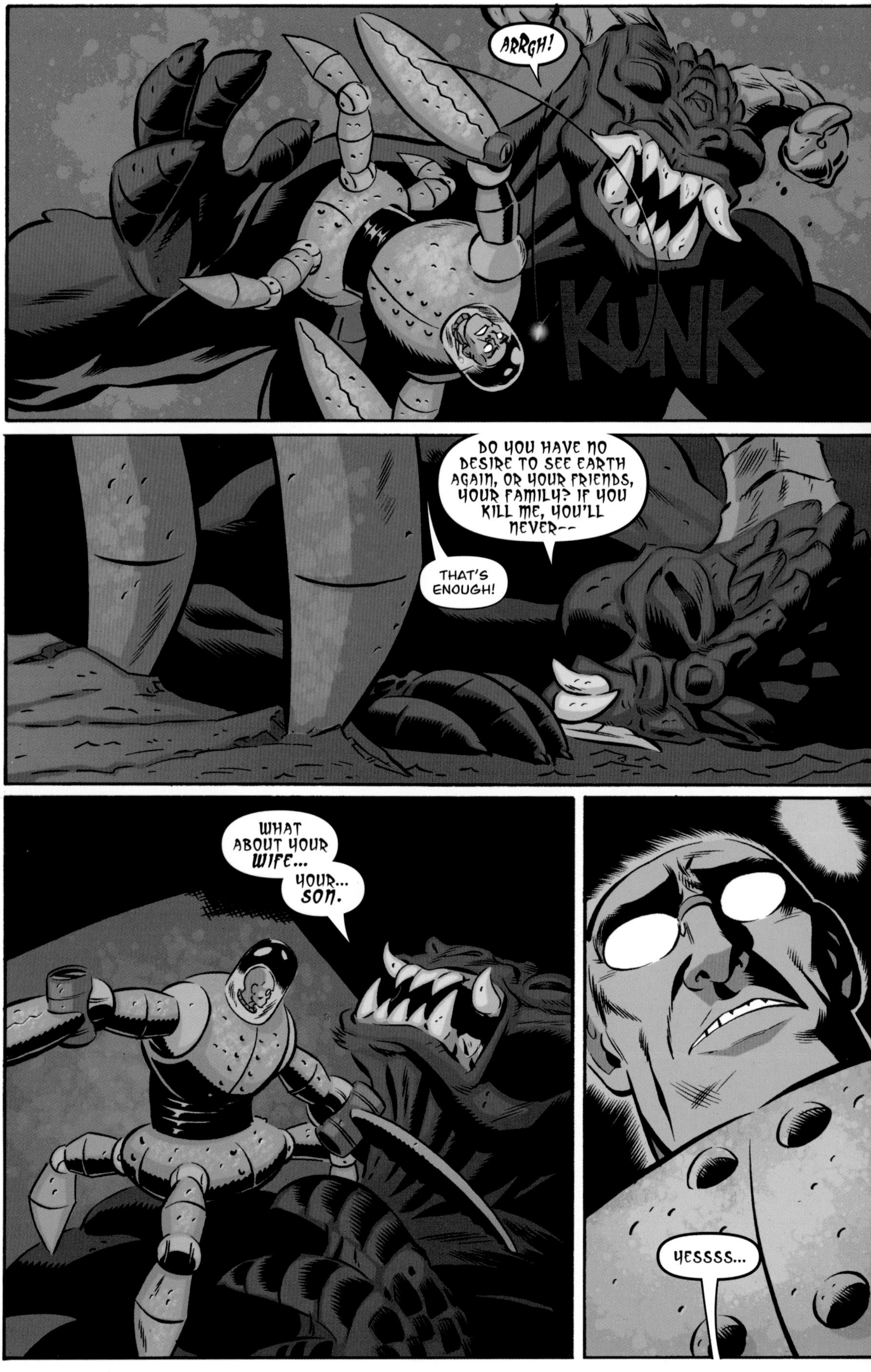
ARRGH!
KUNK
DO YOU HAVE NO DESIRE TO SEE EARTH AGAIN, OR YOUR FRIENDS, YOUR FAMILY? IF YOU KILL ME, YOU'LL NEVER--
THAT'S ENOUGH!
WHAT ABOUT YOUR WIFE...
YOUR... SON.
YESSSS...

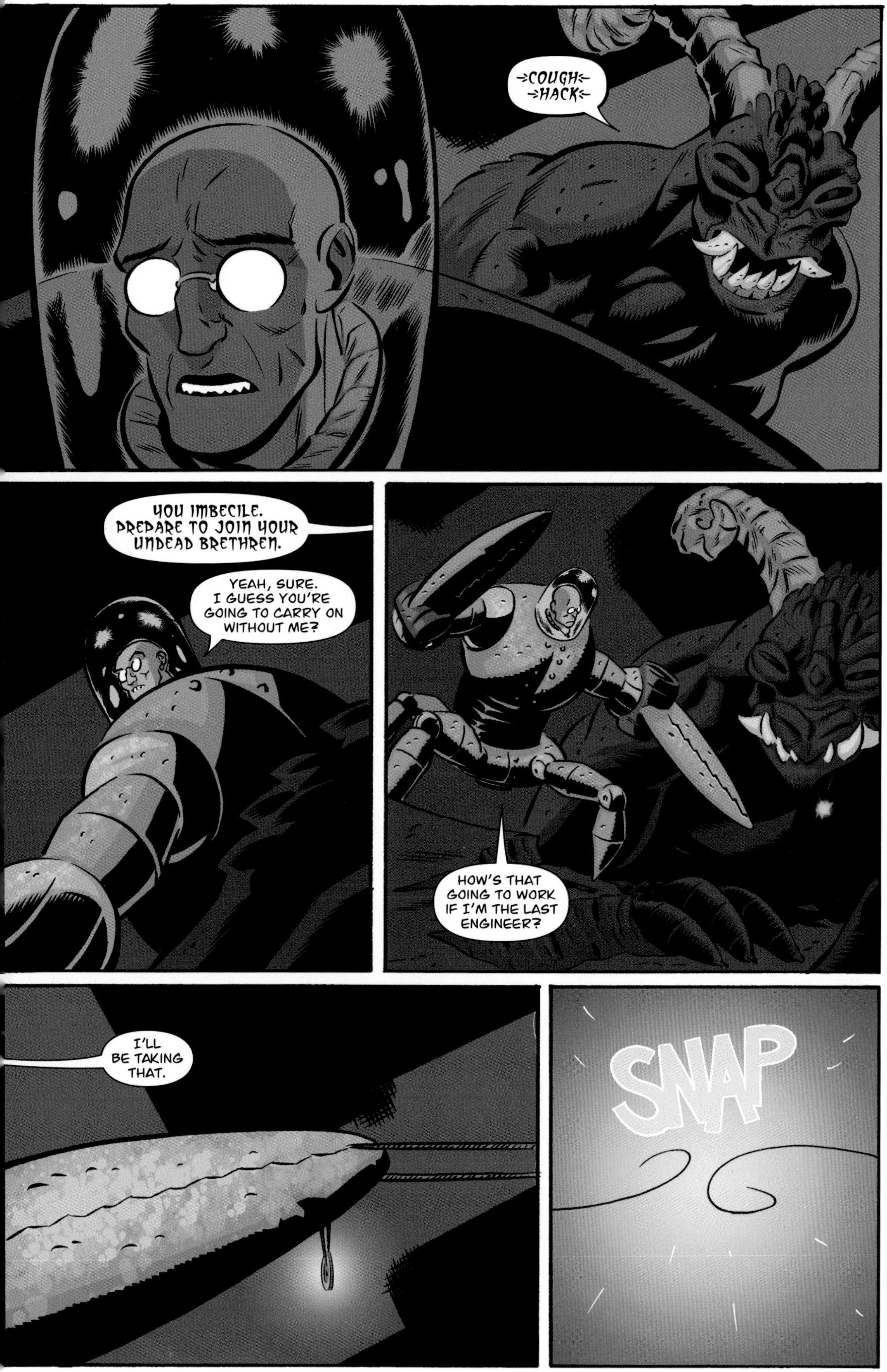

COUGH HACK
YOU IMBECILE. PREPARE TO JOIN YOUR UNDEAD BRETHREN.
YEAH, SURE. I GUESS YOU'RE GOING TO CARRY ON WITHOUT ME?
HOW'S THAT GOING TO WORK IF I'M THE LAST ENGINEER?
I'LL BE TAKING THAT.
SNAP

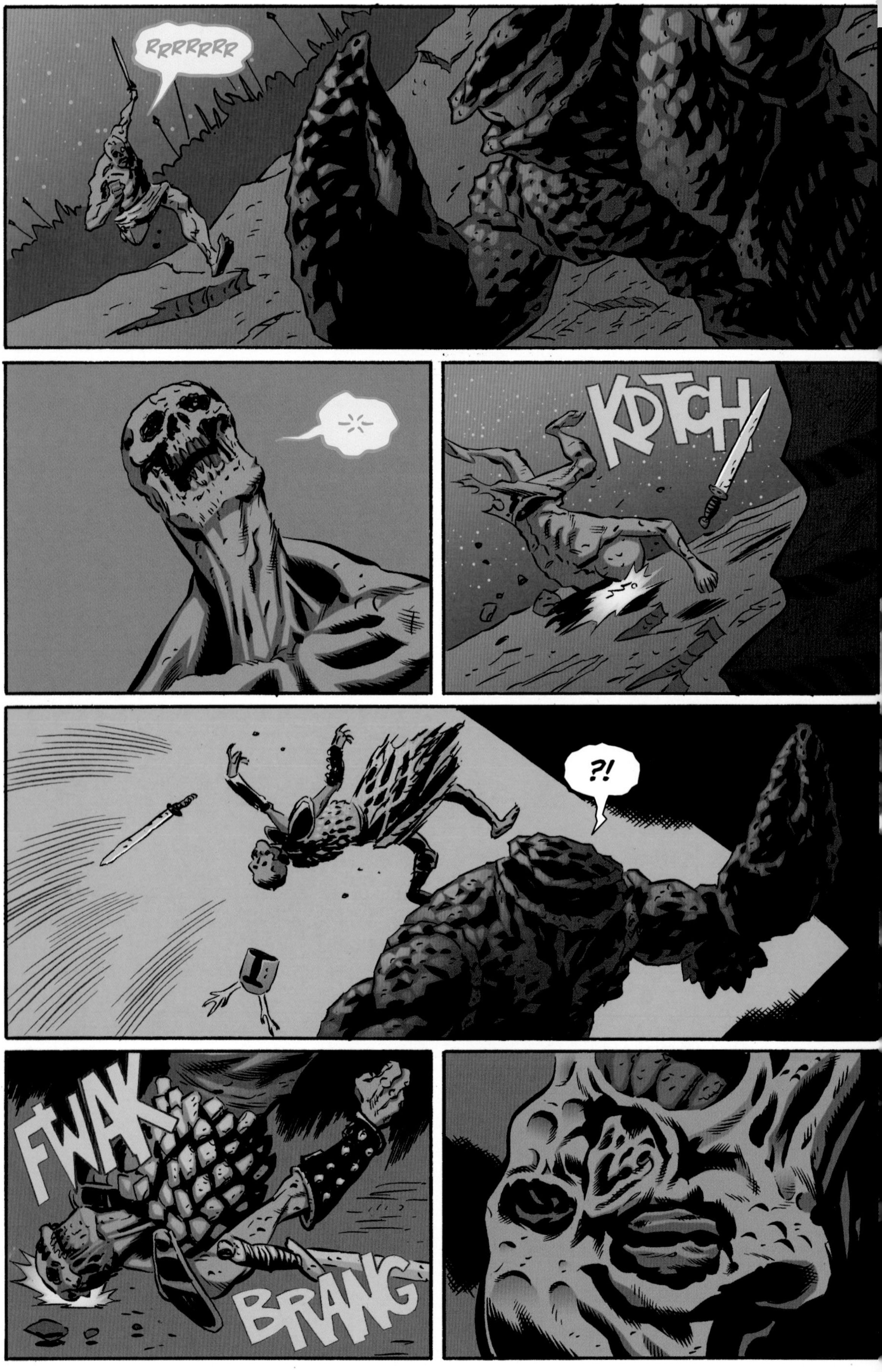
RRRRRRR
KDTCH
?!
FWAK
BRANG

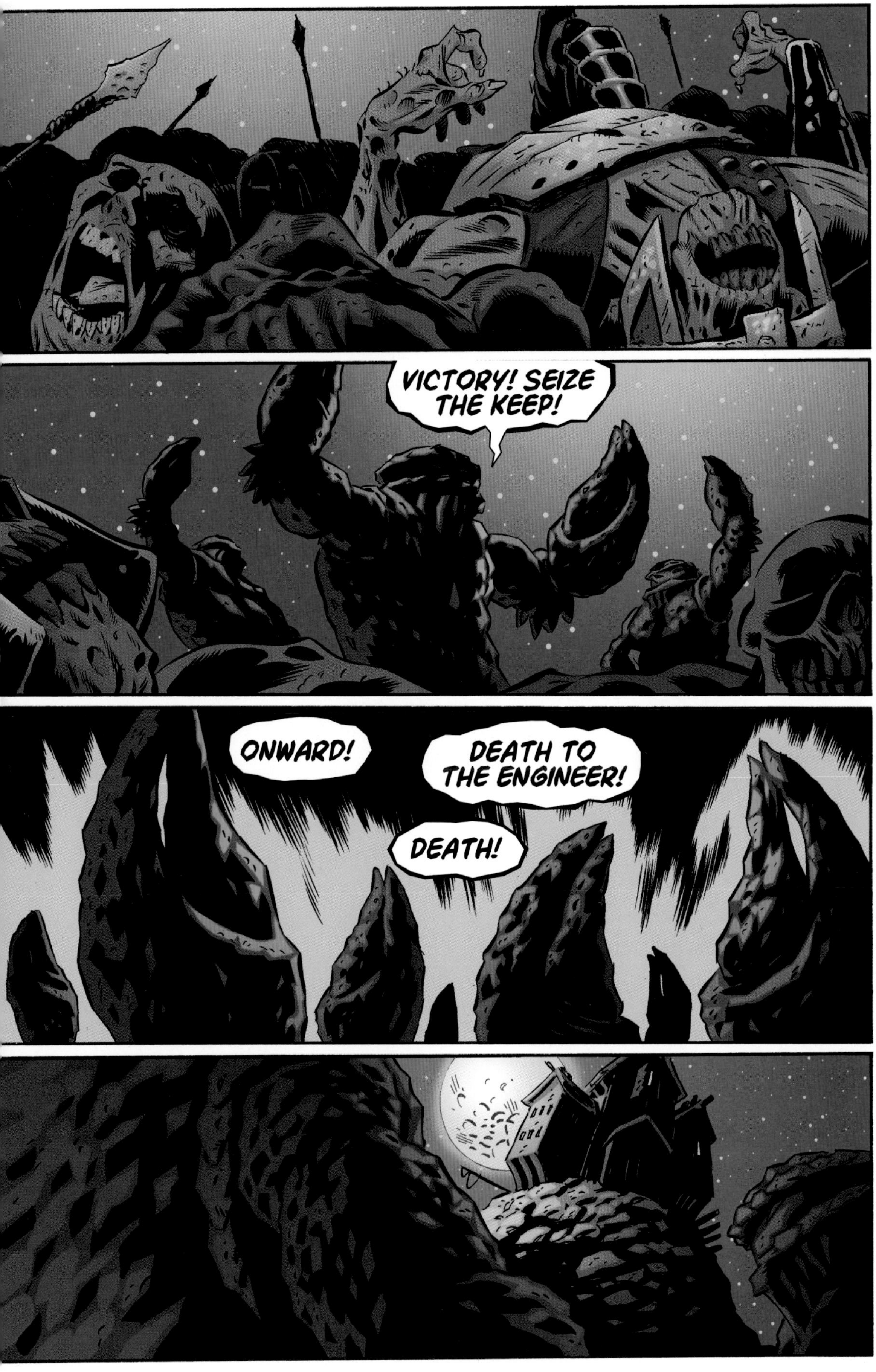
VICTORY! SEIZE THE KEEP!
ONWARD!
DEATH TO THE ENGINEER!
DEATH!

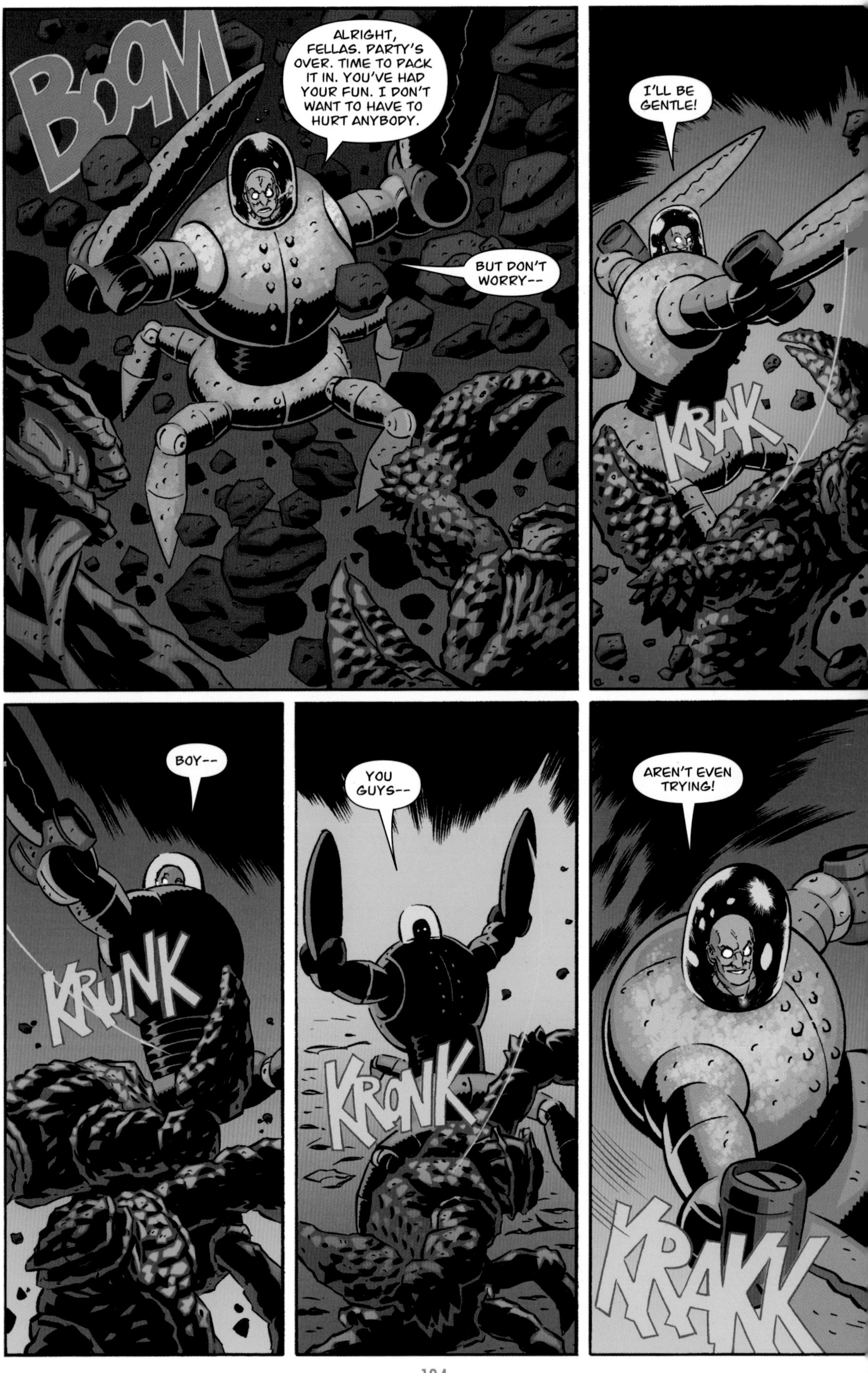
BOOM
ALRIGHT, FELLAS. PARTY'S OVER. TIME TO PACK IT IN. YOU'VE HAD YOUR FUN. I DON'T WANT TO HAVE TO HURT ANYBODY.
BUT DON'T WORRY--
I'LL BE GENTLE!
KRAK
BOY--
KRUNK
YOU GUYS--
KRONK
AREN'T EVEN TRYING!
KRAKK

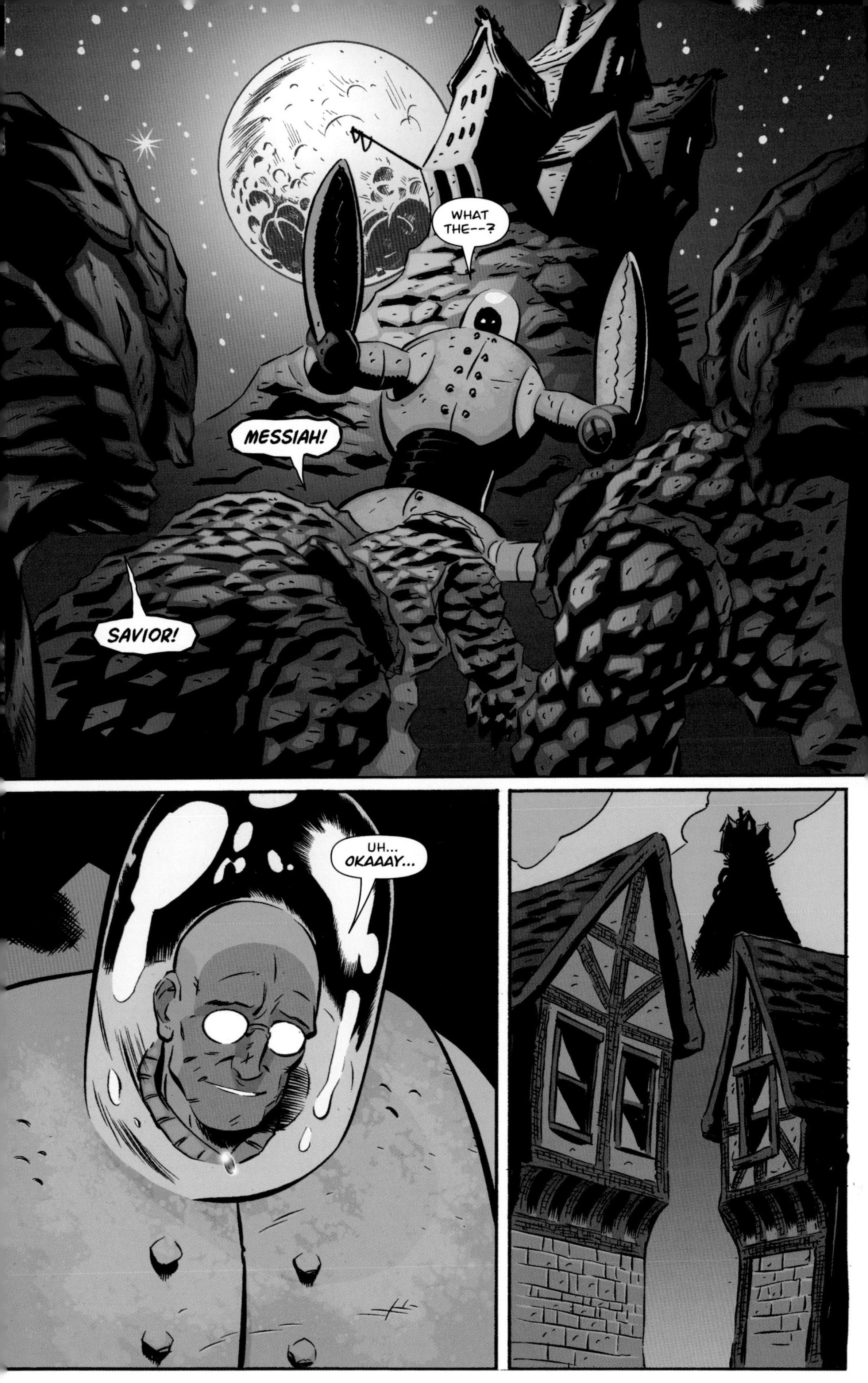
WHAT THE--?
MESSIAH!
SAVIOR!
UH... OKAAAY...

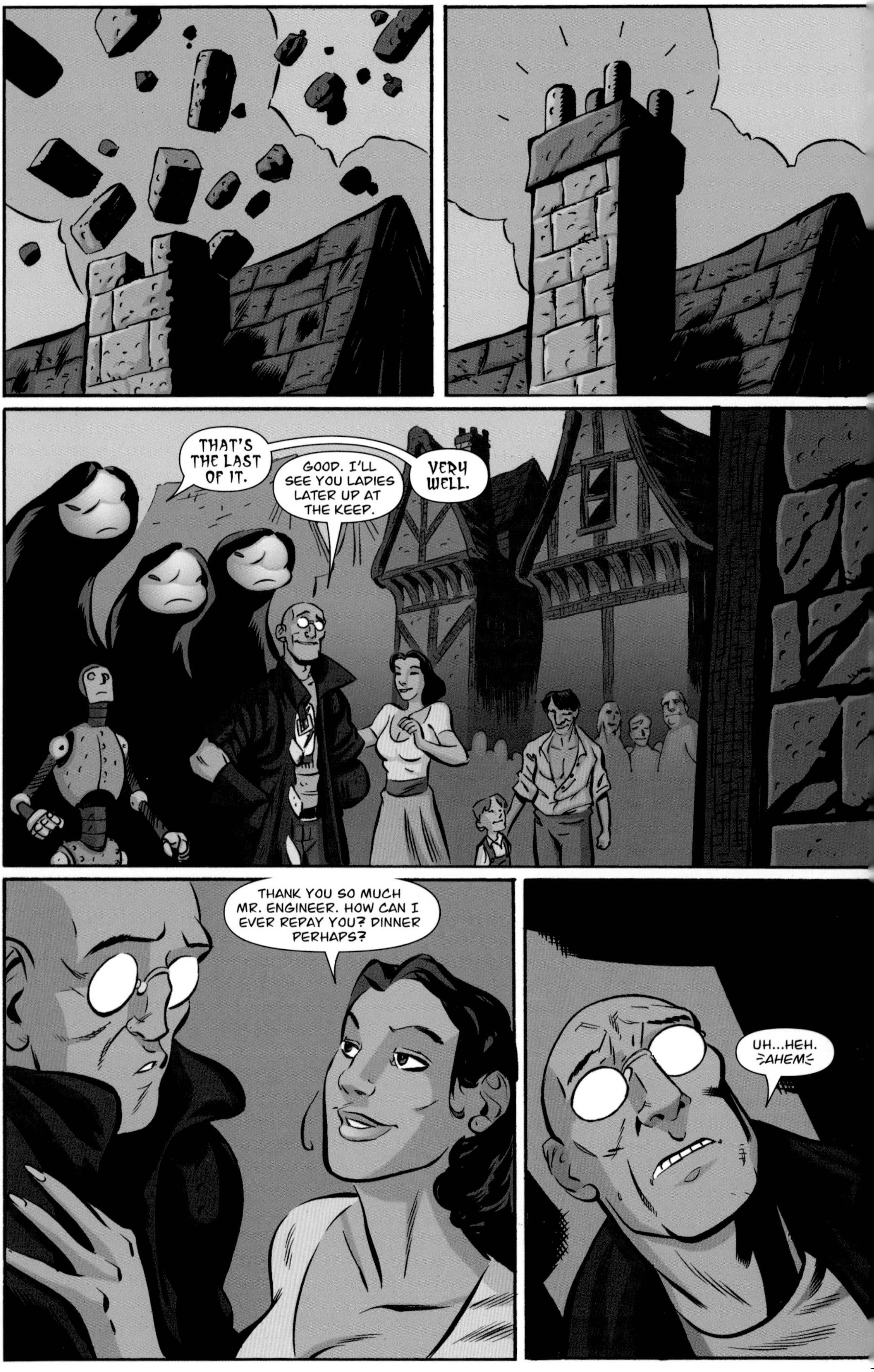
THAT'S THE LAST OF IT.
GOOD. I'LL SEE YOU LADIES LATER UP AT THE KEEP.
VERY WELL.
THANK YOU SO MUCH MR. ENGINEER. HOW CAN I EVER REPAY YOU? DINNER PERHAPS?
UH...HEH.
AHEM

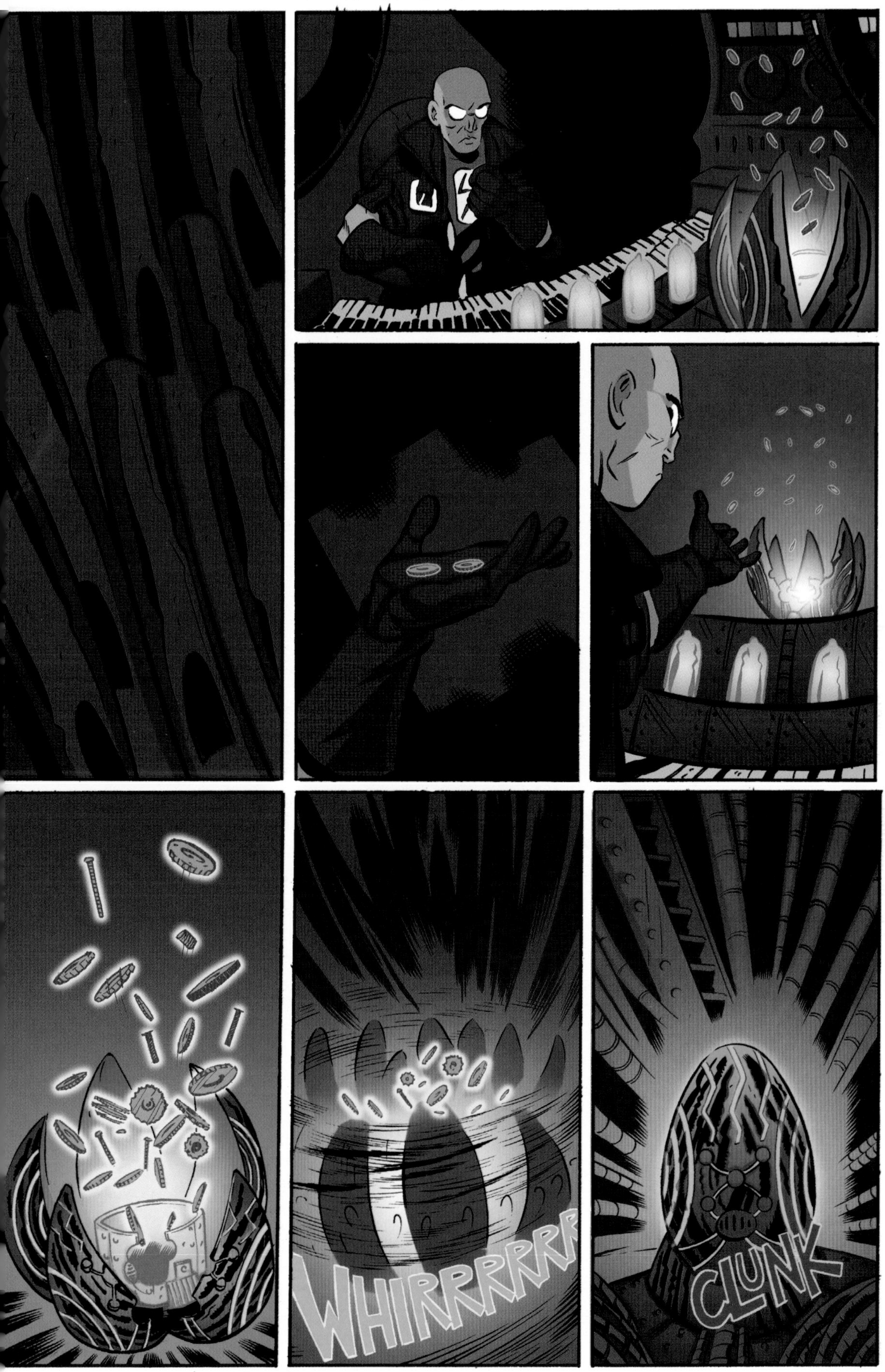
WHIRRRRRRR
CLUNK

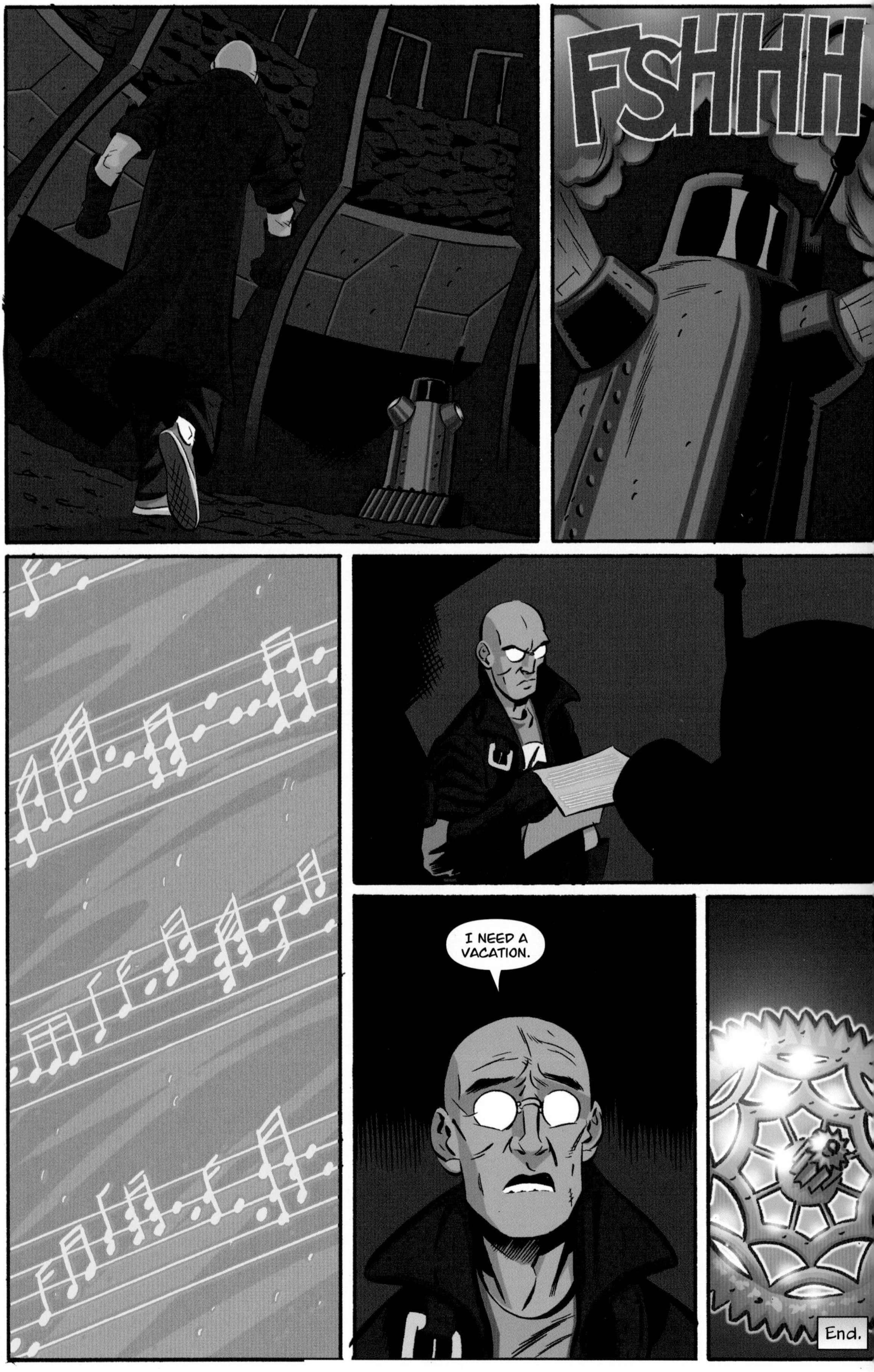
FSHHH
I NEED A VACATION.
End.

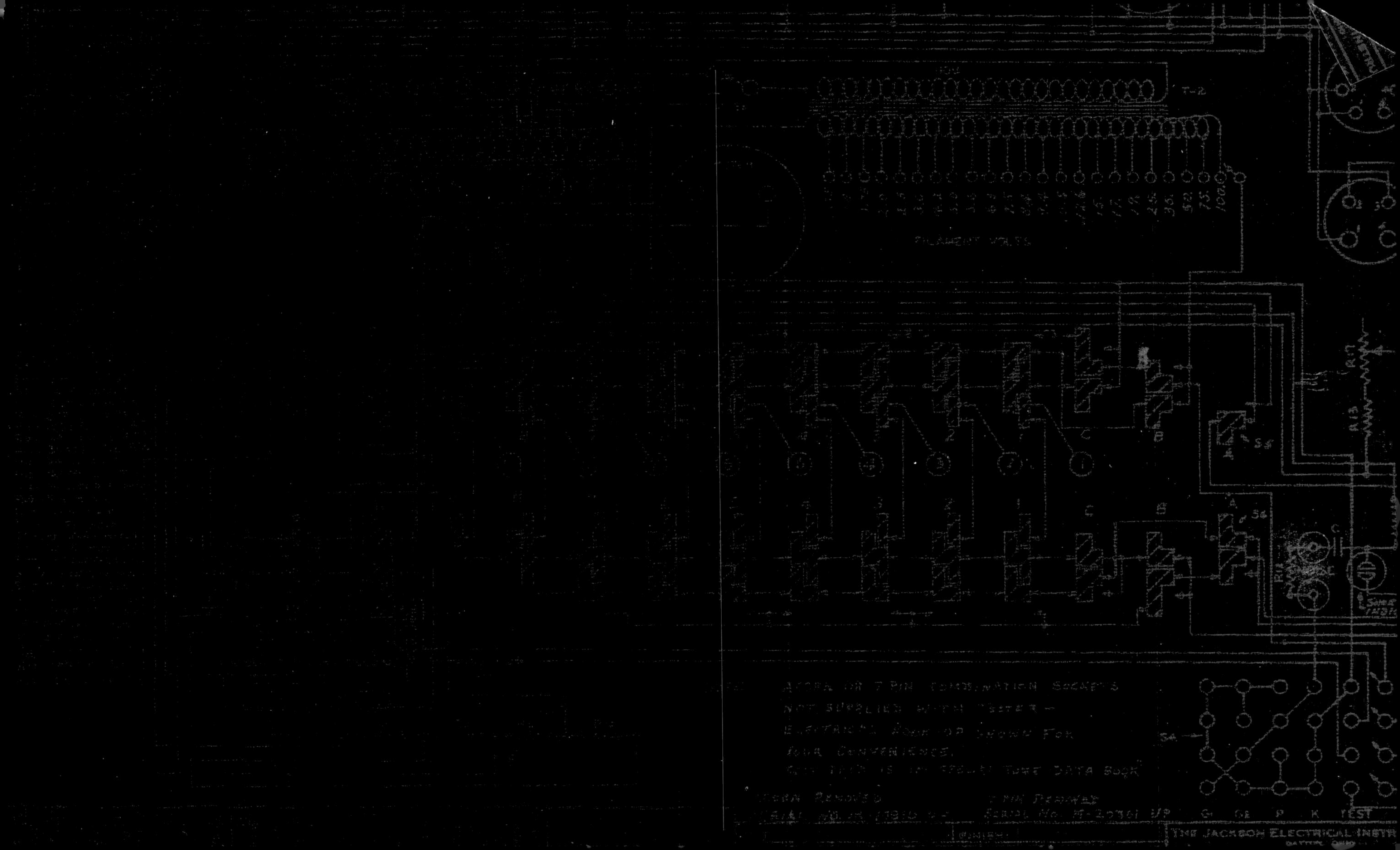

T-2
FILAMENT VOLTS
S4
S5
S6
R11
R13
R17
G
G2
P
K
TEST
NOT SUPPLIED WITH TESTER —
YOUR CONVENIENCE.
THE JACKSON ELECTRICAL INSTR

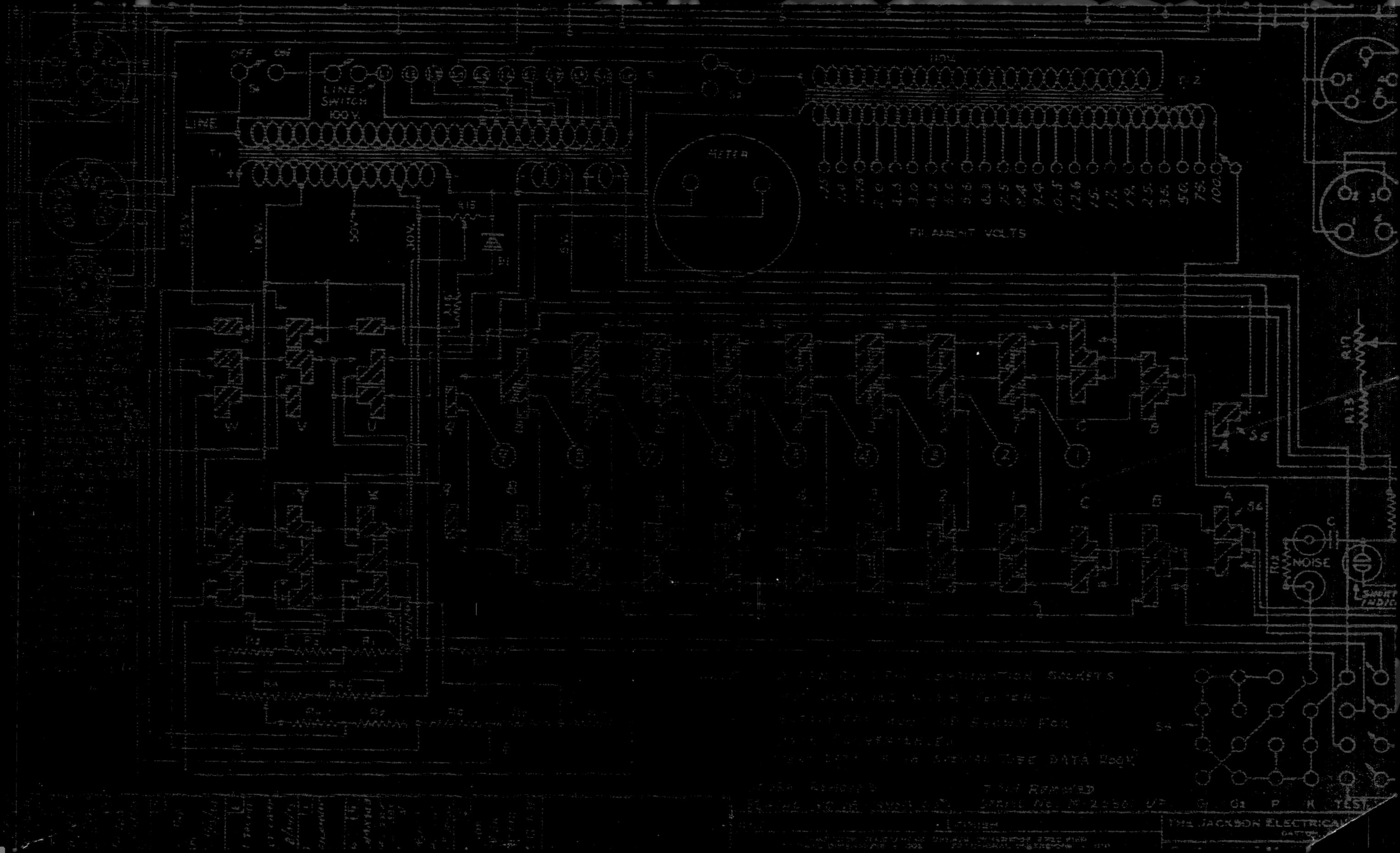
LINE SWITCH 100 V.
FILAMENT VOLTS
METER
NOISE
G G2 P K TEST
THE JACKSON ELECTRICAL

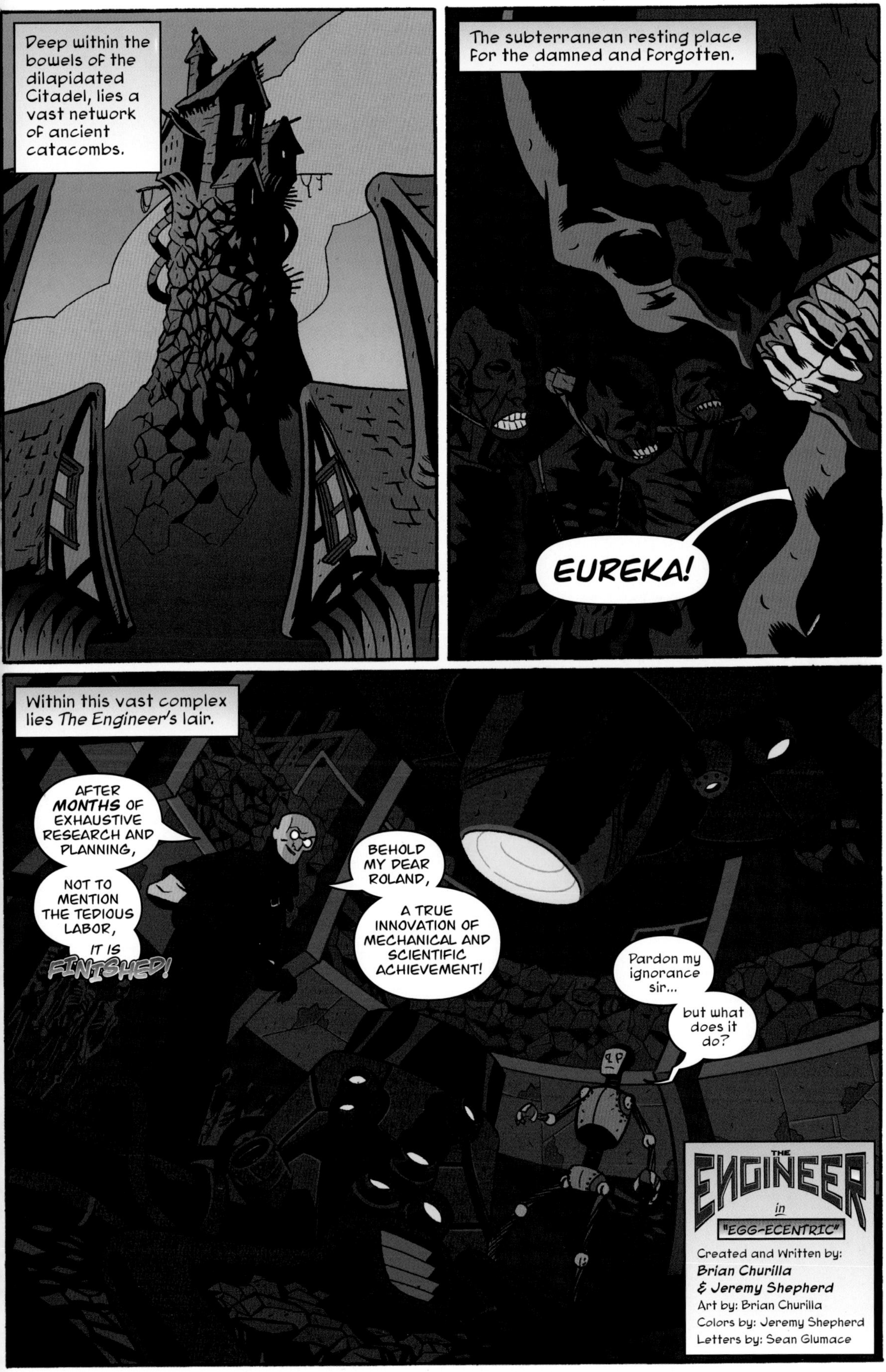
Deep within the bowels of the dilapidated Citadel, lies a vast network of ancient catacombs.
The subterranean resting place for the damned and forgotten.
EUREKA!
Within this vast complex lies *The Engineer's* lair.
AFTER **MONTHS** OF EXHAUSTIVE RESEARCH AND PLANNING,
NOT TO MENTION THE TEDIOUS LABOR,
IT IS FINISHED!
BEHOLD MY DEAR ROLAND,
A TRUE INNOVATION OF MECHANICAL AND SCIENTIFIC ACHIEVEMENT!
Pardon my ignorance sir...
but what does it do?
THE ENGINEER
in
"EGG-ECENTRIC"
Created and Written by:
Brian Churilla
& Jeremy Shepherd
Art by: Brian Churilla
Colors by: Jeremy Shepherd
Letters by: Sean Glumace

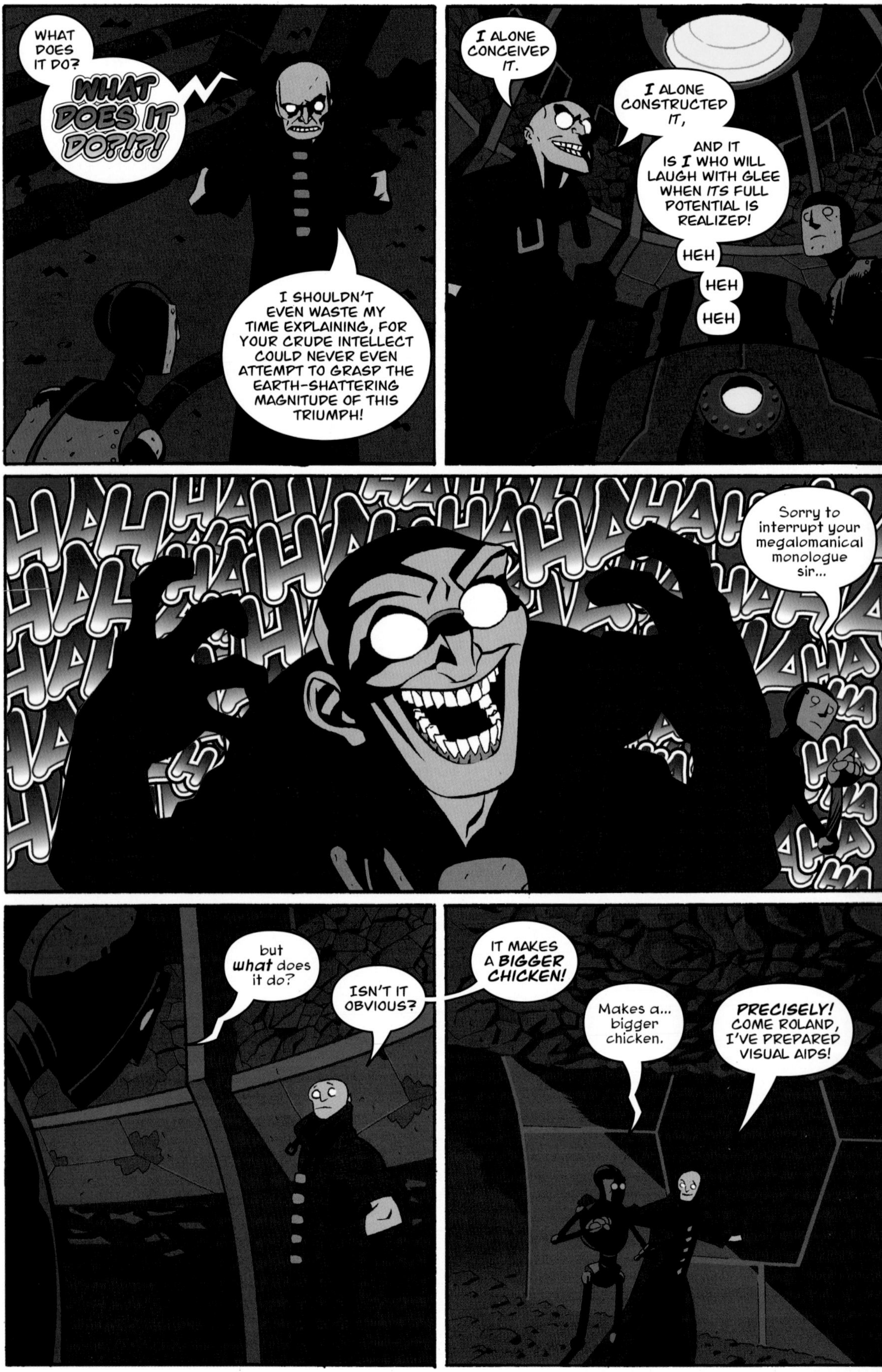
WHAT DOES IT DO?
WHAT DOES IT DO?!?!
I SHOULDN'T EVEN WASTE MY TIME EXPLAINING, FOR YOUR CRUDE INTELLECT COULD NEVER EVEN ATTEMPT TO GRASP THE EARTH-SHATTERING MAGNITUDE OF THIS TRIUMPH!
I ALONE CONCEIVED IT.
I ALONE CONSTRUCTED IT,
AND IT IS I WHO WILL LAUGH WITH GLEE WHEN ITS FULL POTENTIAL IS REALIZED!
HEH
HEH
HEH
HA HA HA HA HA HA HA HA HA HA HA HA HA HA HA HA HA HA HA HA HA HA HA HA
Sorry to interrupt your megalomanical monologue sir...
but what does it do?
ISN'T IT OBVIOUS?
IT MAKES A BIGGER CHICKEN!
Makes a... bigger chicken.
PRECISELY! COME ROLAND, I'VE PREPARED VISUAL AIDS!

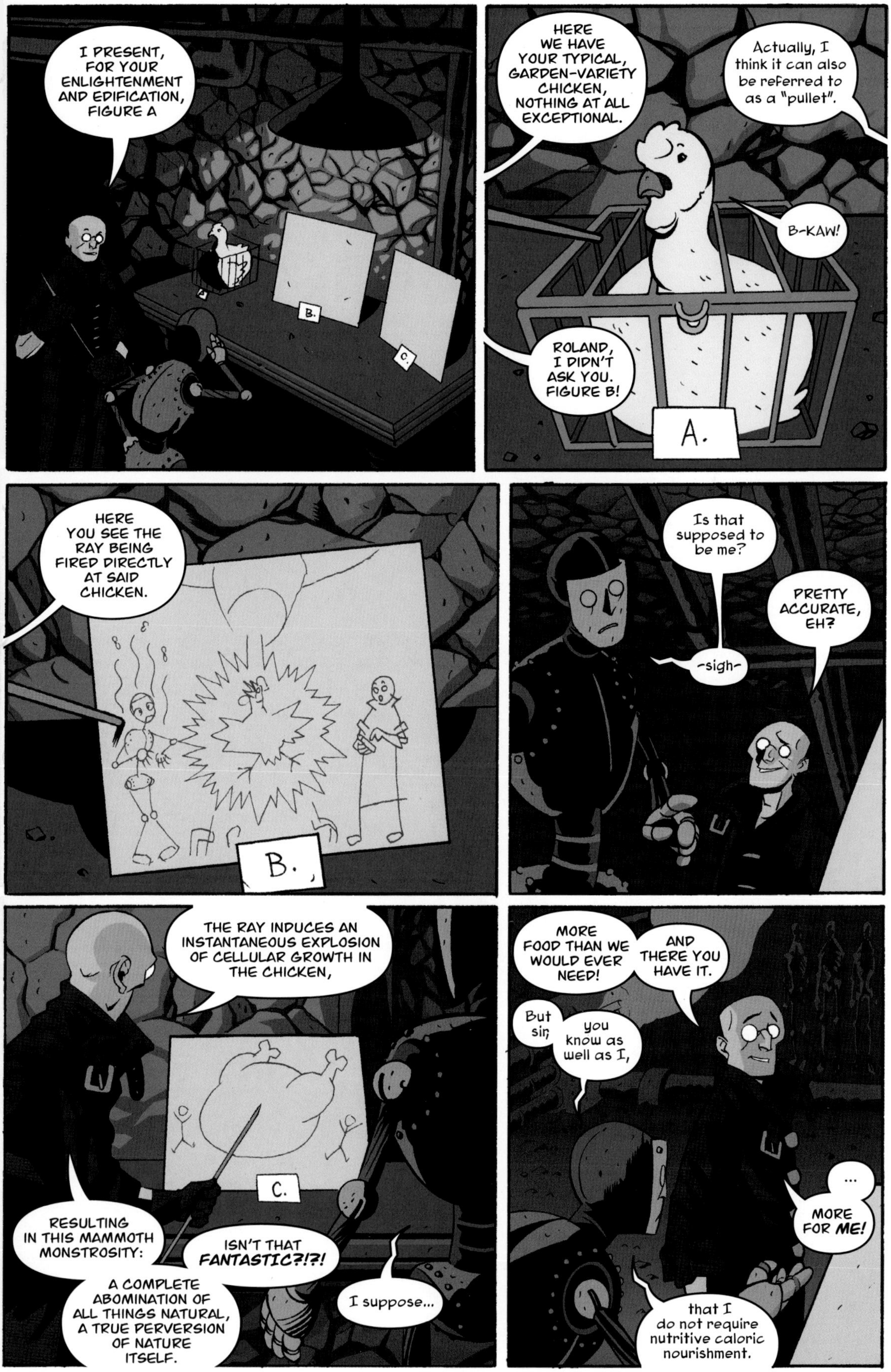
I PRESENT, FOR YOUR ENLIGHTENMENT AND EDIFICATION, FIGURE A
B.
C.
HERE WE HAVE YOUR TYPICAL, GARDEN-VARIETY CHICKEN, NOTHING AT ALL EXCEPTIONAL.
Actually, I think it can also be referred to as a "pullet".
B-KAW!
ROLAND, I DIDN'T ASK YOU. FIGURE B!
A.
HERE YOU SEE THE RAY BEING FIRED DIRECTLY AT SAID CHICKEN.
B.
Is that supposed to be me?
PRETTY ACCURATE, EH?
-sigh-
THE RAY INDUCES AN INSTANTANEOUS EXPLOSION OF CELLULAR GROWTH IN THE CHICKEN,
C.
RESULTING IN THIS MAMMOTH MONSTROSITY:
ISN'T THAT ***FANTASTIC?!?!***
A COMPLETE ABOMINATION OF ALL THINGS NATURAL, A TRUE PERVERSION OF NATURE ITSELF.
I suppose...
MORE FOOD THAN WE WOULD EVER NEED!
AND THERE YOU HAVE IT.
But sir,
you know as well as I,
that I do not require nutritive caloric nourishment.
...
MORE FOR ***ME!***

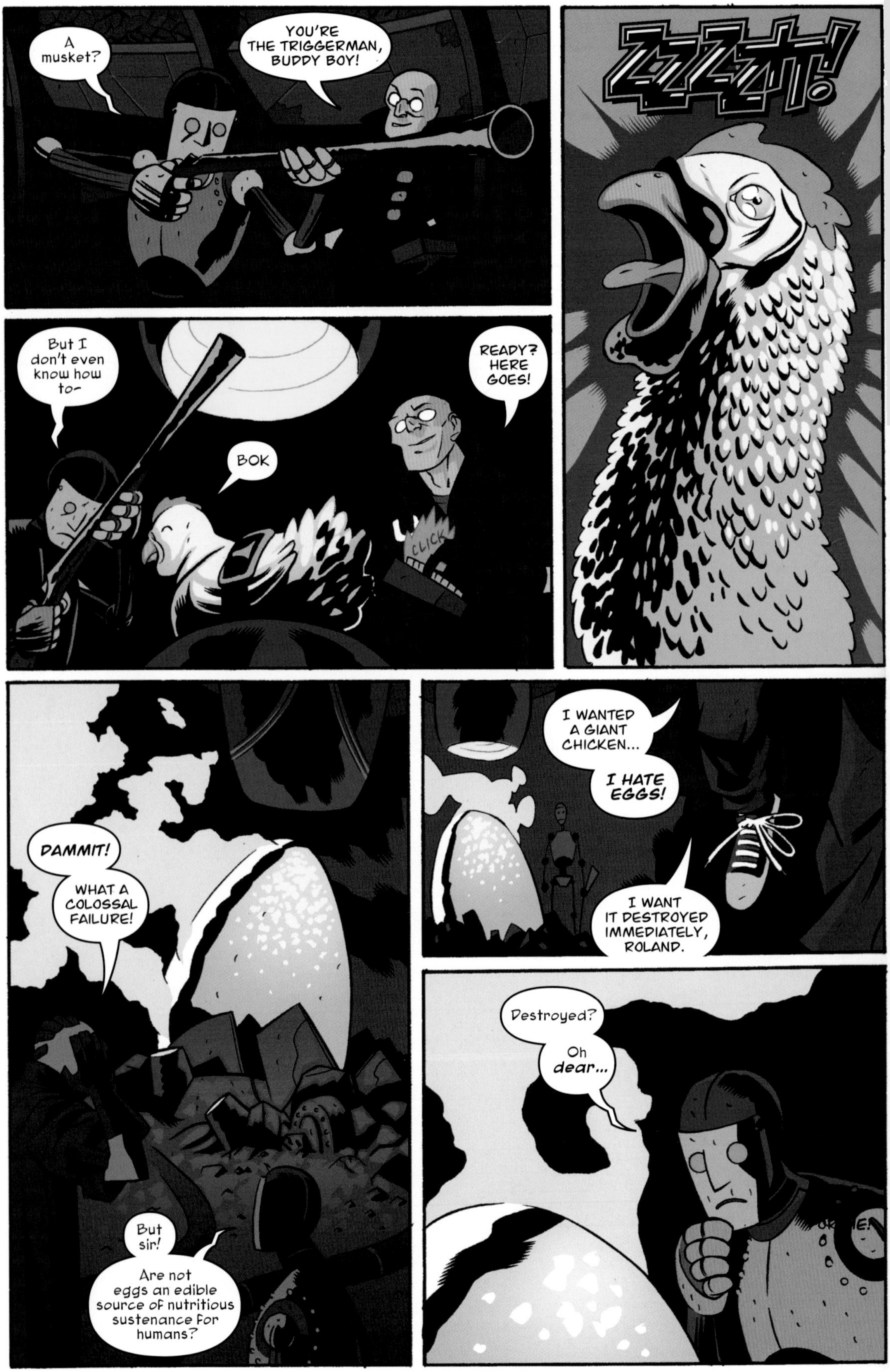
A musket?
YOU'RE THE TRIGGERMAN, BUDDY BOY!
But I don't even know how to-
BOK
CLICK
READY? HERE GOES!
ZZZT!
DAMMIT!
WHAT A COLOSSAL FAILURE!
But sir!
Are not eggs an edible source of nutritious sustenance for humans?
I WANTED A GIANT CHICKEN...
I HATE EGGS!
I WANT IT DESTROYED IMMEDIATELY, ROLAND.
Destroyed?
Oh *dear*...

♪♪

HUH?

One week later...

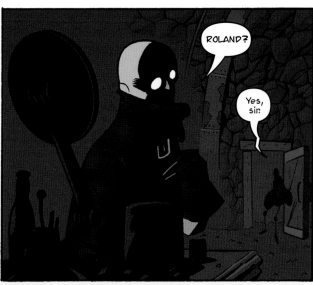

ROLAND?

Yes, sir.

I DON'T WANT TO KNOW WHAT YOUR DOING...

DO I?

ROLAND, I DEMAND TO KNOW WH—

...DEAR GOD.

SLAM!

ROLAND?

ROLAND!

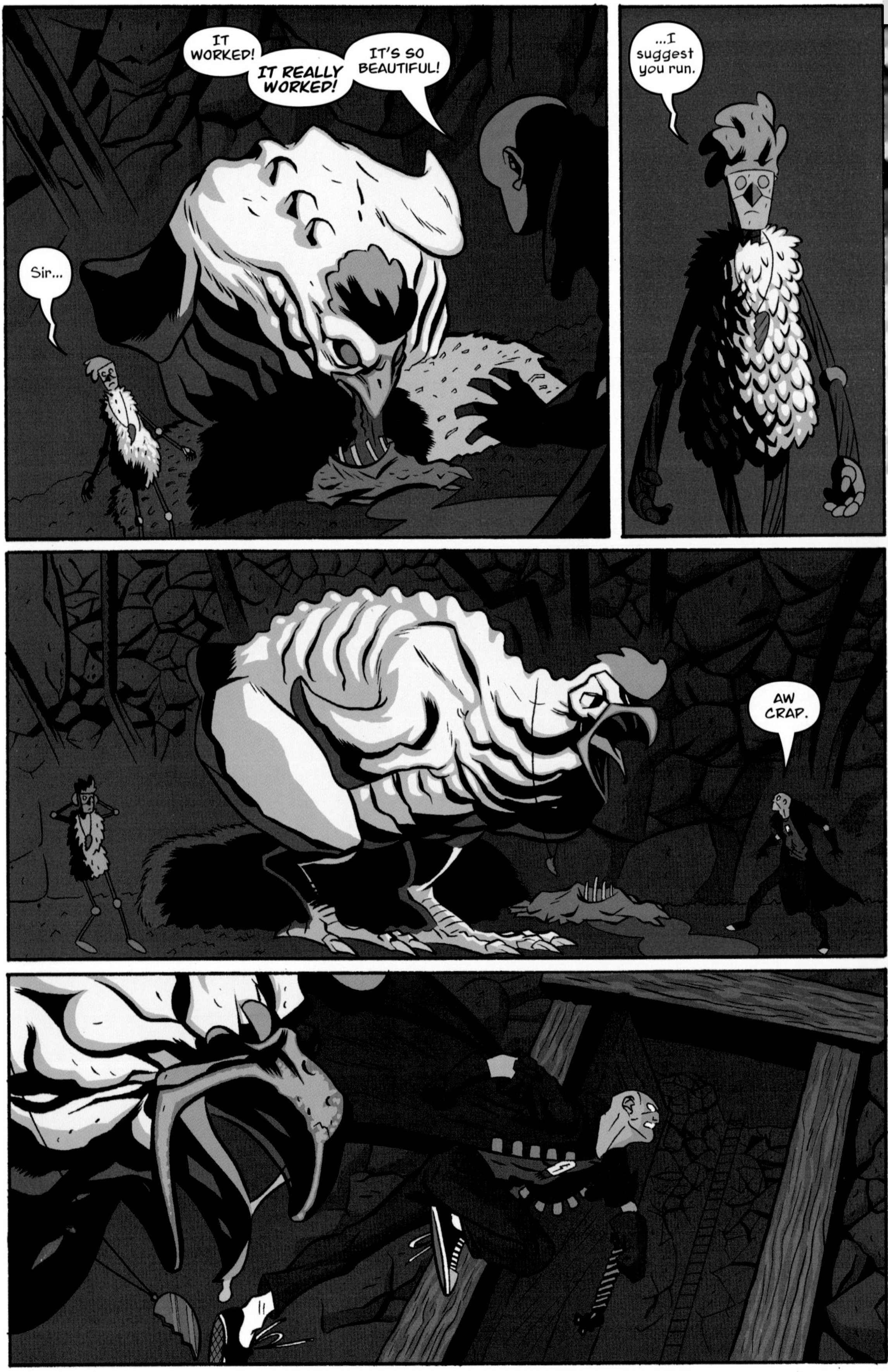
IT WORKED!
IT REALLY WORKED!
IT'S SO BEAUTIFUL!
Sir...
...I suggest you run.
AW CRAP.

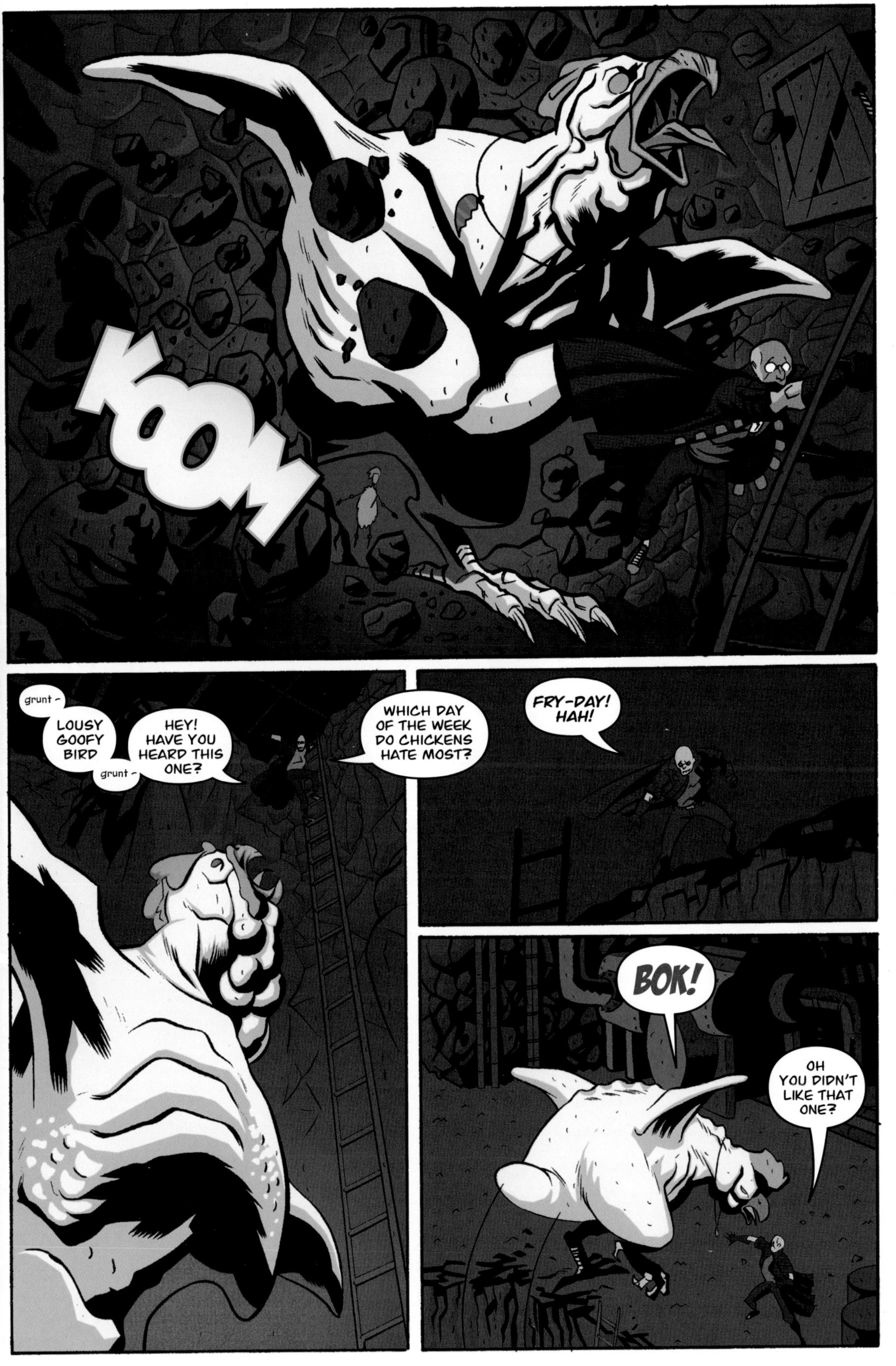

KOOM
grunt -
LOUSY GOOFY BIRD
grunt -
HEY! HAVE YOU HEARD THIS ONE?
WHICH DAY OF THE WEEK DO CHICKENS HATE MOST?
FRY-DAY! HAH!
BOK!
OH YOU DIDN'T LIKE THAT ONE?

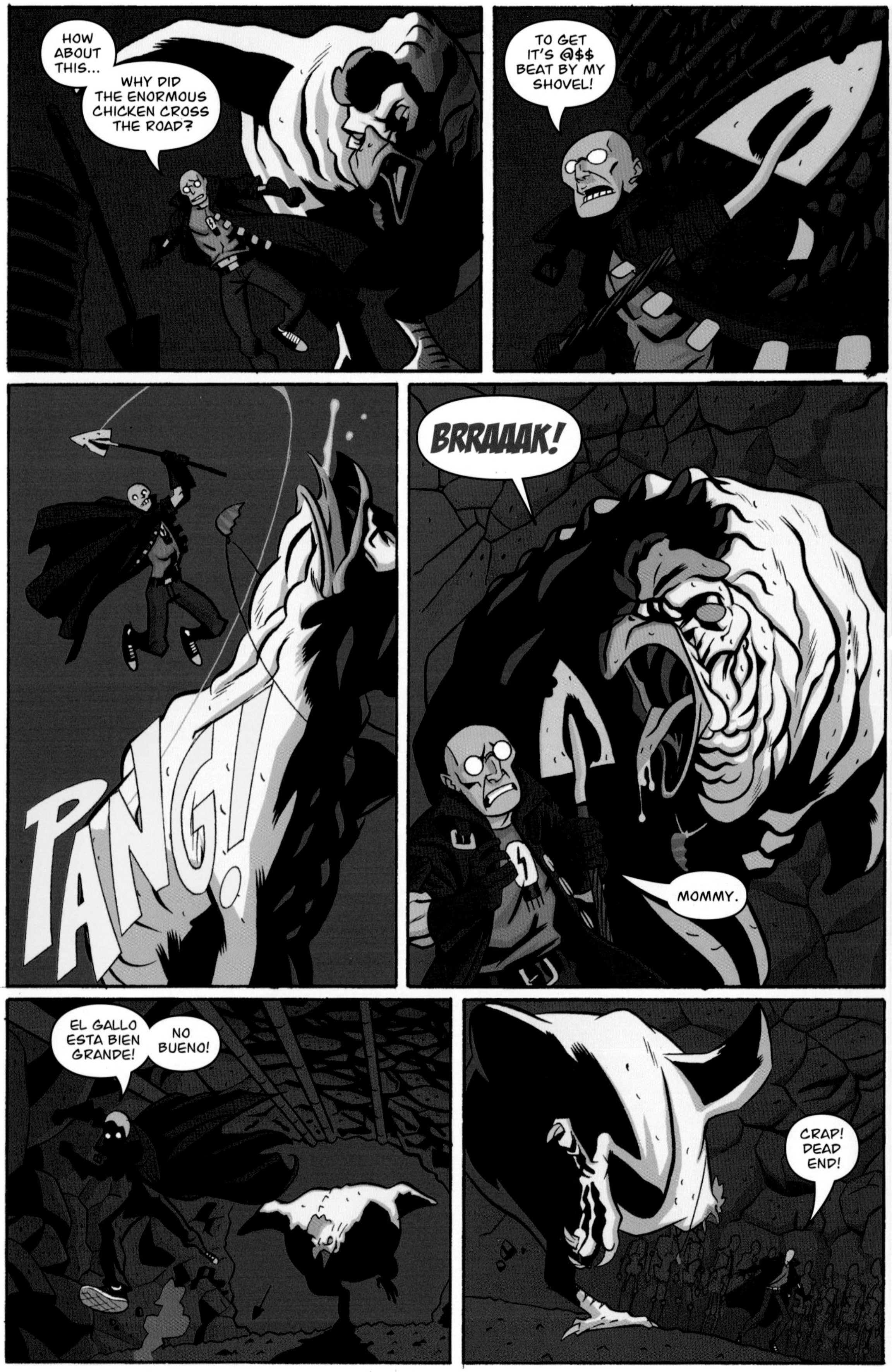
HOW ABOUT THIS...
WHY DID THE ENORMOUS CHICKEN CROSS THE ROAD?
TO GET IT'S @$$ BEAT BY MY SHOVEL!
PANG!
BRRAAAK!
MOMMY.
EL GALLO ESTA BIEN GRANDE!
NO BUENO!
CRAP! DEAD END!

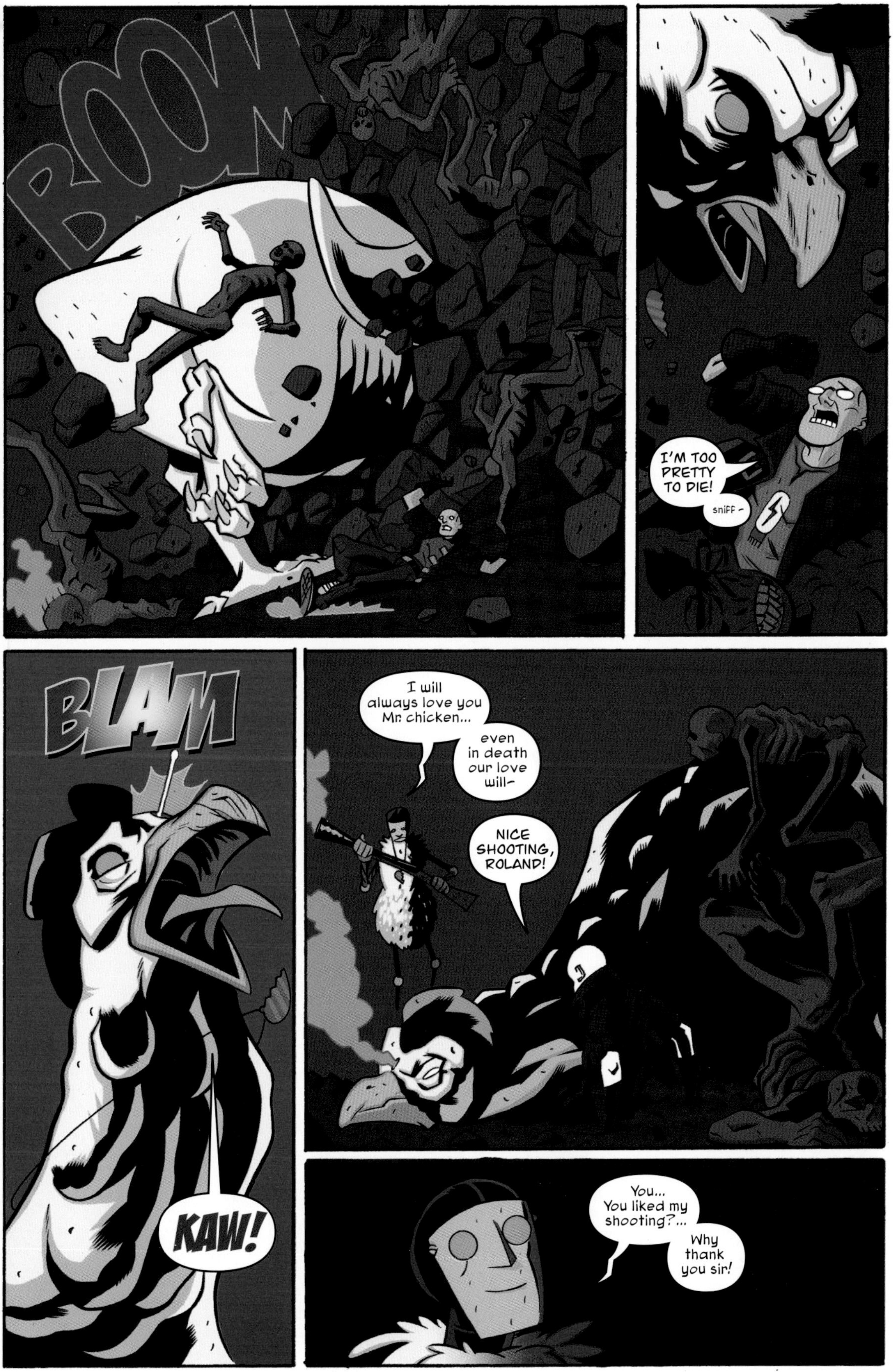
BOOM
I'M TOO PRETTY TO DIE!
sniff -
BLAM
KAW!
I will always love you Mr. chicken...
even in death our love will-
NICE SHOOTING, ROLAND!
You... You liked my shooting?...
Why thank you sir!

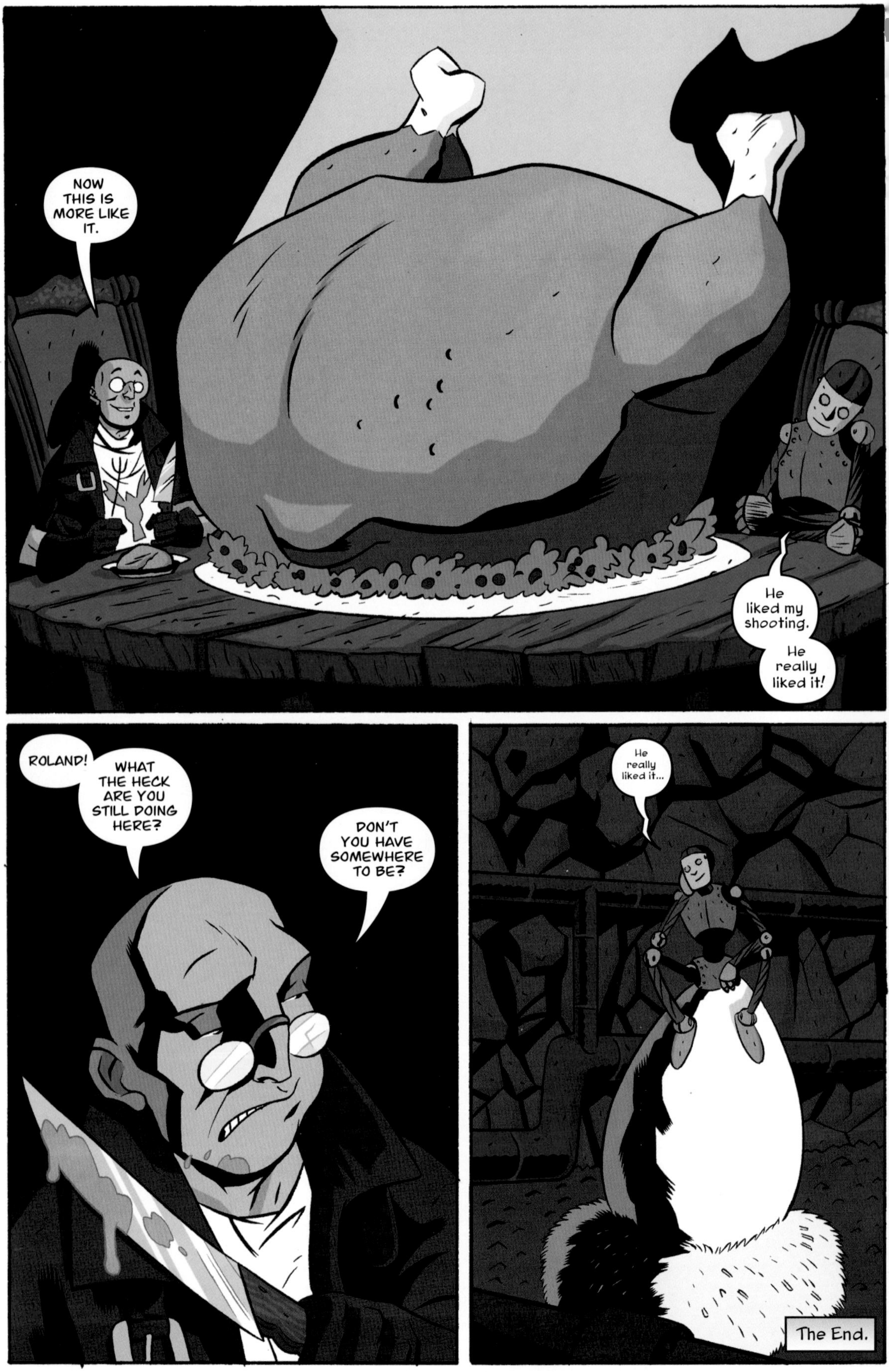
NOW THIS IS MORE LIKE IT.
He liked my shooting.
He really liked it!
ROLAND!
WHAT THE HECK ARE YOU STILL DOING HERE?
DON'T YOU HAVE SOMEWHERE TO BE?
He really liked it...
The End.

THE ENGINEER

sketchbook

When Jeremy and I decided to collaborate on what would eventually become The Engineer, he asked me what kind of stuff I wanted to draw, to which I replied, "Monsters." What better way to enable me to draw loads of creatures than to have a protagonist that travels to different dimensions?! The following pages are some of the conceptual drawings as well as some other random artwork that went into creating this dense tome of creatures and buffoonery (I know, ninety-six pages ain't exactly epic, but when you consider the amount of cool crap shoehorned into it, you'll get where daddy's coming from).

Early concept art of the catacombs and laboratory beneath The Engineer's keep.

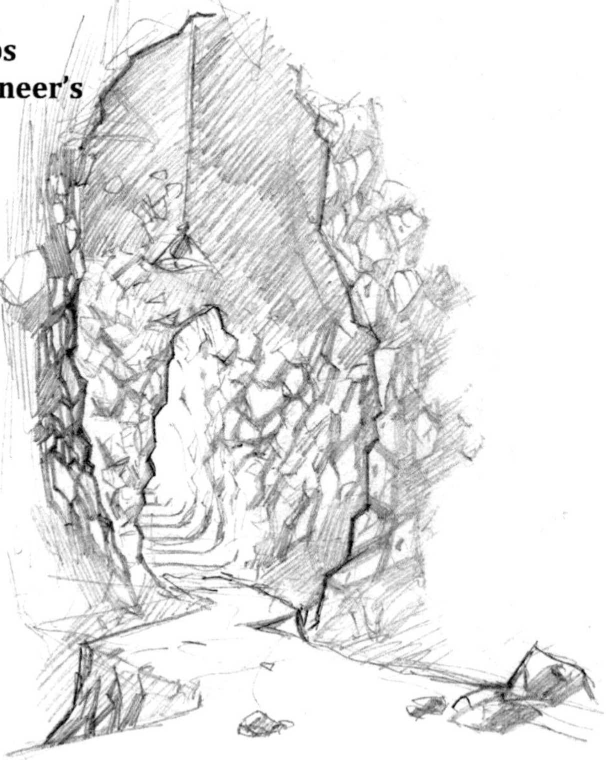

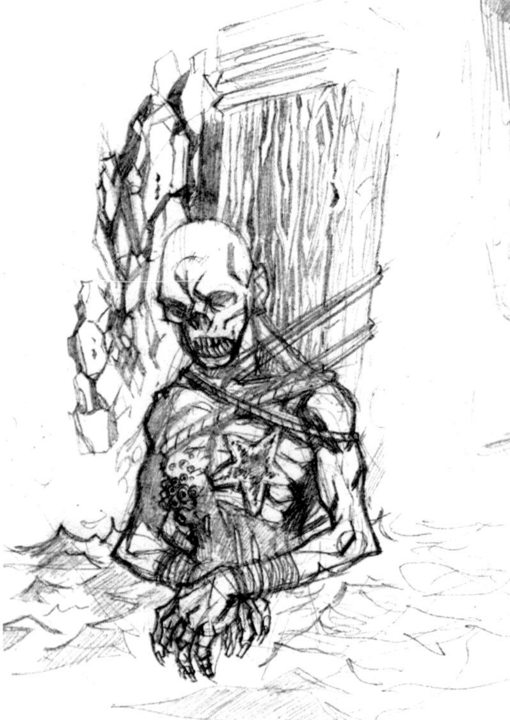

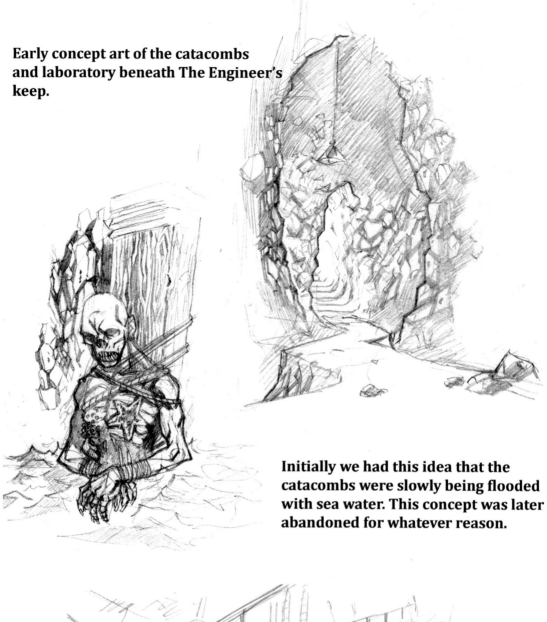

Initially we had this idea that the catacombs were slowly being flooded with sea water. This concept was later abandoned for whatever reason.

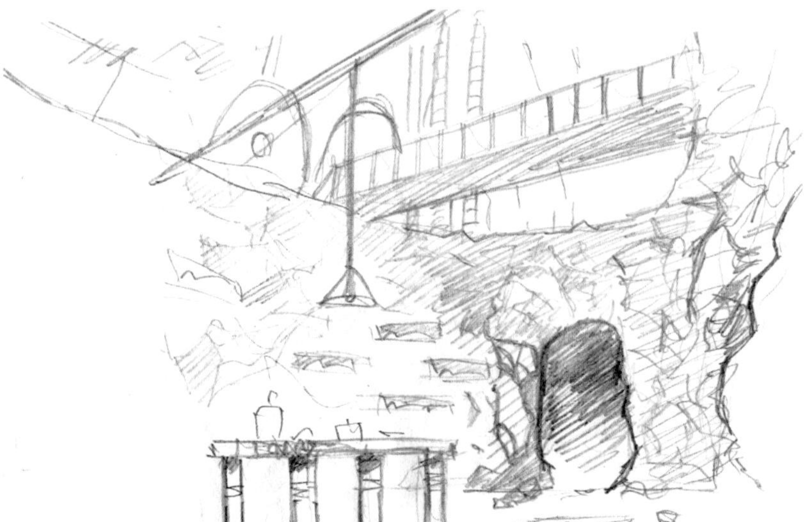

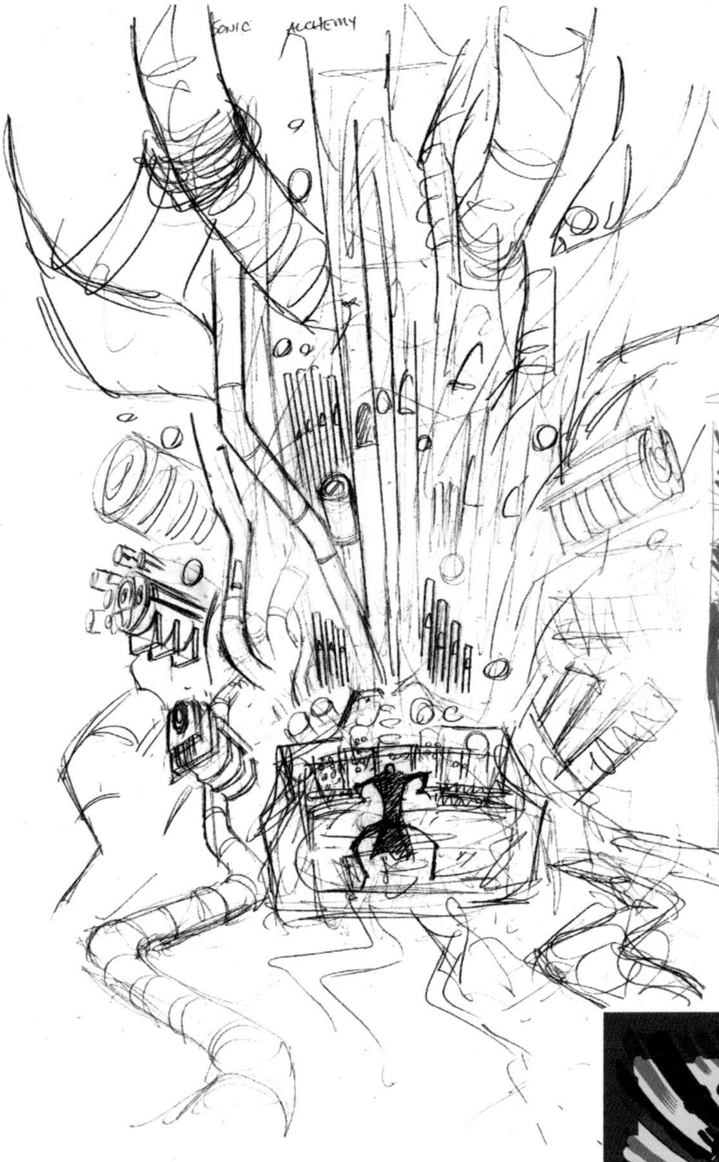
SONIC ALCHEMY

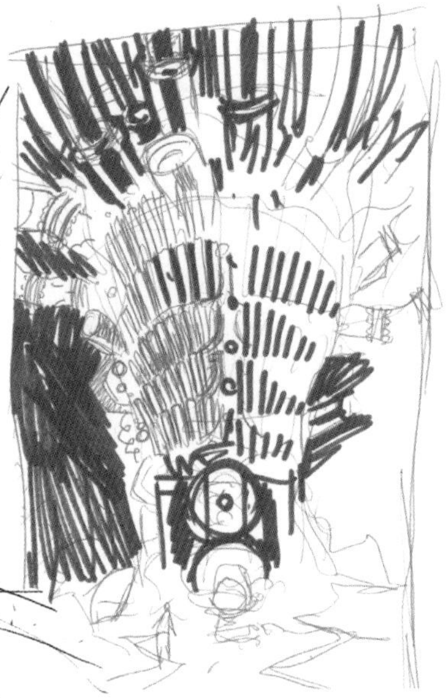

Here we have a few early concepts of Atlas, the colossal steam-powered pipe organ that makes pan-dimensional travel possible. I like my original drawing (top left) better than the final design.

Oh well, It happens.

To the right here is my feeble attempt at expressing a color scheme to Jeremy. I should stick to black and white.

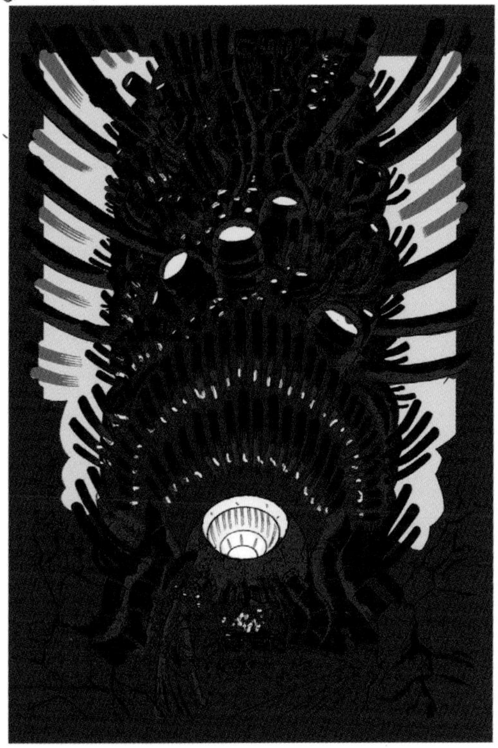

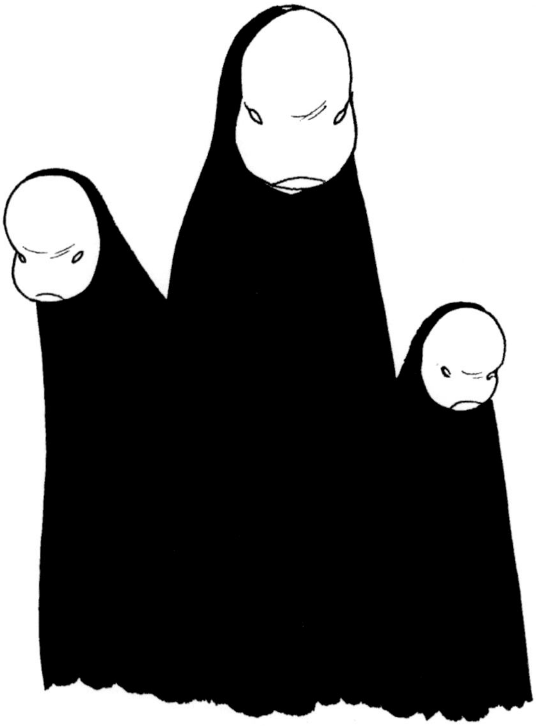

Early concept art for the “Witch Sisters”. In the beginning, they were not nearly as amorphous as they would eventually become. They were inspired by a few things. The cherubic faces were heavily influenced by my cat, a Persian freak of nature by the name of Liri. Persians are typically sweet cats, sure, but centuries inbreeding have produced a profoundly stupid and physically deformed, pitiful animal. Secondly, the Bene Gesserit from Dune. Thirdly, well, there is no thirdly.

Nevermind.

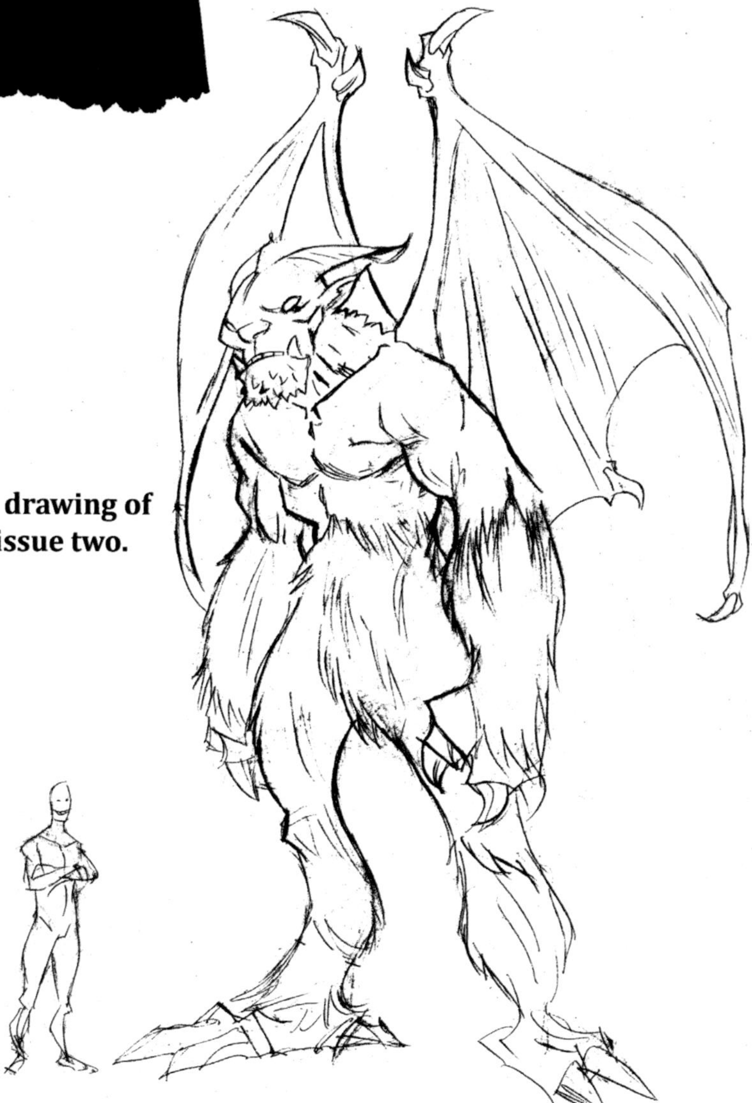

Another early concept drawing of the bat creature from issue two.

The next few pages are some early concept pieces that were used to pitch the book to Archaia.

When we originally conceived the story, there was another doppelganger that with the help of the disgruntled inhabitants of realms that The Engineer had previously visited, was chasing after our bumbling, bespectacled hero. It got a little too convoluted even for us, which is saying something.

Perhaps we'll have to revisit that idea later.

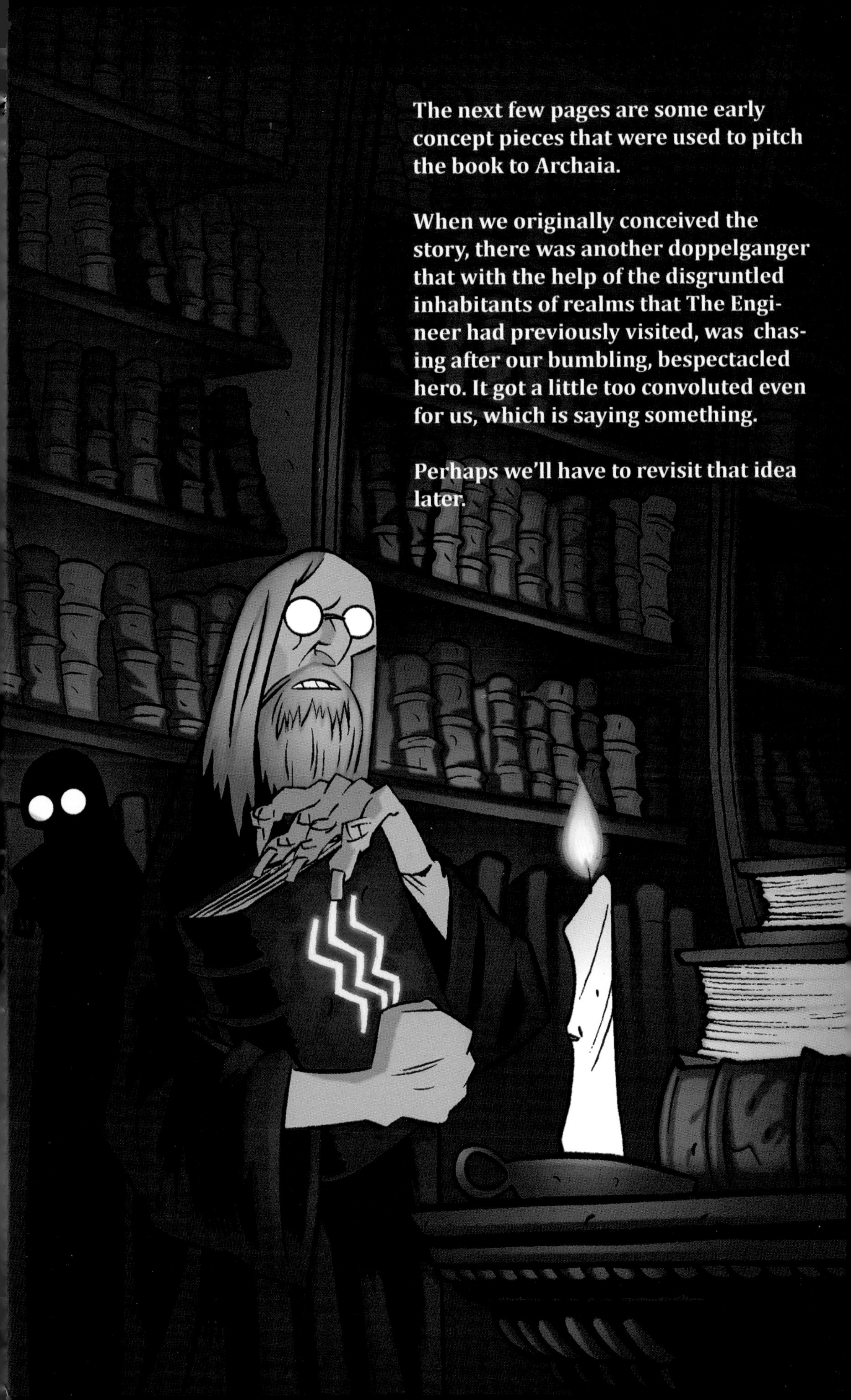

I had originally envisioned the giant bat creature from issue two much, much larger.

It also had a much more bat-like appearance, but because he was nothing more than a larger version of the simian-bat-pug creatures in the beginning of the issue, the design needed to be changed. I'm still quite fond of this piece though.

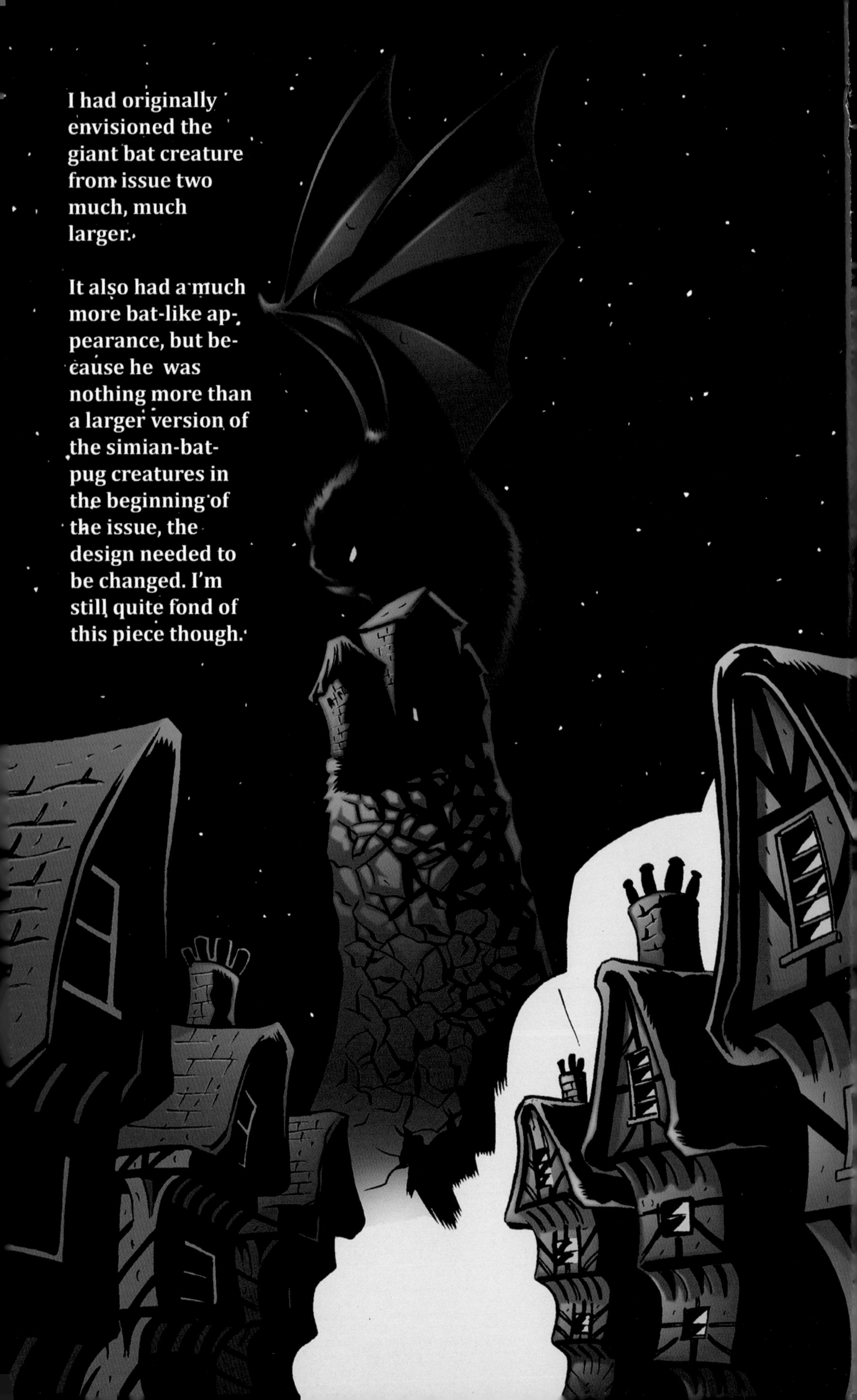

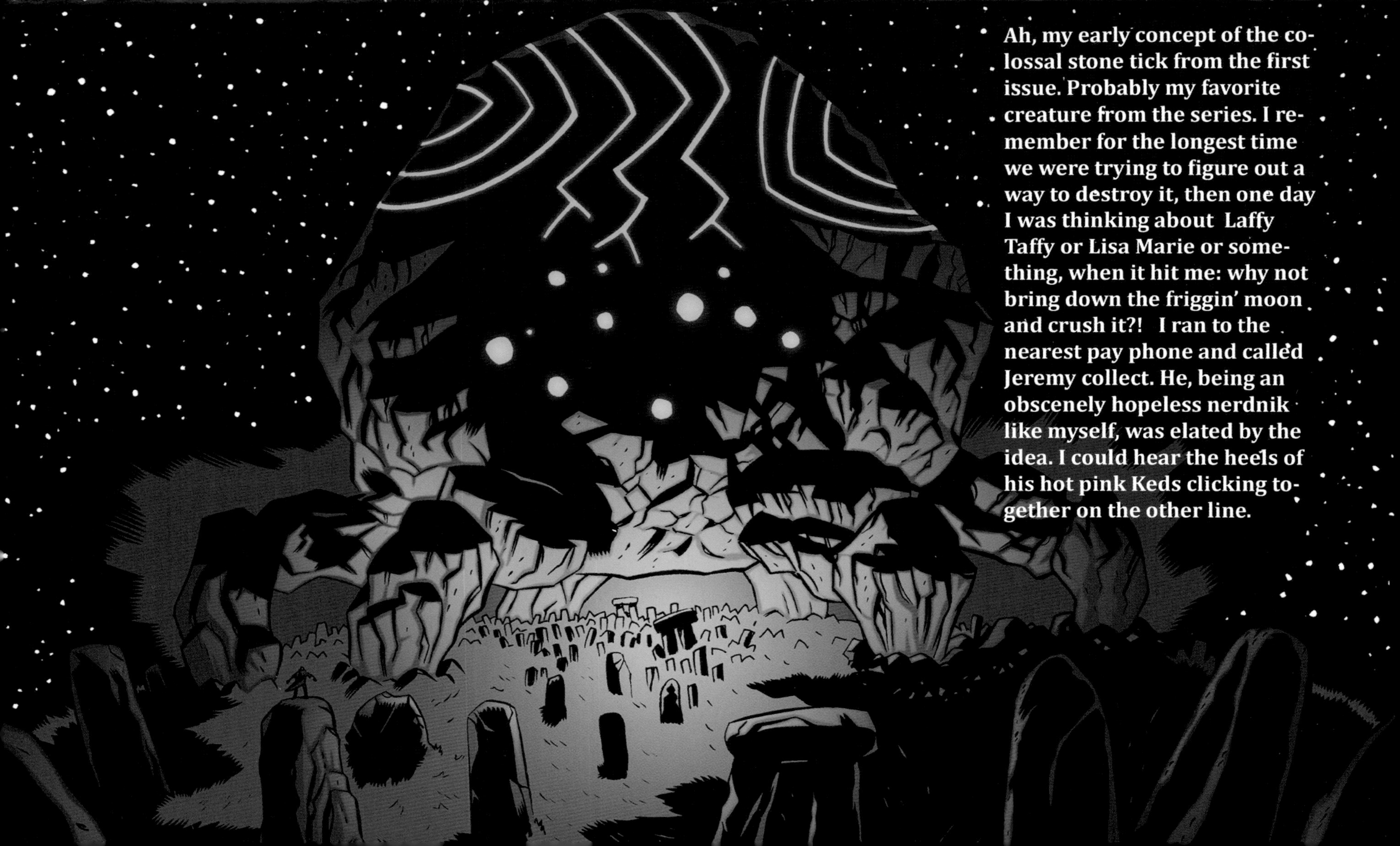

Ah, my early concept of the colossal stone tick from the first issue. Probably my favorite creature from the series. I remember for the longest time we were trying to figure out a way to destroy it, then one day I was thinking about Laffy Taffy or Lisa Marie or something, when it hit me: why not bring down the friggin' moon and crush it?! I ran to the nearest pay phone and called Jeremy collect. He, being an obscenely hopeless nerdnik like myself, was elated by the idea. I could hear the heels of his hot pink Keds clicking together on the other line.

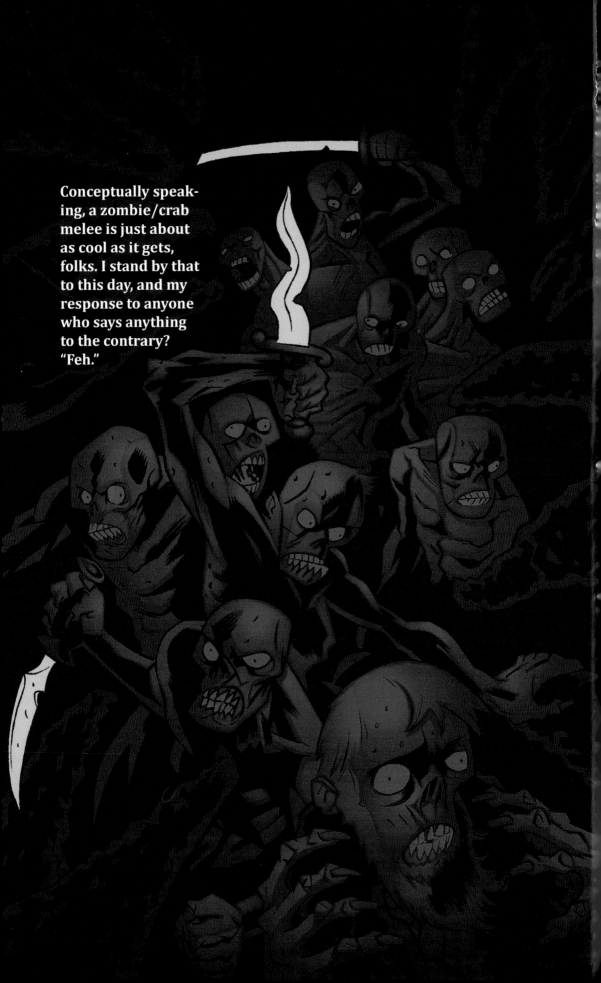

Conceptually speaking, a zombie/crab melee is just about as cool as it gets, folks. I stand by that to this day, and my response to anyone who says anything to the contrary? "Feh."

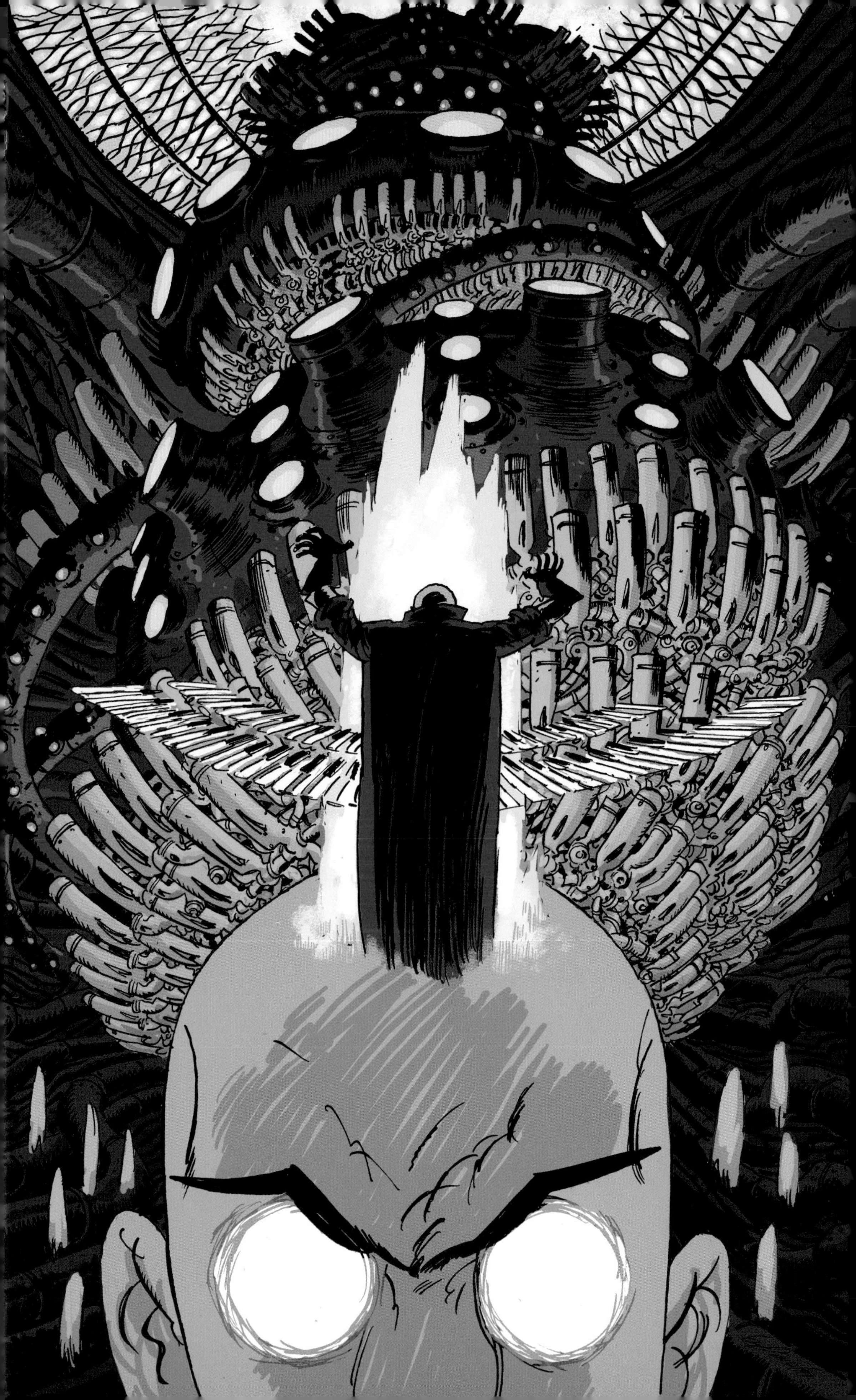

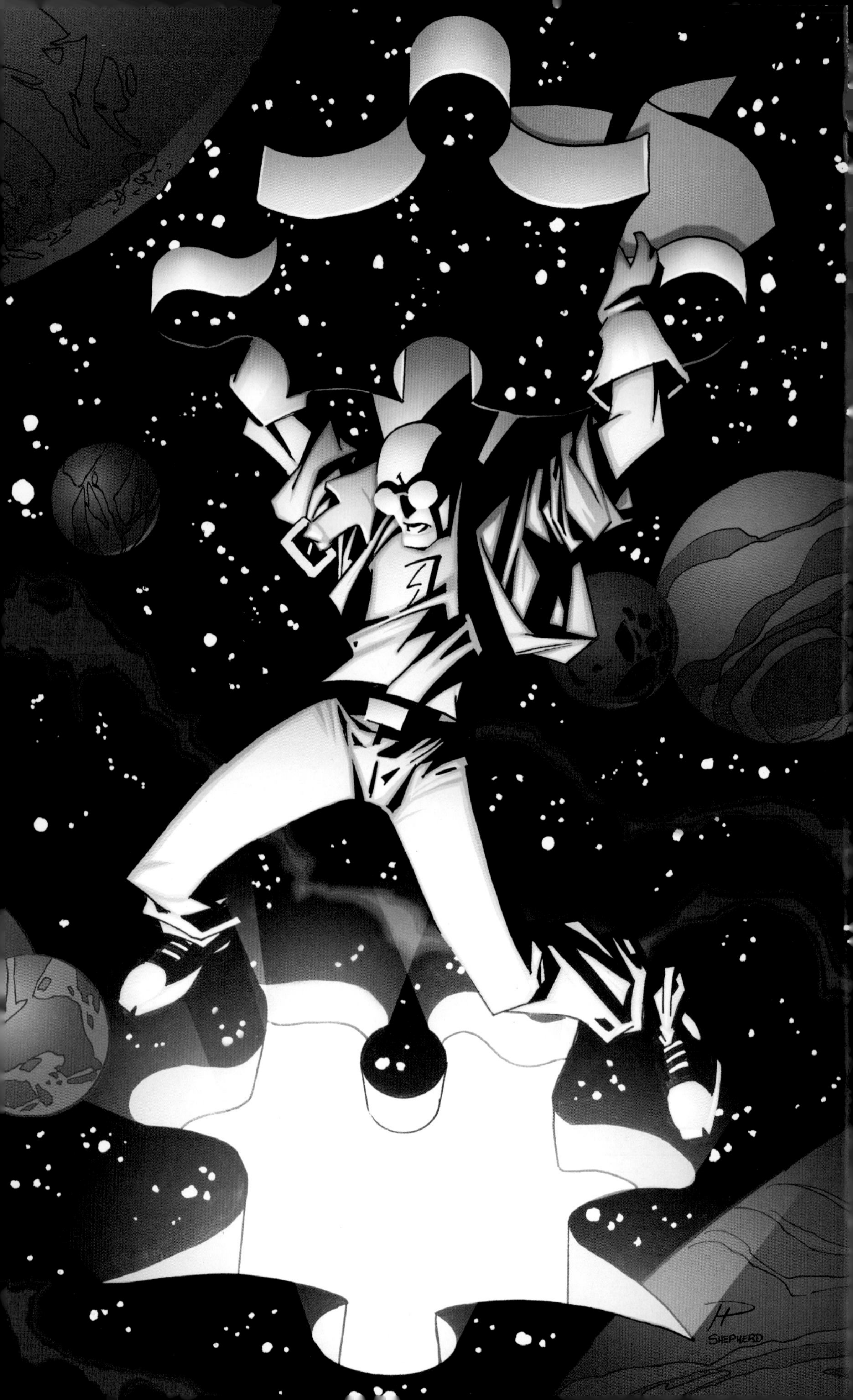
SHEPHERD

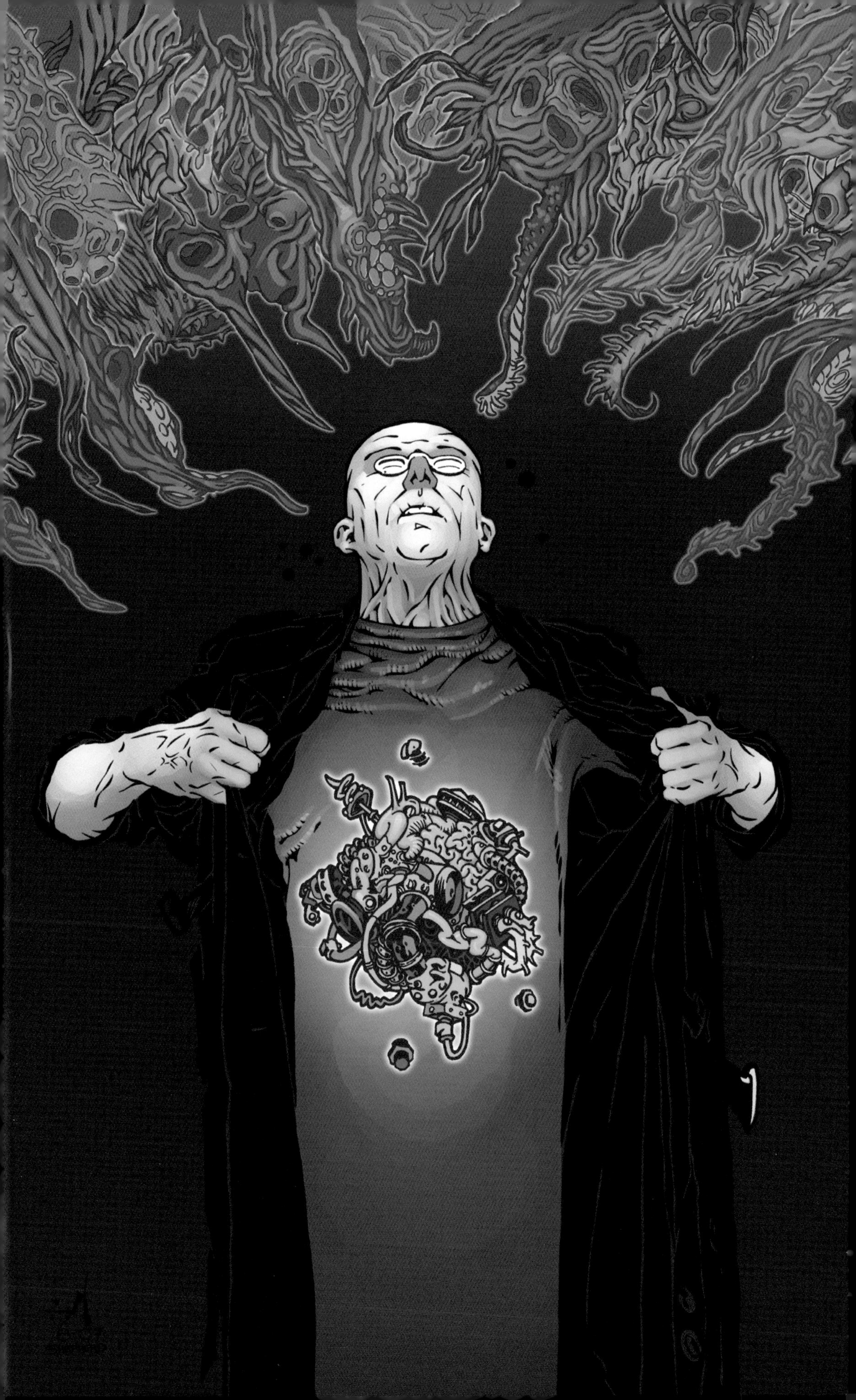

ABOUT THE AUTHORS

Brian Churilla is a cartoonist born, raised and currently residing in Portland, Oregon. He has contributed to the critically acclaimed Dark Horse series *Rex Mundi* (soon to be a major motion picture), the Harvey Award-winning anthology *Popgun, Dark Horse Presents, Creepy, We Kill Monsters*, and the forthcoming ongoing series co-created by Phil Hester, *The Anchor*. He lives with his endlessly patient wife and daughter.

Jeremy Shepherd graduated from the University of Texas at Austin with a BA in Studio Art, where he was introduced to the underground comic community. Not long after, he began his career in comics when he was hired as a colorist for Extreme Studios/Image. While with Extreme he worked on such titles as *Youngblood, Darkchylde,* and *Supreme.* In 1997, Jeremy worked with Liquid! and had the opportunity to work on many Marvel titles including *X-Men, Fantastic Four,* and *Iron Man,* before retiring from comics for almost a decade. During his time away from comics Jeremy managed to squeeze in volunteering in Vietnam for two years, receiving his law degree from the University of San Francisco, and writing children's stories. *The Engineer: Konstrukt* marks Jeremy's return to coloring and his first foray into the world of creator owned comics. Jeremy lives in Portland, Oregon with his assistant/wife/muse Lisa.